A BIRD'S EYE VIEW

AUSTRALIA'S HERON DRONE OPERATIONS IN AFGHANISTAN

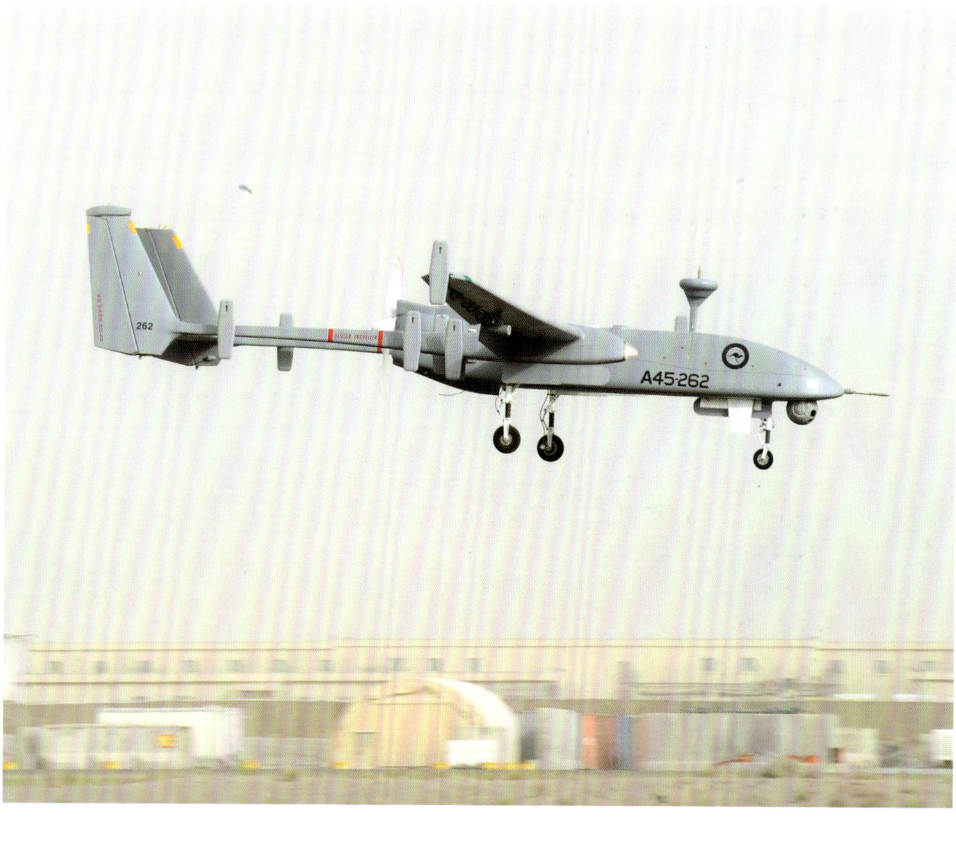

Steve Campbell-Wright
AZ Pascoe

The publishing of this book has been funded and managed by the History and Heritage Branch, Royal Australian Air Force.

All inquiries should be made to the publishers.
Big Sky Publishing Pty Ltd
PO Box 303, Newport, NSW 2106, Australia
Phone: 1300 364 611
Email: info@bigskypublishing.com.au
Web: www.bigskypublishing.com.au

Series: Australian Air Campaign Series; 10

A catalogue record for this book is available from the National Library of Australia

Cover design and typesetting by Think Productions, Melbourne

Front cover and title page: A Royal Australian Air Force Heron Unmanned Aerial Vehicle (UAV) landing at Kandahar Airfield. (credit: Raymond Vance)

CONTENTS

DEDICATION

To the 41 Australians who paid the ultimate sacrifice during the War in Afghanistan, and to those who, along with their families and friends, continue to live with the physical and mental scars of their service.

AUSTRALIAN AIR CAMPAIGN SERIES FOREWORD

The Australian Air Campaign Series produced by Air Force's History and Heritage Branch focusses on four themed sub-series:

- Campaigns, operations and battles
- Capability and technology
- Bases and airfields
- People.

These themed titles explore specific facets of the Air Force from its inception in 1921. What they reveal are unique insights, providing the reader with a greater appreciation and deeper understanding of those aspects that have shaped the Air Force's history and heritage.

Importantly, these publications are sourced from official records and research and often include first-hand accounts. While endorsed for studies in military history, the range of topics in these publications provides an ideal conduit for the broadest of audiences to pursue and learn more about the many aspects that have contributed to the development of Australia's Air Force.

Apart from being a significant point of reference, these publications ultimately acknowledge bravery, ingenuity and resilience – in essence, the service and sacrifice that is the hallmark of those who have served and continue to serve in the Air Force.

Robert Lawson OAM
Air Commodore
Director-General History and Heritage – Air Force

FOREWORD

The Royal Australian Air Force's Heron unmanned aerial vehicle (UAV) was a critical asset in the fight against terrorism and insurgency in Afghanistan. From 2009 to 2014, the Heron detachment provided intelligence, surveillance and reconnaissance (ISR) support to Australian and Coalition forces on the ground, contributing to the mission's success and helping to keep our soldiers safe.

When the Joint Operations Command first put out an urgent operational requirement for a tactical ISR capability for use by the Special Operations Task Group and other Australian forces in Afghanistan in early 2009, the Royal Australian Air Force (RAAF) moved very quickly to make the urgent operational requirement happen. While some circumstances favoured the rapid stand-up of the capability, it was one of few instances where the RAAF has introduced a capability directly into an operational theatre. It also needs to be remembered that this was the Air Force's first medium-altitude long-endurance UAV. The ability to embed our initial cadre of personnel with the Canadian Department of Defense Heron operations was critical to the development of operational tactics, techniques and procedures necessary to fulfil the mission.

This book provides an in-depth look at the RAAF Heron detachment's operations in Afghanistan, offering a rare glimpse into the world of UAV operations in a complex and challenging environment. It provides a detailed account of the Heron's capabilities, the challenges faced by the detachment and the contributions made by the men and women who served in this vital role.

Through the personal accounts of those who served in the Heron integrated project team and the Heron detachment, readers will gain a better understanding of the impact of the Heron UAV on the mission in Afghanistan. They will also gain insights into the unique challenges faced by those who operate UAVs and the critical role they play in modern warfare.

This book is a tribute to the courage, dedication and professionalism of the RAAF Heron detachment and a testament to the enduring spirit of the Australian Defence Force. It is a must-read for anyone interested in the history of the RAAF, the role of UAVs in modern warfare and the sacrifices made by our men and women in uniform.

Air Marshal Geoff Brown AO (retd)
Former Chief of Air Force, 2011–15

ACKNOWLEDGEMENTS

This book has grown from a desire by the ADF drone community to record the experiences and achievements of Australia's first medium-altitude, long-endurance operational drone capability and to tell the story of its acquisition, sustainment, deployment and legacy. With service involving drones in the Australian Army and the RAAF, Keirin Joyce provided the impetus and energy that led to our sponsorship as researchers and authors of the Heron experience. We are grateful for his impetus and ongoing drive to see the project through and for arranging sponsorship through Director General – Air Combat Capability Branch of the RAAF.

Many of the details of the book have come from oral history interviews conducted by History and Heritage Branch of the RAAF. The branch's long-running program has captured first-hand accounts of service by ADF personnel, often many years after the event. However, the interviews of Heron personnel were carried out very soon after the cessation of operations in Afghanistan and offer rare accounts of recent operations. The branch's foresight in capturing these accounts has been of great benefit. We were not able to identify all interview subjects due to privacy reasons, but their voices have contributed significantly to the richness of the story. Others have told us their stories directly. We thank David Riddel, Jonathon McMullan, Sean McClure, Sue Osborn and Andrew Earl for their willingness to share their accounts of service with ADF drones. Special thanks also go to Robert Coorey of Geospatial Intelligence Pty Ltd and Peter McSherry, formerly of MacDonald Dettwiler and Associates, for assistance from the industry side of the story. We especially thank Menachem Schwachter of Israel Aerospace Industries for his tireless search for images and information. For addressing any security concerns, we also thank the staff of RAAF Surveillance and Response Group, especially Group Captain Stephen Hoadley, Warrant Officer Scott Doring, Wing Commander Adam Robinson and Wing Commander Colin Gray.

The ADF employs many fine photographers, and their work features heavily. We are also thankful for the contributions of images by non-professional ADF photographers who, often armed with a mobile phone as well as their personal protection weapons on deployment, have provided some of the more candid images. We also acknowledge the work of the Australian War Memorial in collecting images of service life and making them available, and that of those in the community with aviation interests. We have used some images from the United States, and the appearance of US Department of Defense visual information does not imply or constitute endorsement.

The aircraft illustrations by Juanita Franzi are world class, and we thank her for applying her keen eye and attention to detail to the realm of drones. James Kightly has led us to new sources, notably many outside the usual military sphere, and Andy Wright has supported us as editor with great skill. From the Australian War Memorial, we are also indebted to Gus Garside for access to objects in the collection and to Dr Lewis Frederickson for his advice and unstinting support.

Content advice and fact checking was provided by many in the team of Heron stalwarts mentioned above with further advice from Michael Spencer of Air Force Headquarters. Special thanks go to Andrew Earl for his insights that improved the balance and voice of the text.

If writing history is about drawing the most likely conclusions from the available evidence of the past and weaving it into a narrative for a contemporary audience, then any errors in interpretation in this book rest entirely with us.

ACRONYMS

131 STA	131st Surveillance and Target Acquisition Battery
20 STA	20th Surveillance and Target Acquisition Regiment
ADF	Australian Defence Force
ADMINO	administration officer
AIA	air intelligence analyst
ANSF	Afghan National Security Forces
ASAP	as soon as possible
ASLAV	Australian Light Armoured Vehicle
ASOR	aviation safety occurrence report
AT	Aerial Target
ATOL	automatic take-off and landing
AUTRY	airborne UHF transmitter receiver relay
AVO	aerial vehicle operator
A/WGCDR	acting wing commander
BACN	Battlefield Airborne Communications Node
BCE	before the common era
CENTRIXS	Combined Enterprise Regional Information Exchange System
CO	commanding officer
CONOPS	concept of operations
CRM	crew resource management
DGPS	differential global positioning system
DGS-AUS	Distributed Ground Station Australia
DLOC	directed level of capability
DMO	Defence Materiel Organisation
DND	Department of National Defense
DSTO	Defence Science and Technology Organisation
DTC	Dynamic Targeting Cell
EOIR	electro-optic infra-red
EW	electronic warfare
FE	force element
GAF	Government Aircraft Factories

GDT	ground data terminal
GCS	ground control station
GIA	geospatial imagery analyst
GMS	ground mission station
GPS	global positioning system
HALE	high-altitude, long-endurance
HERTI	high endurance rapid technology insertion
HOTO	handover-takeover
IAI	Israel Aerospace Industries
ICAT	International Coalition Against Terrorism
IDF	Israel Defense Forces
IED	improvised explosive device
INTELO	intelligence officer
IPT	integrated project team
ISAF	International Security Assistance Force
ISR	intelligence, surveillance and reconnaissance
ISRO	intelligence, surveillance and reconnaissance officer
ISTAR	intelligence, surveillance, target acquisition and reconnaissance
JP129	Joint Project 129
JTAC	joint terminal attack controller
KAF	Kandahar Airfield
LOGO	logistics officer
MALE	medium altitude, long endurance
MANPADS	man-portable air--defence system
MATLO	maintenance liaison officer
MDA	MacDonald Dettwiler and Associates
mIRC	internet relay chat
MOSP	Multi-Sensors Optronic Stabilized Payload (or Multi-Mission Optronic Stabilized Payload in some IAI publications)
MOTS	military off-the-shelf
MOU	memorandum of understanding
MTF	Mentoring Task Force
NUASDU	Navy Unmanned Aircraft Systems Development Unit
NUASU	Navy Unmanned Aircraft Systems Unit
OPSEC	operational security

OP-UP	operational upgrade
OUR	operational urgent requirement
PED	processing, exploitation and dissemination
PO	payload operator
PTSD	post-traumatic stress disorder
RAAF	Royal Australian Air Force
RAMSI	Regional Assistance Mission to the Solomon Islands
RAPS	remote autoland positioning sensor
RC	South Regional Command South
RIP	relief in place
ROCL	remote out-of-country leave
ROVER	remotely operated video-enhanced receiver
RSO&I	reception, staging, on-forwarding and integration
SAR	synthetic aperture radar
SASR	Special Air Service Regiment
SOTG	Special Operations Task Group
UAS	unmanned/uninhabited aerial system
UCAV	unmanned/uninhabited combat aerial vehicle
UHF	ultra-high frequency
VHF	very-high frequency
VTOL	vertical take-off and landing
WGCDR	wing commander
XO	executive officer

Note: Aviation altitude is expressed in the ISO standard of feet above sea level.

PREFACE

Air power relies on a foundation of technology, people and knowledge. In this book, we aim to provide an account of how Australian aviators applied their knowledge and skills using sophisticated technology to achieve significant air power effects for Australia. We tell the story of defining the need for the Heron drone, acquiring the technology, training the people and applying their knowledge. The Royal Australian Air Force (RAAF) and its associated contractors introduced the Heron into Australian service and provided a highly valuable resource for ground forces in Afghanistan, helping to keep them safe and achieve tactical objectives. The Heron is one of a long line of drones used by the Australian Defence Force (ADF), and it has seen more combat service than any other to date. By way of introduction, we briefly trace the origins of drone use in the Australian military; to conclude, we provide an insight into the future of drones for the ADF.

Herons and their sustainment unit, No 5 Flight RAAF, were part of the ADF story for only a short time compared with most other capabilities and units, operating from 2010 to 2017. Unlike many military histories, our book is about recent military operations. This has the benefit of being able to capture the feel of the operational experience of the Heron more directly. However, some evidence may not yet be available due to its security classification and must be left to be discovered for future histories.

The Chief of Air Force's intent for books in the *Australian Air Campaign Series* is that they are readable, well-illustrated, educative and enduring. With this in mind, we assume readers will already be generally aware of the role of the ADF in providing military options for the Australian Government; while they may not have served in a military force themselves, readers will be interested in exploring aspects of the Australian military way of life. We also assume readers will be broadly interested in world affairs and the role of the Australian military in achieving the nation's strategic objectives. The book, therefore, assumes an Australian context.

Regarding terminology, there are several ways to refer to machines such as the Heron. Officially, the ADF uses the term remotely-piloted aerial system, or RPAS (pronounced 'are paz') for short. RPAS replaced the previous terms of unmanned/uninhabited aerial vehicle (UAV) and unmanned/uninhabited aerial system (UAS). These acronyms are clumsy, and they do not form an unambiguous and euphonious word, in the way acronyms like laser and Anzac do. The popular imagination and the media have long adopted the term 'drone'; for a time, the ADF avoided the term, fearing connotations of an unthinking, autonomously acting machine. As drones have become more commonplace, with roles as diverse as disaster relief and wedding photography, those connotations have lessened, and we are happy to use the term throughout the book.

On the subject of acronyms, defence forces generate what has recently become known as an acronym-rich environment. (We have not taken one editor's suggestion of noting this as an ARE.) Acronyms are so much a natural part of the verbal and written language within defence forces that most members are unaware of the extent of their use. Rather than seek to avoid acronyms altogether, we make use of many of those used in the Heron operating environment to give a more authentic military flavour and to draw readers closer to the people who operated the Heron. Through the foresight of the long-running RAAF oral history program, many of the first-hand experiences of those people are now on record. We have drawn from their accounts and used their own words throughout the book.

Reflecting the opening claim that air power is founded on technology, people and knowledge, we have structured the book around these three main topics as they relate to the ADF experience of the Heron. We precede these with an historical overview of drones in Australian military service. To guide the narrative, each chapter seeks to answer the questions we imagine readers might ask as we recount the ADF's experience of the Heron. In line with our respective backgrounds and experiences as authors and members of the ADF, Steve focused on the main text, and AZ on the breakouts. We hope you enjoy our efforts.

Steve Campbell-Wright
AZ Pascoe
November 2024

Chapter 1

A BIRD'S EYE VIEW

On a hot night in June 2010, an Australian Heron drone launched from Kandahar Airfield on a mission over Afghanistan as part of Operation *Hamkari*. The mission began as a routine combat overwatch for Australian special forces in the follow-up actions after the Shah Wali Kot Offensive in Kandahar Provence. It was the height of the fighting season, and the Australian Special Operations Task Group (SOTG) was tasked with conducting disruptive operations to flush out Taliban insurgents. A United States Army UH-60 Black Hawk helicopter, one of four carrying SOTG members to the attack, crashed and rolled several times before catching fire.[1] Of the ten Australians on board the helicopter, two died at the scene, and one died soon after in the military hospital. An American helicopter crewman was also killed, and several in the crash suffered injuries.

Soldiers from Australia's Special Operations Task Group boarding a US Army Black Hawk helicopter after a town meeting in Shah Wali Kot near Kandahar, Afghanistan, June 2010 (Raymond Vance)

The Heron supporting the airborne assault ended up providing overwatch of the crash site and recovery operations in what was still a contested battle zone.[2] It looked out for insurgent combatants and their spotters, along with clearing landing zones for the medevac helicopters, to provide a safe exit for the rescuers. The critical factor the Heron brought to the situation was live situational awareness. This has been the goal of military commanders, no doubt before the earliest writings on war. The sixth century BCE general and war theorist Sun Tzu said: 'What enables the wise sovereign and the good general to strike and conquer, and achieve things beyond the reach of ordinary men, is foreknowledge.'[3] Knowing what the adversary is doing – or perhaps is planning – provides an exceptional advantage in battle. It helps to see through the fog of war.

At the operational and tactical levels, watching the enemy's pattern of life, assessing their firepower capability, observing them manoeuvre and listening to them as they plan can be very difficult. However, these observations can provide exceptional foreknowledge and help to achieve battlefield, and ultimately strategic, success. Reducing the risk of detection and not placing surveillance and reconnaissance personnel in danger is vitally important. However, before the inherent stealth and safety of unmanned drones, how was battlefield reconnaissance carried out?

Battlefield reconnaissance before the drone era

For centuries, horse-mounted cavalry was the means of choice for battlefield commanders to gain tactical and operational intelligence of opposing forces.[4] Cavalry scouts were able to ride forward to observation positions and gather real-time intelligence about the capability of opposing forces, the terrain of the battlefield and the availability of local resources. Scouts offered the advantages of speed and mobility. Reconnaissance supplemented their roles as shock forces to break through weakened infantry lines and protective elements to guard the flanks during infantry advances and retreats.

However, small arms became more powerful and accurate during the mid-19th century as rifles replaced muskets for general issue to soldiers; early machine guns – such as the 1861 Gatling gun – also vastly increased the lethality and effectiveness of foot soldiers. As a result, from about 1870, cavalry forces placed less emphasis on their role as frontline shock forces and greater emphasis on reconnaissance.[5] With the establishment of trench warfare during the First World War in 1914–18, cavalry reconnaissance became largely impractical. However, it remained part of the training doctrine of some military forces as late as 1939.[6] Manfred von Richthofen, the famous 'Red Baron' fighter pilot, served as a mounted cavalry reconnaissance officer early in the First World War before transferring to the Imperial German Army Air Service in 1915.[7]

Motorised transport on the battlefield during the First World War quickly replaced horse-borne cavalry due to its similar advantages of speed and mobility.[12] Armoured cars, and later tanks, were able to venture forward in reconnaissance roles in relative safety. During the Second World War, non-mounted reconnaissance also came into its own, as armies formed infantry reconnaissance regiments to supplement armoured reconnaissance. Highly specialised units carried out reconnaissance within enemy occupied territory and were the basis of the special forces elements that emerged during the war. Amphibious reconnaissance also developed during the war.

Aerial reconnaissance has its own long history. Height can offer considerable advantage in observing an enemy, but high vantage points in the terrain may not always be well placed or not under the control of a force wishing to exploit them. Reconnaissance balloons have provided the solution at various times. The first known use of a military reconnaissance

Cavalry scout missions

Military use of horse-mounted soldiers in combat stretches back to antiquity, and employing cavalry scouts for military reconnaissance missions is similarly ancient. Scholars argue Greek warfare in the 7th century BCE involved the use of minimally armed riders who were likely conducting scouting missions.[8] Prior to the First World War, horse-mounted cavalry units performed a variety of crucial battlefield roles, typically facilitated by fielding several different kinds of cavalry with their own unique tasks. While heavier units (such as the European Cuirassiers) were tasked in battle with shock actions designed to disrupt enemy formations, lighter cavalry units on small, swift horses conducted scouting missions.[9] Cavalry scouts possessed the speed and mobility to move tactically on battlefields, avoiding enemy detection while gaining crucial information about an enemy's force size and disposition.[10] This fundamentally shaped the conduct – and in some cases, determined the outcome – of military engagements. A well-executed scouting mission and the intelligence it gathered could provide commanders with early warning and allow them to concentrate firepower at a decisive point in time and space to target the enemy's weaknesses and defeat them. In fact, in Britain, by the late 19th century, reconnaissance was widely held to be the cavalry's principal duty.[11] The First World War marked a turning point in warfare, and cavalry was no exception. Cavalry forces today are tech-enabled and look vastly different from their forebears but, as their scouting missions throughout time demonstrate, skilful and timely reconnaissance remains pivotal to modern military conflict.

(National Army Museum)

Battle of Fleurus, 1794

The Battle of Fleurus is the first recorded instance of the decisive military use of an aircraft to influence the result of a battle. On 26 June, as part of a two-year campaign in the Austrian Netherlands, the army of the First French Republic under General Jean-Baptiste Jourdan engaged and defeated the Coalition Army commanded by Prince Josias of Coburg. Central to this victory was the French use of the reconnaissance balloon *l'Entreprenant*, manned by the French Aerostatic Corps. On 22 June, the balloon was dragged across almost 50 kilometres of ground into position on the plain of Fleurus, and over the following three days, an officer ascended daily to observe the disposition of Austrian troops on the battlefield at Charleroi (in modern-day Belgium). During the battle on the 26th, the *l'Entreprenant* remained aloft for nine hours, with the observer recording the Austrian army's composition and movements and relaying them to the French commanders for use in tactical decision-making. They did so by lowering written reports down the tethering ropes in sandbags. With approximately 80,000 men each to their forces, the two militaries were numerically matched. However, the French use of aerial observation enabled them to concentrate their troops against, and defeat, the First Coalition. The victory at Fleurus effectively destroyed the Dutch Republic and proved a watershed moment for the French army, which remained dominant for the remaining three years of the War of the First Coalition, ensuring the survival of the French nation.

(after Thomas Naudet)

balloon was during the French Revolutionary Wars. In 1794, during an engagement known as the Battle of Fleurus, French forces flew a tethered balloon above the battlefield and received real-time intelligence reports of the opposing coalition forces. The French won the battle and ultimately achieved victory in the war, taking possession of the Austrian Netherlands.[13] Tethered, uninhabited balloons remain in use today and were a feature of the skyline of many Coalition camps in the Middle East during the 21st century. They provided platforms for suites of cameras and detection instruments to identify threats against Coalition forces in such places as Camp Victory in Baghdad and Camp Qargha in Afghanistan. Balloons, of course, are generally fixed devices – constrained by their tethers and limited communication ranges – and are unable to roam and carry out wider reconnaissance.

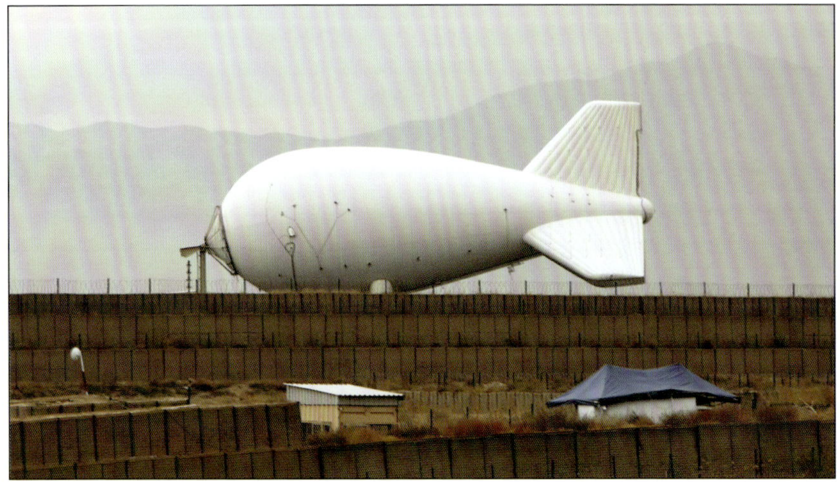

Tethered observation balloon moored for maintenance at Forward Operating Base Qargha, Afghanistan, 2019 (Steve Campbell-Wright)

During the nineteenth century, various experiments were carried out using aerial photography from balloons with and without occupants, as well as from tethered kites.[14] By the early 20th century, there were even tests using very low altitude rockets to take photographs of terrain. However, with the development of practical heavier-than-air flight following the Wright brothers' success in late 1903, military forces were quick to adapt aircraft for reconnaissance. Italian forces did so during the Italo–Turkish War in 1911–12, as did Bulgarian forces during the Balkan Wars of 1912–13.[15] Aerial reconnaissance flights became the mainstay of early flying missions during the First World War that followed.

The use of aerial cameras to photograph enemy positions and terrain provided commanders and planners with intelligence in close to real-time – considering the time it took to land the aircraft, process the film, assess the information and pass it on. The intelligence could, however, also be used in planning future operations. Before the Gallipoli Campaign of 1915, Royal Naval Air Service aircraft conducted photo reconnaissance of the Gallipoli Peninsula used in planning the landing.[16] The aircrew, however, were placed at considerable risk, as opposing forces endeavoured to deny such advantage by bringing aircraft down either by ground fire or aerial attack.

First World War observer from the Royal Air Force demonstrating use of a hand-held aerial camera, 1918 (Royal Air Force)

Photo reconnaissance was also used to great effect during the Second World War, with the ability to fly at very high altitudes with high-resolution camera equipment providing intelligence of a far higher quality than during previous conflicts. However, the information gained was still only, at best, close to real-time, and the risks to the aircrew remained, despite the lower likelihood of attack from ground fire. For example, on 14 August 1942, a German Luftwaffe Focke-Wulf Condor reconnaissance aircraft was gathering information on Allied shipping in the Atlantic near Iceland when it was spotted and shot down by an American Lockheed Lightning fighter.[17]

Second World War photographers from the Royal Air Force preparing cameras to mount in a photo reconnaissance Mosquito aircraft (Imperial War Museum)

The Cold War ushered in a leap in aerial reconnaissance capability, with machines such as Lockheed's U-2 Dragon Lady high-altitude reconnaissance aircraft and SR-71 Blackbird supersonic strategic reconnaissance aircraft. These aircraft and others like them carried a range of sensors beyond standard photographic cameras, such as reconnaissance radars and signals detection equipment. The U-2 aircraft overflew the Soviet Union for four years during the late 1950s to gather intelligence on the Soviet missile program, bomber capabilities and military sites. Famously, the overfly program ceased in 1960, when the Soviets shot a U-2 down with a newly developed surface-to-air missile and captured the pilot.

Reconnaissance satellites take the notion of height for observation to the extreme. They can provide reconnaissance over very wide areas and eliminate the element of human risk in flight. The first reconnaissance satellites – developed in the 1950s – used optical cameras to expose reels of film that were returned to earth for chemical processing. Their role, therefore, was a strategic one that allowed for mid to long-term surveillance rather than use as an operational or tactical level tool. Newer generations of reconnaissance satellites relay digital images as well as information gained from non-optical sensors, such as radar and radio sensors. Typical current day uses also include detecting nuclear test explosions and ballistic missile launches. The intelligence gained by modern satellites, nonetheless, takes time to process, interpret and exploit. Reconnaissance satellites are, therefore, very useful as a strategic tool, but their use in providing real-time tactical reconnaissance to troops on the ground is limited.

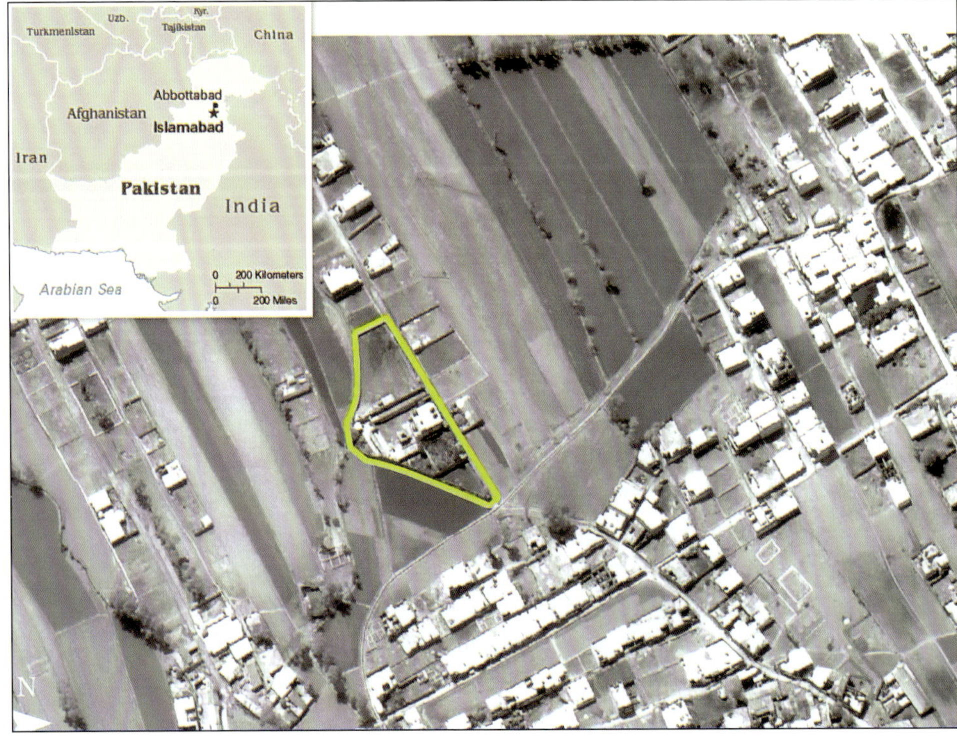

Aerial photo of Osama bin Laden's compound in Abbottabad, Pakistani, 2011 (US Central Intelligence Agency)

The beginning of military drones

Military commanders and their planning staffs, along with personnel engaged in direct combat, require reconnaissance precisely tailored to their needs. It needs to be as close to real-time as possible and not place those gathering it at undue risk. This is where drones come into their own. What factors then led to the development of military drones? Drones did not have a single inventor and were not invented at a single time or place. Instead, various technological innovations over many decades ultimately came together to provide the basis for modern drones. Their main military use was as 'clay pigeons' then target towing aircraft for gunnery practice before drones developed into the significant reconnaissance assets they are now.

English engineer and inventor Archibald Low is known as the 'father of radio guidance systems.'[18] Low was active in many fields throughout his working life; in 1915–17, he worked with Britain's Royal Flying Corps on the invention of radio-guided aircraft to be fitted with warheads. The intention was to launch them against German Zeppelins as they attempted to bomb mainland Britain. These drones were termed an 'Aerial Target' to give the impression they were to be used simply for gunnery practice. Low's radio control system provided rudimentary commands to the drone to allow a ground operator to steer the aircraft. The radio control signals were even encrypted.[19]

A wide range of experimental Aerial Target designs were developed by the Royal Flying Corps, including ones made by Sopwith Aviation, de Havilland and Ruston Proctor. The Ruston Proctor Aerial Target of 1916 was one of the most successful and is credited with leading to the development of the American-made Kettering Bug of 1918. Also in the United States, the Hewitt-Sperry Automatic Airplane, first test flown in 1917, added gyroscopes to radio-controlled aircraft to increase stability. During the late 1920s, the Royal Aircraft Establishment experimented with a radio-controlled flying anti-ship weapon for the Royal Navy named Larynx. The drone had greater speed and payload capacity than any of its predecessors; it was actually faster than fighter aircraft of the time.[22]

These drones were in fact the precursors to cruise missiles. Nonetheless, the technology they employed was critical to the success of drones in the sense they are known today. The main difference is cruise missiles are lost on detonation of their warhead, while drones are designed to return after releasing their munitions or employing their sensors.

The 1932 experimental Fairey Queen was, however, one drone always intended as an aerial target. It was based on the Fairey Aviation Company's existing IIIF floatplane. Only three were made, and they failed in trials. Where Fairey failed, however, De Havilland succeeded in 1935. They adapted their existing D.H.82A Tiger Moth trainer aircraft to be a radio-controlled drone designated the D.H.82B Queen Bee. More than 400 were built, and most were used in realistic anti-aircraft gunnery training by the Royal Navy.[23] In 1937, the Airspeed aircraft company also made a successful radio-controlled floatplane called the AS30 Queen Wasp. However, only a handful were made.[24]

Ruston Proctor Aerial Target

In 1916, English engineer Archibald Low – widely recognised for his pioneering work in radio navigation systems – launched the Ruston Proctor Aerial Target, the world's first unmanned, winged aircraft. After joining the British Army in 1914, Low had been rapidly promoted to captain, then moved to the Royal Flying Corps. Sometime later, as the head of the corps' Experimental Works, he began working on an unmanned, radio-controlled aeroplane. His work was known simply as the 'Aerial Target' (AT) project – an attempt to mislead the Germans into believing it was simply a project to test naval anti-aircraft capabilities. In reality, the AT had two intended functions. Firstly, it was designed to defend against German Zeppelins, under the command of a ground-based radio controller. Secondly, it served as a flying bomb, controlled from a nearby piloted aircraft, to be flown into enemy planes. Low believed the AT would also be effective against ground targets. His hand-selected team of roughly 30 men quickly designed and built a prototype that launched from the back of a truck using compressed air and flew for several minutes before the engine failed.[20] Low later added an electrically driven gyroscope but, after several other prototypes met the same fate, his project was discontinued, the British Government seeing little value in unmanned aerial vehicles (unlike the Germans, who twice tried to assassinate Low).[21] Despite this outcome, the Ruston Proctor Aerial Target is the earliest precursor of today's combat drones, and the project opened the path for ongoing development of this technology.

(Royal Aircraft Establishment)

D.H.82B and the term 'drone'

The 1932 Fairey Queen sparked greater understanding of the need for target aircraft to support realistic anti-aircraft gunnery training and led to the development of the world's first truly successful unmanned aircraft – the de Havilland D.H.82B Queen Bee.[25] Featuring the wings, engine, tailplane and undercarriage of the de Havilland D.H.82A Tiger Moth, the Queen Bee appeared almost identical to the famous trainer. However, its lighter and more buoyant wooden fuselage mimicked that of the D.H.60 Gypsy Moth, allowing the Queen Bee to float so it could be retrieved and reused after naval gunnery training.[26] While the forward cockpit position had a set of manual controls to enable manned flight, more important was the rear seat. Fully enclosed, it held radio-control gear and pneumatic servos linked to the aircraft's rudder and elevator controls.[27] A huge ground transmitter, roughly the size of a delivery van, sent radio signals to the aircraft's servos using a simple rotary dial, where the numbers corresponded with commands for the Queen Bee.

The Queen Bee inspired use of the term 'drone' in reference to unmanned aircraft. Admiral William Standley, the United States Navy's Chief of Naval Operations, attended a demonstration of the Queen Bee in 1935 and, upon his return to the USA, directed the establishment of the US Navy's Radio-Controlled Aircraft Project. In his 1936 semi-annual report, Officer in Charge Lieutenant Commander Delmar Fahrney referred to the aerial targets as 'drones', purportedly coining the term in homage to the de Havilland Queen Bee.[28]

(Aero Illustrations)

Denny Radioplane OQ-2

In November 1939, Hollywood movie star and aviation enthusiast Reginald Denny demonstrated his fourth Radioplane prototype, the RP-4, to the United States Army. Its successful flight ushered in the first mass-produced drone in the United States, the Denny Radioplane OQ-2. Denny had spent four years trying to refine his prototype as an anti-aircraft gunnery training tool, first demonstrating the RP-1 in 1935, then the RP-2 in 1938, and the RP-3 in early 1939.[29] His timing was ideal. In the late 1930s, various drone experiments by the United States Navy precipitated the United States Army's initiation of its own service-specific projects exploring the potential of radio-controlled targets and weapons.[30] Denny's radio-controlled aircraft business, the Radioplane Company, was commissioned to provide 53 drones for the United States Army. Over the next two years, the United States Air Corps supported Denny's continued refinement of the drone and, in 1941, began mass production of the Radioplane RP-5A, designated by the United States Army as the OQ-2A and OQ-2B, and as 'Target Drone, Denny' or TDD-1 by the United States Navy.[31] The OQ-2 was catapult launched and, if it survived the gunnery training serials, later recovered by deploying a seven-metre diameter parachute.[32] From 1941 to 1945, the Radioplane Company supplied almost 15,000 drones for the United States military forces in many variants, and the Denny Radioplane effectively provided the foundation on which drone technology development in the United States was predicated.[33]

(Luca Mariotti)

A significant step in the path to modern drones was the miniaturisation of radio-control components. Reginald Denny, a British aviator, inventor and Hollywood film star, made a commercial scale model aircraft in the 1930s – called the Dennyplane – intended for hobbyists. In 1935, he bought the designs for a radio-controlled model aircraft from Walter Righter and began manufacturing what he called the Radioplane – this time intended for military use as a target drone. They were meant to be destroyed, but any that survived gunnery practices were able to be recovered using a parachute fitted to the drone. The United States Army and Navy ordered around 15,000 Radioplanes in several variants during the Second World War. At about the same time, American inventor Edward M Sorensen patented an improved ground control system that displayed information sent back from the drone. This allowed the pilots to see flight characteristics such as speed and direction, which meant drones were able to fly out of sight of the pilot.

Several experiments in full-scale attack drones were carried out during the Second World War, but they did not prove sufficiently effective to go into service. During the post-war and Cold War eras, the United States used several variants of the piston-engine Radioplane in target drone roles, with one variant, the RP-71 Falconer, being used for aerial photo reconnaissance.[34] As these small drones made by various manufacturers evolved, some were powered by pulsejet and turbojet engines to keep pace with the jet fighters they were simulating as targets. The success of the Falconer led to further developments in reconnaissance drones, and the jet-powered Ryan 147 Lightning Bug was used in photo and signals reconnaissance missions over China and North Vietnam during the 1960s and 1970s.[35]

Tadiran Mastiff reconnaissance drone made by Israel's Tadiran Electronic Systems and used by the Israeli Air Force during the 1982 Lebanon War. This example is preserved in the Evergreen Aviation & Space Museum, Oregon, USA (Magnus Manske)

These roles were largely as strategic surveillance assets. However, a significant step in the use of drones as operational and tactical assets took place during the 1982 Lebanon War. The Israeli Air Force used Tadiran Mastiff and Israel Aerospace Industries (IAI) Scout drones for real-time aerial reconnaissance, as electronic jammers and as decoys to deceive Syrian forces into activating their surface-to-air missile system radars, thus giving away their locations.[36] The placement of sophisticated sensors and communication equipment on remotely piloted aircraft provided a massive leap in capability and is the basis for modern drones. They became aerial systems, rather than simply aircraft. That is, flight is not their main reason for being; what they do while flying is more important. What then are modern drones capable of?

Modern drone capabilities

Digital electronics allow the rapid two-way passing of data between drones and their ground control stations. This in turn has allowed for the development of flight control interfaces that mimic flight controls of normal aircraft. The drone responds to flight control inputs from pilots in the way an aircraft they might normally sit in does. Pilots can also select autopilot for phases of the mission, including landing. They are, therefore, intuitive for pilots to fly. This brings significant advantages in military settings, where military pilots operate in dynamic congested airspaces, often in contested environments. They naturally emulate being in the battlespace, complete with situational awareness, without actually being there.

Aside from advances in flight controls, modern drones can carry a wide range of sensing equipment. Electro-optical cameras capture light in the visible spectrum, while infra-red cameras detect movement and heat without the aid of visible light. Thermal imaging cameras capture heat information and allow the discovery of abnormal heat signatures. Radars can detect objects at a distance, even underground in the case of ground-penetrating radar. When used in conjunction with gyroscopes, aerial sensors can provide extremely high-resolution data.

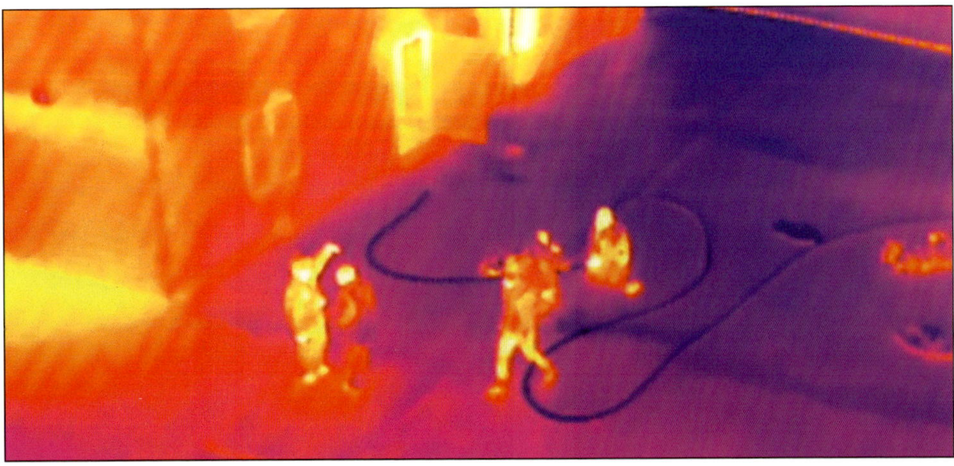

Infra-red thermal camera image of a firefighting event showing the heat signatures of firefighters and residual heat after the fire (DJI FLIR Systems Zenmuse XT)

Drones have important uses in the civil sphere. The ability to mount sensors on drones and fly to places too dangerous for people is used in a variety of situations, such as firefighting, disaster relief and mining. Drones are also cost-effective in industrial and commercial settings, such as resource management, agriculture, infrastructure management, archaeology, filmmaking and product delivery.[37] Police forces also use them for crime detection, surveillance and investigation.

Electricity companies, for example, use drone-mounted thermal imaging cameras to inspect generation and distribution infrastructure, seeking out abnormal heat nodes that might indicate high-resistance points and, therefore, potential failures. Facilities maintenance companies use drones to visually inspect situations as diverse as high roofs and solar panel farms. Firefighting coordinators have used infra-red cameras on drones to keep track of emergency services personnel in smoke-filled situations. Search and rescue services can use drones with thermal cameras to detect a missing person in low visibility environments, say due to cloud or foliage cover.[38]

In modern military conflict, the term battlefield reconnaissance has been replaced by intelligence, surveillance and reconnaissance (ISR), which encompasses the broader purposes and uses of reconnaissance. The Australian Defence Force (ADF) definition of ISR is that it 'synchronises and integrates the planning and operation of sensors, assets, and processing, exploitation and dissemination systems in direct support of current and future operations.'[39] This more sophisticated way of describing the older notion of reconnaissance recognises that information is of limited use if it is not interpreted and passed to those who need it in a meaningful and timely manner. ISR contributes to the warfighting function of situational understanding – essential for one force to prevail over another. ISR aims to enable what is known in military terms as 'information superiority', which is intended to lead to 'decision superiority'.[40] That is, commanders and battle planners will be able to out-think and out-manoeuvre their opponents if they have better intelligence. In the context of Australian Army doctrine, ISR also includes target acquisition and is termed ISTAR (intelligence, surveillance, target acquisition and reconnaissance).

ISR gathers information by a range of means that includes airborne early warning and control aircraft, satellites, human intelligence and drones. Drones have played an increasing role in ISR in recent times, and they offer significant advantages. Some can loiter for very long periods, well over comfortable and safe times for aircrew in manned aircraft. They can venture into airspace that poses higher risks than might normally be acceptable for airborne early warning and control aircraft. With live communication between active ISR assets, drones can integrate into a system that produces a more complete intelligence picture. Meanwhile, small tactical drones allow ground troops to gain local battlefield intelligence through close-range reconnaissance and surveillance.

Beyond their roles in ISR, modern military drones can play an important part in directly attacking the enemy, known in military terms as strike. Drones can be used in support of strike operations or can be used to carry out strike directly. In the support role, some unarmed drones can give target designations via GPS coordinates or laser line-of-sight as

NATO drone classifications

The North Atlantic Treaty Organisation (NATO) published its *Strategic Concept of Employment for UAS in NATO* in 2010. It seeks to describe drones and their capabilities to facilitate NATO planning and execution of drone operations at all levels. The document identifies and describes drones in three classes, as shown in this table.

Class	Category	Normal employment level	Normal operating altitude	Normal mission radius	Primary supported commander
CLASS I (less than 150 kg)	MICRO less than 2 kg	Single operator or tactical section	Up to 200 ft	Line-of-sight up to 5 km	Platoon or section
	MINI 2 to 20 kg	Tactical sub-unit (manual launch)	Up to 3,000 ft	Line-of-sight up to 25 km	Company or squadron
	SMALL 20 to 150 kg	Tactical unit (requires launch system)	Up to 5,000 ft	Line-of-sight up to 50 km	Battalion, regiment or brigade
CLASS II (150 kg to 600 kg)	TACTICAL	Tactical formation	Up to 10,000 ft	Line-of-sight up to 200 km	Brigade
CLASS III (more than 600 kg)	MALE	Operational or theatre	Up to 45,000 ft	Beyond line-of-sight	Joint task force
	HALE	Strategic or national	Up to 65,000 ft	Beyond line-of-sight	Theatre
	UCAV	Strategic or national	Up to 65,000 ft	Beyond line-of-sight	Theatre

Operation Cast Lead, Gaza 2008–09

The capability of drones, both armed and unarmed, was clearly demonstrated when the Israel Defense Forces (IDF) used unmanned aircraft in support of Operation *Cast Lead* from December 2008 to January 2009. *Cast Lead* was a two-phase military operation conducted in response to increased rocket and mortar attacks by Palestinian militant group Hamas.[41] The first phase of *Cast Lead* was a week of aerial bombing, and around midday on 27 December 2008, Israeli F-16 fighter jets, Apache helicopters and unmanned drones struck more than 100 locations. During the 22-day period, in which Israel prevented the media and aid agencies from entering the area, 1,383 Palestinians were killed, including 333 children.[42] Crucial to this operation, however, was the way in which the IDF used unarmed drones to inform their targeting plan, not only during the air and air-ground phases of *Cast Lead*, but in the prior long-term surveillance of Gaza. Today, most drones used by the IDF are unarmed and designed for intelligence gathering via 'loitering surveillance'.[43] Importantly, in the years preceding Operation *Cast Lead*, Israel gathered drone-captured imagery to aid in developing the Israeli Air Force's targeting plan. With their highly advanced visual sensors, high loitering altitudes and long loiter times, IDF drones were able to continuously gather data with minimal risk. This enabled discriminatory targeting – in other words, specific and detailed decision-making about what to target and why – during both phases of Operation *Cast Lead*, and however this information may have been used, there can be no denying the battlefield advantage of such intelligence.[44]

(International Solidarity Movement)

D.H.82B Queen Bee in Australian service

After it was fielded for service by the Royal Navy in 1935, the de Havilland D.H.82B Queen Bee quickly made its way into Australian military operations. HMAS *Australia* (II), one of two 10,000-ton County-class heavy cruisers commissioned for the Australian Government's naval development program of 1924, was the first to fly the Queen Bee.[45] In 1935, *Australia* sailed to the Mediterranean to serve with the 1st Cruiser Squadron of the British Mediterranean Fleet. During this 14-month period, *Australia* entered the Portsmouth Dockyard on 25 August and was fitted with a light rotating Catapult Type S IIL, designed to launch the Supermarine Seagull V, a British amphibious single-engine reconnaissance aircraft.[46] Not long after, in February 1936, it was discovered HMS *Shropshire* was not fitted with the light catapult necessary to launch the Queen Bee, and *Australia* was called upon to embark the aircraft as part of the fleet's anti-aircraft gunnery exercises. The crew of *Australia* fitted the Queen Bee's front cockpit with a dummy pilot, whom they christened 'Fearless Fred' and who was later replaced by 'Daring Dan' (shown in image above). Despite some initial challenges with getting the Queen Bee loaded aboard the ship, and some inclement weather, the crew acquitted itself admirably. The fleet's Commander-in-Chief later commended *Australia* for her 'willingness and promptitude' in assuming these duties for the Queen Bee, which were 'equalled by her efficiency in these duties.'[47] It was a fruitful beginning to Australia's employment of drones in military service.

(Australian War Memorial P00604.013)

an adjunct to their ISR role. These target designations are used by crewed strike aircraft to drop bombs with high precision. In a direct strike role, armed drones are capable of similar precision bombing. Therefore, the true value of drones in modern warfare lies in their ability to achieve ISR and strike effects like, and in some cases better than, those achievable from crewed aircraft but without placing lives unnecessarily at risk. In this way, drones have proved their value time and again in battle. They are a significant asset in the armoury of a military force. What has been Australia's experience of drone operation and development, and what significance has it had on the world stage?

The Australian experience of military drones

The ADF and Australian industry have been along for much of the journey of military drone use and development, notably in the post–Second World War era. In fact, Australia has played a significant part in the development and manufacture of drones internationally.

Australia's first experience of military drones was when Royal Australian Air Force (RAAF) and Royal Australian Navy operated D.H.82B Queen Bee drones from HMAS *Australia* (II) in the Mediterranean Sea in 1935. *Australia* was serving with Britain's Royal Navy and provided the aircraft launch capability for deploying the drones during naval gunnery trials.

Remains of De Havilland D.H.82B Queen Bee radio-controlled target aircraft K5103 being winched on board HMAS *Australia* (Australian War Memorial P03551.008)

In line with its alliance with Britain since Federation, Australia had access to British technology, particularly for military training and combat. Most aircraft purchased by Australia until the beginning of the Second World War were of British manufacture. The RAAF had experimented with the designing and building of a small number of aircraft locally during the 1920s and 1930s, and the Australian Government had formed a highly successful aircraft manufacturing plant by 1939. That plant – known for most of the war as the Department of Aircraft Production – was supported by hundreds of local manufacturers and suppliers. Two major private aircraft manufacturers or assemblers, the Commonwealth Aircraft Corporation and de Havilland Aircraft, also played a significant part in wartime aircraft production.

Soon after the Second World War, the Department of Aircraft Production was restructured to become the Government Aircraft Factories (GAF). It continued aircraft production, manufacturing Avro Lincoln heavy bombers and English Electric Canberra jet-powered medium bombers. Australia, therefore, had experience in designing and manufacturing airframes and aircraft components in the immediate post-war period, and building the Canberra provided valuable experience with jet engines. Further, the perceived threat to Australia of communism ensured continued Government support for aircraft production, and links to the British and American aviation industries, developed during the war, were maintained.[48]

One outcome of this environment was the call to design and manufacture a radio-controlled target drone for use in the development of surface-to-air missiles under the Anglo–Australian Joint Project. The project was established in the wake of the success of Germany's Second World War V1 flying bombs and V2 ballistic rockets and the new Cold War threat posed by intercontinental ballistic and nuclear weapons.[49] Surface-to-air missiles were seen as an effective way to counter such weapons and a credible deterrent to their use. The project chose Australia, with its vast expanses of sparsely inhabited desert, as the location for developing and testing British missiles.

Part of that test program was to design and manufacture a drone to simulate a missile threat. This drone was the GAF Jindivik, thought to be an Australian First Nations word meaning 'hunted one'. The project carried out most of its tests at Woomera in South Australia. Appropriately, Woomera is a Dharug word for a spear throwing device. Weapons such as the Bloodhound radar-guided surface-to-air missile and a host of others were developed and tested in Australia and the United Kingdom using the Jindivik.[50] The Jindivik was also used by a range of navies and air forces in other countries for defensive missile launch training and practice. More than 500 Jindiviks were made between 1951 and the mid-1990s, and they were used by the ADF, the Swedish Air Force, the Royal Air Force and the United States Navy.[51] They saw service into the late 1990s.

The Royal Australian Navy operated 42 Jindiviks between 1966 and 1998 from its Jervis Bay Range Facility, allowing operators of the Seacat and Tartar surface-to-air anti-aircraft missiles to train with live targets. The Jindivik could also simulate an enemy aircraft or cruise missile attack on ships.[53] The Royal Air Force acquired more than half of the total production of Jindiviks and operated them in Wales. Britain ordered a further fifteen Jindiviks that were produced on the reopened production line in 1997. In British service alone, the Jindivik carried out more than 7,000 sorties.[54]

In operation, a team flew the Jindivik from a ground control station. The Jindivik spent most of its mission under the control of an autopilot, while the ground control team sent

Naval gunnery target drones

Throughout their existence, drones have proved invaluable as training targets for anti-aircraft gunnery. The development and subsequent successes of the Queen Bee and the Denny Radioplane, among others, demonstrates the importance of drones as a training tool. As one naval aviation magazine from 1945 noted, many of the downed enemy aircraft throughout the Second World War were destroyed due to the drone-facilitated training for anti-aircraft gunners, pilots and air-crewmen who honed their targeting skills.[52] This continues to the current day. Numerous military forces around the world employ unmanned aircraft to facilitate more challenging and realistic training for their personnel than would otherwise be possible. Target drones are usually made to closely resemble real-world aircraft, as providing this realism is central to their purpose: to develop and test military systems (such as the efficacy of anti-aircraft systems) and to train military personnel in threat aircraft identification skills. To maximise their effectiveness in these roles, contemporary target drones are usually complex systems able to perform difficult manoeuvres and adapt to differing needs. Some feature smoke and infra-red flares to provide visual and heat source cues for weapons systems. The Royal Australian Navy began training at sea with the GAF Jindivik Pilotless Target Aircraft in 1952 as part of a bilateral missile testing agreement between Australia and Britain. Since that time, target drones have become a key aspect of naval gunnery training in Australia.

(QinetiQ AirAffairs)

A typical Jindivik mission

A typical Jindivik mission began with launch from a self-steering trolley that accelerated along a runway until it reached a speed of 110 knots (200 km/h). Reaching this speed, the drone deployed its flaps, pushed its elevators up and released from the trolley to begin the mission. Rather than the ground controller maintaining direct control of the drone throughout its flight, the Jindivik operated via an autopilot that received radio commands. There were 24 commands in total, 18 for various autopilot flight commands and another 6 to operate the other onboard equipment. Used mainly by the Royal Air Force, the RAAF and the Royal Australian Navy, later versions of the Jindivik operated out of the Jervis Bay Range Facility in New South Wales for training in live missile and gunnery practice. Surface-based missile systems, such as the Tartar and Seacat, used Jindiviks as targets. This was invaluable for the Seacat, which used a human operator to guide the missile onto its target. The Royal Australian Navy's A4 Skyhawk fighter-bombers used the Jindivik as a target for their Sidewinder air-to-air missiles; the drone could also be fitted with countermeasure systems for more realistic training or to simulate enemy missile or aircraft attack on ships. When the training phase of the mission was complete, azimuth and elevation vectors were used to align the drone onto the runway and initiate landing. Landing at 125–150 knots (230–280 km/h), as the Jindivik touched down on its single fuselage skid, operators commanded it to bank. This made 'shoes' on either wingtip touch the runway so operators could control its path along the ground as the drone slowed to a stop.[57]

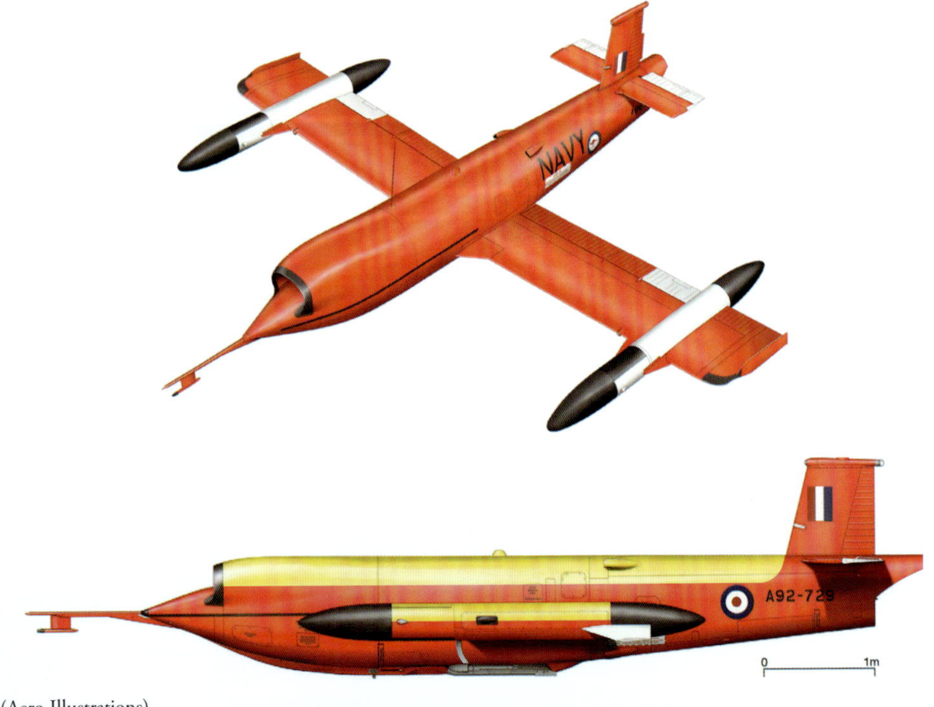

(Aero Illustrations)

Flying the Pika

In 1948, the Australian Government entered a bilateral agreement with Britain for a guided-missile testing project that required an unmanned target aircraft capable of 15-minute sorties at 40,000 ft. Australia began developing a drone called the Jindivik;[62] two years later, the first flight of the project's manned prototype, the Pika, took off from South Australia's Woomera airfield. Two Pikas were produced by the Government Aircraft Factories in Melbourne, Victoria as a proof-of-concept to test the Jindivik's aerodynamics, engine and radio control systems.[63] They remain the only Australian-designed and built manned jet aircraft to date. Like the Jindivik 1, the Pika was powered by a single Armstrong Siddeley Adder turbojet and could reach a maximum speed of more than 400 knots (755 km/h). Although the addition of a pilot reduced the fuel load and thus decreased flight endurance to 30 minutes, the Pika provided an invaluable training opportunity. Capable of being piloted manually or remotely, it enabled the future Jindivik ground station operators to train with an aircraft while having the added assurance of a pilot in the cockpit to take control if necessary. John Miles, one of the three Pika test pilots, said: 'While it may not have been ideal from a pilot's viewpoint, it provided a most useful test bed.'[64] Over the next four years, the two Pikas logged more than 100 flying hours in testing, and despite some minor accidents, the trials were successful. As well as vital operator training, this stage of the project proved the Jindivik did not need a rudder; this saved cost and weight in the drone's production. The Pika was a crucial step in creating the Jindivik: Australia's first national drone.[65]

(Aero Illustrations)

commands to alter its flightpath and speed. Pilots did, however, control the launch and landing sequences. Weighing more than 1,500 kilograms on take-off, these jet-powered drones could fly at a maximum altitude of 66,000 feet during their 15-minute sortie time.[55] Like the Queen Bee before it, the Jindivik could self-destruct on command from the ground or from a chase aircraft if flight control was lost.[56]

Most of the Jindiviks were shot at directly – resulting in their destruction in case of a hit. As missiles became more accurate, there was a danger of losing all Jindiviks to practice strikes. So, by the 1990s, a system was devised whereby the drone trailed either a flare pod, infra-red or radar target that acted as a decoy for heat-seeking and other missiles. This avoided the missiles hitting the actual drone, and the near miss was recorded on a camera mounted on the Jindivik to confirm the accuracy of the strike.[58] The Jindivik played a very important part in the international development and introduction of a range of surface-to-air and air-to-air missiles.

Part of the story of the GAF Jindivik is the inhabited test version of the drone used to check its aerodynamics, flight performance and control systems. Two of these were built and designated the GAF Pika, an Australian First Nations word meaning 'flier'.[59] The first one flew in 1950, and they hold the reputation as the smallest piloted jet aircraft ever made. Australian test pilots flew 214 flights in the Pika between 1950 and 1954.[60] The aircraft proved invaluable as the test bed for the remote-control equipment to be fitted to the pilotless Jindivik. While very similar in design to the Jindivik, the Pika had a cockpit with manual flight controls and a retractable undercarriage installed in the centre section of the fuselage. The jet engine air intake, which normally ran through the that area, was split to enter the fuselage from each side. The pilot was able to fly the aircraft in the conventional manner or use the autopilot functions as they would have operated in the Jindivik.[61] One of the two Pikas survives and is on display at the RAAF Museum, Point Cook, Victoria.

A deficiency of the Jindivik was the small target size it presented – either visually or as an infra-red heat signature – to pilots, ground radar stations and the missiles themselves compared with the size of actual fighters and bombers. A solution developed during the late 1950s was to convert obsolete Gloster Meteor jet fighters to remote control. These flew between 1957 and 1974, carrying out 477 sorties at Woomera. A total of 81 Meteors were destroyed during the program – 59 were destroyed by missile strikes, while the remainder succumbed to flight malfunctions. Also, 17 Canberra bombers were converted to remote control in Northern Ireland during 1959–65 and flown to Woomera. The first target flight was successful, with the Canberra drone being shot down at 50,000 feet by a ground-fired missile.[66]

Prior to the introduction of the Jindivik into service with the Royal Australian Navy, a small piston-engine radio-controlled drone helped to train shipborne operators of the Navy's Seacat air-defence missiles. The Navy acquired and operated 54 Northrop Radioplane KD2R5 Shelduck target drones between 1963 and 1973. The disposable target drone, made in the United States in several variants, served 18 nations, and more than 60,000 went into service.[67]

The Shelduck

In 1962, the Royal Australian Navy placed an order with American firm Northrop for ten KD2R5 Shelducks to be delivered in 1963. Over the next decade, the Navy used the drone predominantly to train Seacat operators in anti-aircraft surface-to-air missile and gunnery practice. Unlike the Jindivik, which later replaced it in naval gunnery training, the Shelduck was operated entirely onboard ships at sea. During its service, it flew from any ship capable of operating these aircraft, including HMAS *Sydney* and HMAS *Duchess*. The operating team for the drone was small, consisting of only six personnel who had to work together to get the Shelduck into the air. The drone was mounted on the horizontal launch ramp while the crew powered up the four-stroke piston engine, attached equipment (such as the parachute used for recovery) and conducted final checks. The launch ramp was then elevated to the launch angle, and the solid-fuel boost rocket was activated. Once airborne, the Shelduck had roughly an hour-long flight time, and operators had to maintain visual contact throughout the sortie, as the air and ground systems frequently lost contact. In the early June 1964 trials, a Seacat fired from HMAS *Derwent* successfully hit a Shelduck launched from HMAS *Anzac*. However, over the drone's service life, the majority were recorded as lost at sea during training missions.[68] The Jindivik soon replaced the Shelduck. Northrop later evolved into Northrop Grumman, which today produces the MQ-4C Triton drone being acquired by the RAAF.[69]

(Australian War Memorial NAVY06622, NAVY10559)

The propeller-driven Shelduck could climb to 23,000 feet and had a maximum speed of 200 knots (370 km/h). It was launched with either a bungee catapult or from a rocket-assisted-take-off ramp. It was able to simulate attacks by aircraft against ships and could be fitted with wing-tip reflectors to appear as an attacking aircraft on ships' radars. During a trial in 1964, a Shelduck launched from HMAS *Anzac* was brought down by a Seacat missile fired from HMAS *Derwent*.[70] The Shelduck was also used as an anti-aircraft gunnery target. If a Shelduck survived its sacrificial mission, it could deploy a parachute and be recovered from the water. The drone was effectively a stopgap used for missile defence training while the Jindivik was being brought into operational service with the Navy. Unlike the Jindivik, the Shelduck could be launched from ships in the open sea, which gave added realism to the training.[71]

Government Aircraft Factories (GAF) embarked on another Australian-made target drone in the late 1960s. The Turana – thought to be named after an Australian First Nations word for 'rainbow' – was a jet-engine target drone that could be launched from ships using the existing Ikara anti-submarine missile launchers fitted to Royal Australian Navy River-class frigates and Perth-class destroyers. Following its development and testing phase at Woomera, the Turana was intended for use as a target drone for ship-based missile defence system training and gunnery training.[72] The drone was recovered by boat after parachuting to the water at the completion of its mission. Twenty-three Turanas were built before the manufacturing program was cancelled in 1979. Technical problems and cost overruns contributed to the cancellation. The Jindivik, therefore, continued as the Navy's gunnery and missile defence training drone.[73]

GAF Turana P1-023 was the last built (below), and P1-011 is shown with its rocket boost motor fitted (Aero Illustrations)

Significantly, the skills and experience gained in Australia through the Anglo–Australian Joint Project between 1946 and 1980 built on those gained by the nation's aircraft manufacturers during the Second World War and have provided the basis for Australia's aerospace industry ever since. Manufacturing itself is no longer in government hands; private industry has played the major role in aircraft manufacture, supply and maintenance for some time.

GAF, renamed Aerospace Technologies Australia, moved into private hands in 1995, when it became Boeing Australia. Australian company de Havilland Aircraft, which was formed in 1927 as a subsidiary of Britain's de Havilland Aircraft Company, was taken over by Hawker-Siddeley in 1960. The de Havilland Aircraft company was renamed Hawker de Havilland from 1965. The Commonwealth Aircraft Corporation, which was formed in 1936, became part of Hawker de Havilland in 1985, and both companies ultimately became part of Boeing Australia in 2000.

Beyond local aircraft manufacture and assembly, several aircraft have entered Australian service since the Second World War through overseas suppliers. American company Lockheed began its Australian connection with the introduction of the Hudson light bomber into RAAF service in 1940. The company continues as a major contributor to Australian aerospace as Lockheed-Martin Australia. Two British companies, the Bristol Aeroplane Company and the English Electric Company, provided aircraft for use on the Woomera test range as part of the Anglo–Australian Joint Project and amalgamated to become the British Aircraft Corporation in 1960. The company now serves the Australian defence sector as BAE Systems Australia.

Air Target Services Australia technician Matthew Odd preparing a Phoenix jet before launching in support of a 16th Regiment, Royal Australian Artillery missile firing exercise at the Woomera Range Complex, South Australia, 2018 (Craig Barrett)

The Australian aerospace industry sector is also rich in component manufacturers and providers of aviation services. The sector manufactures products such as airframes, avionics and ground support equipment. It provides services encompassing maintenance, design, research and training, and it has increased its rate of exports over time. The sector is highly regarded for its technical expertise and standards and is, therefore, strongly placed in global aviation supply chains.[74] Further, rather than being locked in fierce competition, aerospace companies in Australia have often cooperated to provide different aspects of the one project. Participation by the aerospace industry sector in the acquisition of new capabilities is a very good way to ensure the ADF is well supported in the development, maintenance, modification and sustainment of its capabilities.[75] 'Gun runners' – as the employees of most aerospace industry companies are affectionately known – are often ex-military members who have moved on to a new aspect of their career. This is only natural, as they have spent many years, often in operational environments, gaining the knowledge and skills required to assist in the development of new military technology.

One major benefit of the sector's standing is that it increases Australia's access to military off-the-shelf (MOTS) aerospace products. These are military hardware items and any associated software made by commercial suppliers for immediate use by many military organisations worldwide. MOTS can allow for the rapid acquisition of military capabilities by being ready to meet anticipated military needs, rather than being supplied after designing and manufacturing a bespoke capability to meet a specification laid down by a military organisation.

Kalkara guided target system launching from the Gilbert Point launch site, HMAS *Stirling* Garden Island, Western Australia, 1999 (Defence)

One such acquisition was the BAE MQM-107E Kalkara Unmanned Aerial Target. The Kalkara, given an Australian First Nations name meaning 'storm bird', began trials with the Royal Australian Navy in 1998 and ultimately replaced the Jindivik as the Navy's aerial target for missile defence training.[76] BAE Systems supplied 20 of these jet-engine drones to the Navy. They were able to simulate a missile or aircraft about to attack a ship in order to test the ship's detection and defence systems and to train the systems' operators. They flew in a similar speed range to missiles and jet fighters and at similar altitudes – 100 feet to 40,000 feet. Typical Kalkara flights lasted between 30 and 60 minutes.[77] The drones were launched from a stand with rocket assistance and were recovered by stopping the engine and parachuting them into the ocean by for retrieval by boat. Each drone was expected to perform a minimum of 17 flights.[78]

The Kalkara could be fired at directly, or it could tow a Hayes drogue-type target behind it.[79] These targets can project an infra-red or radar signal that mimics an aircraft. The drones operated at Jervis Bay in New South Wales, HMAS *Stirling* in Western Australia and Woomera in South Australia. At Woomera, the drone proved valuable in trials for the introduction of air-to-air missile systems into service with the RAAF.[80]

In an arrangement similar to other highly technical MOTS acquisitions, the Kalkara was operated by a defence support provider, in this case Boeing Australia. Boeing provided all maintenance and repairs for the drone and its ground control stations. It prepared the drone for flight, and Boeing staff members operated the drone during its mission. The Kalkara served the Royal Australian Navy until 2008, and the Navy has not acquired a new drone to perform its role.[81]

Israel Aerospace Industries Scout drone being refuelled by Australian Army and contractor staff during evaluation trials, 1993 (Defence)

As light drone capability progressed throughout the 1970s and 1980s, notably with developments in military drones in Israel, the Australian Army began to take an interest in acquiring them for use on the battlefield. Project Land 53, also known as Project *Ninox*, sought to improve the Army's night fighting and surveillance capabilities. An aerial surveillance drone capability was part of that effort.[82] In 1993, the project invited Israel Aerospace Industries (IAI) to demonstrate two types of drones in Australia to prove their value. These were the IAI Scout and Searcher. Both types were powered by a piston engine, and take-offs and landings were controlled by a pilot using a radio-control aircraft-style handset. These corporal-ranked pilots passed control of the drones to commissioned officer pilots for the navigation phases of the flight once airborne. The drones' sensor operators were artillery soldiers.[83]

Canadian CL-327 Bombardier Guardian during Australian trials, 1999
(Federation of American Scientists)

The trials – conducted at Kununurra in Western Australia and Tindal in the Northern Territory in conjunction with the Defence Science and Technology Organisation (DSTO) – were a success, and they demonstrated the ability to share drone sensor data with ground and airborne assets.[84] However, the process of acquiring a drone capability for the Army ran into bureaucratic delays. In 1997, the drone aspects of Project *Ninox* became a separate joint project. Project *Warrendi* – named for the Narungga-Kaurna word meaning 'to seek' – was officially known as Joint Project 129 (JP129).[85] This new project was also carried out in conjunction with the DSTO and sought to bring tactical surveillance drones into service in the ADF, including the eventual installation of synthetic aperture radar. Its first drone trial used a Canadian-made Bombardier Aerospace CL-327 Guardian vertical take-off and landing (VTOL) drone carrying electro-optical infra-red (EOIR) sensors for tactical surveillance.[86] The successful trial was conducted in 1999 during Exercise *Crocodile 99*, based at RAAF Base Tindal in the Northern Territory, and led to JP129 Phase 2 in 2001 that sought to introduce the first tactical drones for deployed use in the ADF, the IAI Malat I-View 250A. The contract to provide two of these was awarded to Boeing Australia in December 2006.[87] This acquisition, however, did not eventuate for a range of technical reasons, and the project began the long search for an alternative after seven years in planning and development.[88]

Meanwhile, the Army had adopted a range of interim military-off-the-shelf (MOTS) drones for use in trials and on operations during the lead up to the eventual cancelation of JP129 Phase 2. The first such interim drone was the CX-1 Avatar. The Army made a rapid acquisition purchase of five to assess their use in battlefield aerial reconnaissance in 2000. The Avatar is a small, electric-powered, close-range drone that is launched and recovered by hand. The drones were made in Queanbeyan by Codarra Advanced Systems.[89] They were allocated to infantry regiments, the Special Air Service Regiment (SASR) and an artillery locating battery. Inexperience as drone operators led to the Army damaging most of them during trials, and one was last seen heading towards Parramatta after being launched from Holsworthy Barracks in New South Wales.[90] Despite these issues, the SASR did deploy them briefly in 2000 to Timor-Leste in support of Operation *Astute* and during the Sydney Olympics. The Army purchased more Avatars of an upgraded design in 2002. The surveillance troop of the 131st Surveillance and Target Acquisition Battery (131 STA) took on the Avatars for further trials and training before finally disposing of them.[91]

Codarra CX-1 Avatar (Defence)

The DSTO also conducted experiments in autonomous flight controlled by artificial intelligence using Avatars at the Army's restricted Graytown Range north of Melbourne between 2004 and 2008. The AI software, developed by Melbourne company Agent Oriented Software, controlled the drone's autopilot during flight and modified its route to meet set waypoints as efficiently as possible considering real-time weather conditions. This was claimed to be a world-first achievement for a drone.[92]

In the tradition of Australian aviation and technical innovation, an Aerosonde Mark 1 drone, named *Laima*, was the first drone to cross the Atlantic Ocean, which it did in 1998 in 26 hours and 45 minutes. The drone was made by Environmental Systems and Services in Melbourne, Victoria and was brought to operational status by a consortium of international industry and government partners. At only 13 kilograms, it was also the smallest aircraft to make the crossing at the time.[93]

The Aerosonde range of drones is primarily for use in government and industry survey and inspection roles in areas such as mining and meteorology. However, a version of the Mark 3, known as the AeroGuard, was put into military use when 131 STA deployed four of them on Operation *Anode* in 2003 as part of the Regional Assistance Mission to the Solomon Islands. The drones were employed in an Army ISTAR role as well as for relaying communications to ground troops in remote areas. Commanders in the field also noted the presence of a drone had a psychological effect on the activities of local militia groups.[94]

The deployment of the AeroGuards was managed as part of the DSTO's Project *Nervana*, and the team comprised military members, scientists, imagery specialists and Aerosonde staff.[95] The project aimed to examine aspects of the battlefield that could be automated, particularly by providing live video images to ground commanders.[96] The five-week deployment was used to trial drones under operational conditions, after tests in Victoria and the Northern Territory, and it aimed to build on the ADF's drone expertise and provide data for future drone acquisitions.[97] Importantly, the air traffic control of the drones at Henderson Airfield in the Solomon Islands, in conjunction with normal international airfield operations, was a first for RAAF air traffic controllers.[98]

The deployment to the Solomon Islands in 2003 was widely claimed to be the first time the ADF had used a drone on operations.[99] At the time the claim was made, the use of the CX-1 Avatar by the SASR in Timor-Leste in 2000 was still classified secret.

A soldier of the US Army 27th Infantry Regiment preparing to launch a Raven drone during a joint US and Iraqi cordon and search operation, Patika Province, Iraq, 2006 (Michael Guillory)

AeroGuard missions in the Solomon Islands

In 2003, the 131st STA Battery detachment commenced daily Aerosonde operations by ensuring positive airspace de-confliction with all military and civilian airspace users in the area. Their base at Honiara International Airport on Guadalcanal in the Solomon Islands was ideal both for facilitating this de-confliction and for allowing the detachment to site the ground control station (GCS) close to the runway for efficient launch and recovery phases. One of the detachment's four AeroGuard drones – deployed in support of the Regional Assistance Mission to the Solomon Islands (RAMSI) – was loaded onto a launch frame on the roof of a Land Rover in preparation for take-off before the vehicle accelerated to 80 km/h down the runway. After travelling 500 metres, the drone separated from the frame and took flight under the manual control of the aircraft operator before being handed over to the GCS to commence the pre-programmed, automated flight plan.[100] Over five weeks, the detachment flew 22 sorties and accumulated 106 flying hours, covering more than 4,100 nautical miles.[101] During these missions, the Aerosonde flew to remote RAMSI areas of interest to capture imagery the detachment aimed to analyse and provide to the Combined Task Force Headquarters within 60 minutes of the aircraft's recovery.[102] At times, the detachment also relayed communications for remote ground-based forces.[103] The effects were far reaching. As mission commander Lieutenant Colonel Frewen wrote in *Defence* magazine: 'Our tactical UAVs were also a potent psychological tool that clearly played on people's minds. We openly displayed our abilities, and the imagination of the locals took over from there.'[104] The use of the Aerosonde in the Solomon Islands for Operation *Anode* in 2003 was the Australian Army's first official operational deployment of a drone and provided a valuable experience from which to continue developing the ADF's drone capability.

(Gary Ramage)

Another interim drone purchased directly from the manufacturer under a rapid acquisition arrangement was the AeroVironment RQ-11 Raven. They were purchased in 2004 under Project *Redfin* for the SASR, which used them to conduct trials of their observation capabilities.[105] Widely used by United States special forces, the Raven is hand launched and powered by an electric motor that drives a propeller. It weighs less than two kilograms and operates at heights below 500 feet, carrying an optical and infra-red camera and a thermal imager.[106] The SASR is reported to have used the Raven with the Special Operations Task Group (SOTG) in Afghanistan.[107]

The next interim drone capability to enter service with the ADF while awaiting the outcomes of JP129 was the Israeli-made Elbit Systems Skylark 1. These were purchased directly from the manufacturer in 2005 as another rapid acquisition. The Skylark was an electric-powered, hand-launched drone weighing only 4.5 kilograms and with a wingspan of two metres. It had a flight duration of up to an hour. The payload could be changed between an electro-optic camera and an infra-red camera. In each case, unlike the Raven, the cameras could be locked onto a target to provide a constant video feed of a point on the ground. The Army deployed the Skylark to southern Iraq in early 2006 in support of the Al Muthanna Task Group, which later became the Overwatch Battle Group (West).[108] The Skylark also deployed to Timor-Leste as part of the United Nations Integrated Mission in East Timor on Operation *Astute* in 2007. It did so with the former 131 STA, which had become part of the 20th Surveillance and Target Acquisition Regiment (20 STA) in the previous year. Their use of drones on the deployment was not widely publicised until one crashed into the wall of a suburban house in Dili in May 2007.[109] Between 2007 and 2014, the SOTG also deployed the Skylark to Tarin Kot in Afghanistan in support of the NATO-led International Security Assistance Force (ISAF). [110]

Sergeant Kev Waugh (left) holding a Skylark drone used for reconnaissance missions in discussion with a British Army general, Iraq (Defence)

The Skylark proved the value of tactical drones for the Army, but it highlighted the need for a more persistent surveillance and target acquisition drone. This low-altitude, long-endurance Insitu ScanEagle, weighing 15 kilograms and with a flight duration of up to 18 hours, proved to be the answer. The petrol-powered drone was based on the Insitu SeaScan commercial drone, which was developed for collecting weather data and helping fishermen locate schools of tuna. It was already being used by the United States Marine Corps and United States Navy and could range as far as 100 kilometres from the controller. Like the Skylark, it could carry a sensor payload, interchangeable between an electro-optic camera and an infra-red camera. This reduced their potential 18-hour flight times, as the cameras were only suited to either day or night.[111] The ScanEagle was launched by a pneumatic launcher and captured, rather than landed, by flying it into an arrestor wire that caught the wingtip. This eliminated the need for runways and allowed the drone to operate from forward areas.[112]

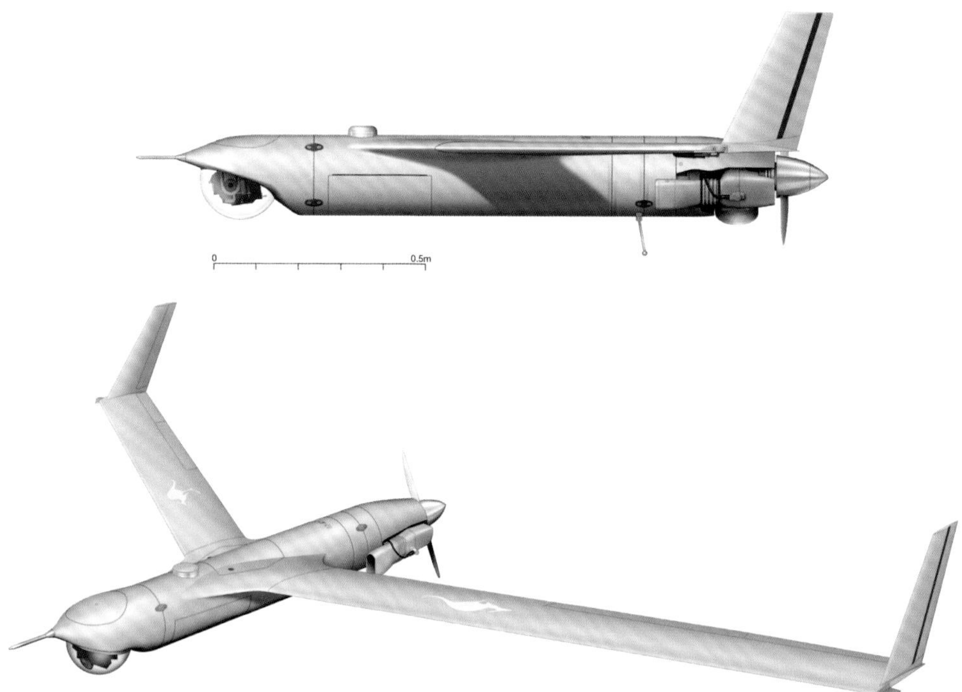

Boeing Insitu ScanEagle drones from 20th Surveillance and Target Acquisition Regiment: 07-455 used at Tarin Kot Air Base, Afghanistan (perspective) and 06-274 used at Talil Air Base, Iraq (profile) (Aero Illustrations)

The increased size and complexity of the ScanEagle meant expert civilian contractors were needed for take-off, landing and maintenance. These civilian operators were included in the partnered contract with InSitu Pacific and Boeing Australia to lease and operate the ScanEagle. They deployed with soldiers from 20 STA in Iraq in late 2006 in support of Overwatch Battle Group (West) during Operation *Catalyst*. The drones operated from Talil Air Base and were controlled through dedicated ground control stations. These were sometimes mounted in armoured ASLAV and Bushmaster tactical vehicles. The drones accompanied convoys and were used to searched for improvised explosive devices.[113]

Boeing contractor operating a ScanEagle at Ali Air Base, southern Iraq, as part of the Overwatch Battle Group (West), May 2008 (Michael Cecil, Australian War Memorial P10237.030)

The ScanEagle proved to be a major step forward in real-time ISR support to Australia's deployed troops, and the ADF established a second contract in mid-2007 to use them at Kandahar Airfield in Afghanistan in support of the Reconstruction Task Force and the SOTG during Operation *Slipper*. The innovative team in Afghanistan developed a means of powering the ground control stations to make them portable.[114] The ScanEagle remained in service with the Army until mid-2012, when it was replaced by the RQ-7B Shadow.

Arrestor wire rig used to recover ScanEagle drones from flight, Tari Kot, Afghanistan, 2009 (Nick Fletcher, Australian War Memorial P09831.119)

With the success of the partnership between the ADF and InSitu Pacific, the company established its own operations in Brisbane, Queensland, which further reinforces the organic links between defence and industry in Australia. Alongside working with the ADF, InSitu's Australian base trains civilian drone operators and works with commercial and civil organisations to meet their drone requirements.[115]

Following the five-year success of the ScanEagle in ADF hands in Afghanistan, the Army sought a more modern replacement. In a foreign military sales agreement that involved the United States Army, Textron Systems Australia and American company AAI Corporation, the Army acquired the RQ-7B Shadow 200 tactical reconnaissance drone.[116] Variants of the Shadow were already in operational service with the United States Army in Iraq and Afghanistan.[117] Between late-2011 and 2013, the Army acquired 18 Shadow drones.[118]

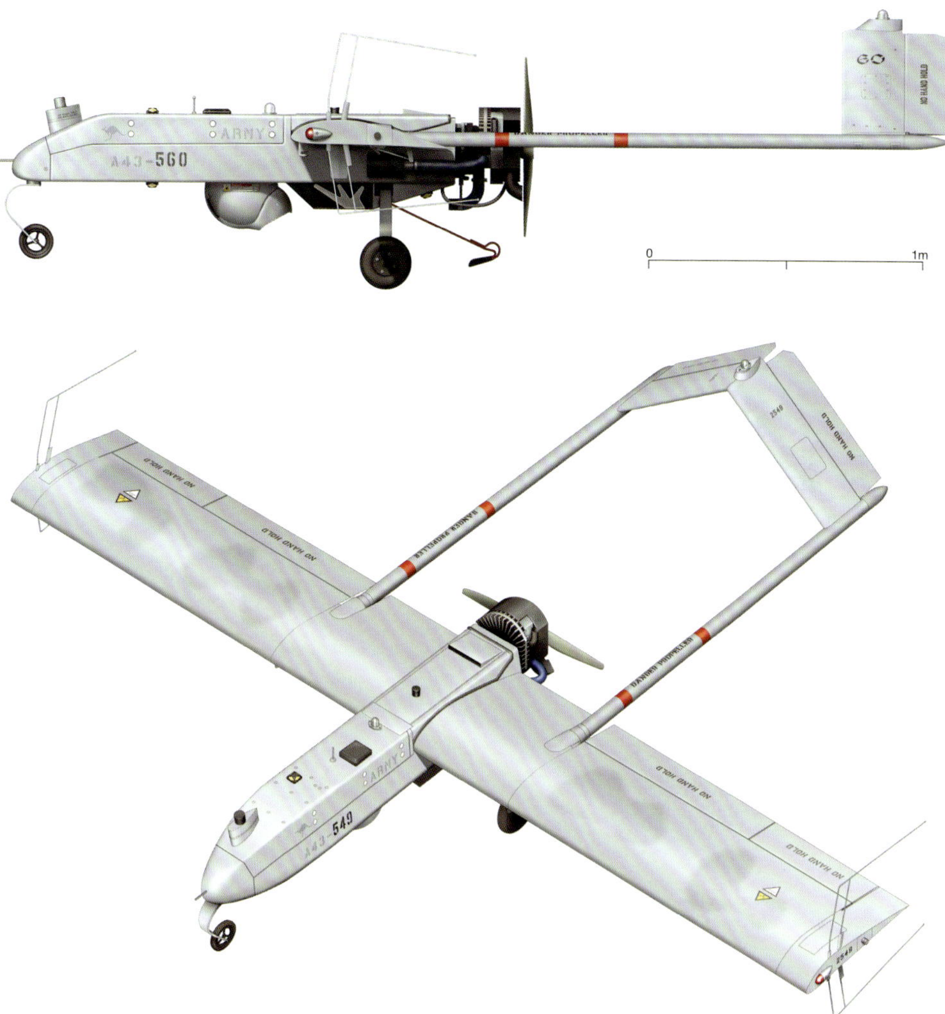

RQ-7B Shadow 200 drones: A43-549 shown as tested at Woomera in 2011 (perspective) and A43-560 used by 20th Surveillance and Target Acquisition Regiment at Tarin Kot Air Base, Afghanistan, 2012 (profile) (Aero Illustrations)

The Shadow is launched by a pneumatic catapult mounted on a trailer and is captured during landing by an arrestor wire laid on the ground between two weights; the drone's tail hook catches the wire. The 200-kilogram drone is powered by a rotary internal-combustion engine driving a propeller. As a primary payload, the Shadow carries a sensor suite that comprises an infra-red camera, an electro-optical camera and a laser system. It can fly for up to eight hours.[119] While this is significantly less than its ScanEagle predecessor, the capability of the sensor payload was greatly increased. Overall, the image quality was better, it was able to relay communications to areas otherwise out of range, and it carried a laser target designator.[120] The laser designator was able to guide munitions, including artillery shells and bombs, onto targets. The version of the Shadow acquired for Australian use differed from the standard United States Army version. Australian radios and intelligence processing were used instead of the American equipment; rather than Humvee support vehicles, the Australian Shadows used ADF Unimog trucks. Nonetheless, the ADF used the United States Army logistics support system, training and simulators.[121]

Shadow drone being prepared for launch at the staging and operating area, Tarin Kot Airfield, Afghanistan, 2012 (Stephen Dupont, Australian War Memorial P10950.469)

The Army's 20 STA operated four Shadows from Tarin Kot from early 2012,[122] conducting ISTAR missions for the SOTG in support of the NATO-led ISAF mission in Afghanistan.[123] They operated the Shadow there until November 2013, providing ground troops with near real-time video imagery for more than two years. Typical Shadow missions included route reconnaissance, point reconnaissance and surveillance flights to monitor pattern-of-life activities.[124] At the time of writing, the Shadow continues as an ISTAR drone with 20 STA at its home base of Enoggera Barracks in Queensland and is due to be replaced under Project Land 129 Phase 3, which JP129 has subsequently been renamed.

In 2012, the Royal Australian Navy began trials with the ScanEagle, previously only operated by the Army.[125] The Navy formed the Navy UAS Development Unit (NUASDU) in that year to conduct drone experimentation and gain an in-depth understanding of their use in the maritime environment. NUASDU began flight trials with a leased InSitu ScanEagle from Jervis Bay Airfield in March 2013, and by May, Navy crew members of the unit, in conjunction with InSitu contractors, gave a demonstration of flying the ScanEagle from HMAS *Parramatta*.[126] NUASDU was renamed as the Navy UAS Unit (NUASU) when it acquired two more ScanEagles for further sea trials in 2015. NUASU acquired the two drone systems from the Army at a nominal price of $1 by transferring the lease.[127] One was subsequently flown for operational evaluation purposes from HMAS *Newcastle* while deployed on Operation *Manitou* to the Middle East Region in 2017.[128] Significantly, the ScanEagle was the first drone to operate simultaneously in the same airspace as a manned Royal Australian Navy aircraft – an MH-60R Seahawk helicopter. This achievement, which occurred during Operation *Manitou*, demonstrated the possibility of operating drones and manned aircraft safely in close proximity in the military environment.[129]

ScanEagle drone being launched from the flight deck of HMAS *Newcastle* in the Middle East region, 2017 (Nicolas Gonzalez)

NUASU went on to become the Navy's first experimental drone squadron, commissioned as 822X Squadron, in 2018. The squadron seeks to develop the Navy's familiarity and experience with maritime tactical drones, notably for their ISR capabilities in support of surface, amphibious and anti-submarine warfare, and search and rescue, along with a range of personnel protection activities.[130] The squadron began evaluation trials with the Schiebel S-100 Camcopter in 2017. This Austrian-made drone was already in service with other military forces worldwide. Streamlined like a fish in appearance, this 200-kilogram VTOL drone can operate from unprepared areas without launch or recovery infrastructure, such as runways, launchers or arrestor wires.[131] Driven by an internal combustion engine, the Camcopter can be configured in several different ways and can be flown directly by a pilot or with an autopilot. Its standard endurance is up to six hours, and it can operate up to 18,000 feet.[132] At the time of writing, the Navy is also evaluating ScanEagle drones for further uses in relaying communications, ocean mapping and electronic warfare.[133]

Schiebel Camcopter S-100 drone from the Royal Australia Navy's 822X Squadron landing on the flight deck of MV *Sycamore* off the coast of New South Wales, 2020 (Defence)

Until 2004, the RAAF had little experience with drones since the Queen Bee of the late 1930s. However, in that year, the RAAF quietly began gaining drone expertise through being involved with the BAE Systems HERTI drone during its secretive flight trials. HERTI – 'high endurance rapid technology insertion' – was developed in the United Kingdom and made its first flight in December 2004 at Woomera.[134] Tests of the HERTI drone flying in civil airspace took place at West Sale aerodrome in Victoria in 2007. In another collaboration, between the British Ministry of Defence and Australian aerospace industry,[135] BAE Systems also later tested their Mantis and Taranis drones at Woomera.[136] Drones take considerable time to develop; while the Australian aerospace industry has been successful with significant elements of drone innovation over time, it has largely been left to supporting, operating and maintaining roles for foreign-made systems in recent years.[137]

Battlefield reconnaissance has evolved over the past two centuries, notably in response to developments in technology that have allowed military commanders and tacticians increasingly to take a bird's eye view. Engaging with those technological advances has always held an element of physical risk to those who operate them. However, the advent of modern, sophisticated military drones has brought a new era that keeps observers safer than ever before while providing high standards of ISR and strike capabilities. For more than eight decades, Australia's military forces have been engaged with drones, and the nation's defence industry has been there to support them and provide innovation, often at the leading edge of technology. Initially used by the ADF in naval gunnery training, drones developed to match the performance of the potential attack aircraft and missiles they simulated. The advances of the digital age have brought new uses for the ADF's drones, which range from ISR to target identification and even laser target designation.

HERTI drone flying over Woomera during Australian trials, 2004 (Defence)

Chapter 2

CATCHING A BIRD

Before the tragic Black Hawk helicopter crash that took three Australian lives and injured a further seven at Shah Wali Kot in 2010, Australia had been fighting in Afghanistan for almost a decade. The War in Afghanistan began on 7 October 2001, when the United States invaded the country and toppled the Taliban government. It had refused to hand over terrorist leader Osama bin Laden, who was responsible for al-Qaeda's September 11 attacks on the United States. Australia joined the United States-led International Coalition Against Terrorism in November 2001 to help disrupt the use of Afghanistan as a terrorist base and to remove the influence of the Taliban and al-Qaeda in the country.[1] With the success of the Coalition's initial attacks, the Taliban leadership had relocated to southern Afghanistan and into adjoining Pakistan.

ADF members were assigned to warlike operations in Afghanistan under Operation *Slipper*, which ran from 2001 to 2014. The operation was Australia's military contribution to the International Security Assistance Force (ISAF) of the same time period. The primary goal of ISAF was to train the Afghan National Security Forces (ANSF) and assist in rebuilding the country's government and national institutions, with an ultimate aim of transitioning security responsibilities to the ANSF. By the beginning of the second decade of the War in Afghanistan, ISAF had 400 military bases in the country. Most Australian forces held the counterinsurgency role in the southern provinces of Uruzgan and Kandahar. They were right in the thick of the Taliban's insurgency operations. What role did drones play in ISAF's effort to meet it aims?

By 2010, there was a proliferation of drones in a variety of roles. A wide range of ISAF contributing nations were using a bewildering number of drones in the skies over Afghanistan. The war was dubbed 'the drone war' for good reason. The non-exhaustive table below gives some idea of the range.

Nation	Drone	NATO Class	Category	Role
Canada	Heron Sperwer ScanEagle Maveric Silver Fox Skylark	III II I I I I	MALE Tactical UAV Small UAV Mini UAV Mini UAV Mini UAV	ISR ISR ISR ISR ISR ISR
Czech Republic	ScanEagle Raven	I I	Small UAV Mini UAV	ISR ISR
Denmark	Puma Raven	I I	Mini UAV Mini UAV	ISR ISR

Nation	Drone	NATO Class	Category	Role
France	Harfang Sperwer	III II	MALE Tactical UAV	ISR ISR
Germany	Heron KZO Luna Aladin Mikado	III II I I I	MALE Tactical UAV Small UAV Mini UAV Micro UAV	ISR ISR ISR ISR ISR
Hungary	Skylark	I	Mini UAV	ISR
Italy	Predator Reaper Shadow Bramor Strix-C	III III II I I	UCAV UCAV Tactical UAV Mini UAV Mini UAV	Strike/ISR Strike/ISR ISR ISR ISR
Netherlands	Aerostar Sperwer Aladin Raven	II II I I	Tactical UAV Tactical UAV Mini UAV Mini UAV	ISR ISR ISR ISR
Norway	Raven	I	Mini UAV	ISR
Poland	ScanEagle Orbiter	I I	Small UAV Mini UAV	ISR ISR
Romania	Shadow ScanEagle	II I	Tactical UAV Small UAV	ISR ISR
Singapore	Searcher	II	Tactical UAV	ISR
South Korea	RemoEye-006	I	Mini UAV	ISR
Spain	Searcher ScanEagle Raven	II I I	Tactical UAV Small UAV Mini UAV	ISR ISR ISR
Sweden	Shadow Skylark	II I	Tactical UAV Mini UAV	ISR ISR
United Arab Emirates	Seeker 200	II	Tactical UAV	ISR
United Kingdom	Reaper Hermes 450 Desert Hawk T-Hawk Black Hornet	III II I I I	UCAV Tactical UAV Mini UAV Mini UAV Micro UAV	Strike/ISR ISR ISR ISR ISR
United States	Predator Reaper Global Hawk Hunter K-MAX Pointer	III III III III III I	UCAV UCAV HALE MALE RC Helo Mini UAV	Strike/ISR Strike/ISR ISR ISR Air mobility ISR

Winning hearts and minds

The Australian mission in Afghanistan lasted 20 years, ending in 2021. During much of that time, 'winning hearts and minds' in the region was a cornerstone of Australia's counter-insurgency approach. Winning hearts and minds refers to efforts to provide civil support and reconstruction assistance to build ties with local communities. Seen as a way of improving stability in a region, the hearts and minds approach in Afghanistan also encouraged Afghan civilians to support and look favourably on Australian troops and their mission, increasing Afghan civilians' resilience against, and lack of support for, Taliban insurgents.[2] More than 26,000 Australian personnel served in Afghanistan during Operation *Slipper* from 2001 to 2014. Many of these personnel – as part of the Reconstruction Task Force (RTF) and Mentoring and Reconstruction Task Force (MRTF) rotations – were directly involved in tasks designed to rebuild Afghanistan's struggling infrastructure and empower its people. Engineer elements helped to construct and improve provincial infrastructure, such as schools, hospitals and bridges, while also aiding in the detection and disarming of countless improvised explosive devices placed near civilian roads and villages. RTF soldiers provided skilled-trade training to the local population and members of the Afghan National Army (ANA), while also mentoring their ANA counterparts in tactics, field skills and other essential military skills. These efforts focused on trying to reassure the people of Afghanistan that Australian soldiers were there to help and were trying to rebuild Afghanistan.[3]

(Mick Davis)

These drones served their nation's forces as national assets – looking after their own personnel, for the most part at a tactical level. The strike-capable drones were shared more broadly, as they carried a theatre-wide operational role. The War in Afghanistan had another distinct characteristic. Due to the nature of the weather and agriculture in the region and the roles played by Taliban sympathisers as farmers and combatants, there was a fighting season. The season started in spring and ran from April to October. Snow thaws in April each year and roads, including those into neighbouring Pakistan, reopen. Opium poppies are planted from October and harvested in April, and that workforce is available for fighting from April until the next planting season. Different types of drones came into their own depending on the season.

For the ADF, the ScanEagle drone used by the Army in Afghanistan from 2007 was serving well in an overwatch role to help protect route convoys and to provide a visible presence to act as a deterrent to insurgents. They did not, however, have persistence, and their low altitude and noise could sometimes give them away. They were useful in their role as a tactical local intelligence, surveillance and reconnaissance (ISR) asset.

An urgent problem

From 2008, the rate of improvised explosive devices (IED) attacks on Coalition forces in Afghanistan increased dramatically. IEDs had always been a feature of the conflict in Afghanistan – in fact, throughout the 20 years of the war, more than 800 American and 200 British military personnel were killed by IEDs. This number accounts for close to half the deaths of combatants from those nations. IED attacks were mounted against a total of 117 armed bases in Afghanistan, and most of those attacks were attributed to the Taliban.[4] By August 2008, the Australian Government became concerned about the escalating rate of IED attacks. The situation became increasingly urgent when Defence and Boeing Australia mutually terminated the Joint Project 129 (JP129) Phase 2 contract to provide the two Malat I-View 250 surveillance drones in September 2008, citing technical issues that made it difficult to provide the full scope of the contract in sufficient time.[5]

Members of the Mentoring Task Force forming a catafalque on the body of 22-year-old combat engineer Corporal Richard Atkinson during a memorial service at Tarin Kot, Afghanistan, after he was killed by an improvised explosive device on 2 February 2011 during a partnered Afghan National Army patrol in Uruzgan's Tangi Valley (Christopher Dickson)

A ScanEagle mission to remember

Retired Warrant Officer Class Two (WO2) Sue Osborn was a sergeant with the 20th Surveillance and Target Acquisition Regiment when she deployed to Afghanistan in 2010 as a ScanEagle mission commander. One mission, during which she was in direct support of American forces conducting a key leadership engagement (KLE) with local Afghan officials, remains a highlight of her deployment. Osborn had a stellar crew to work with. She had an excellent soldier, with whom she had strong rapport, as the air vehicle operator and an experienced image analyst. She remembered: 'It started the day prior, when a specialist signaller came into my GCS to install a US tactical satellite radio so I could have direct comms with the ground forces.' On the morning of the highlight mission, she had the aircraft on station at the required time and conducted a radio check with the ground call-sign. The ScanEagle crew's mission was to keep the aircraft ahead of the convoy, providing battlefield commentary and early warning. Once the road move was complete, Sergeant Osborn and her team scanned for suspicious activity; after almost half an hour, they found some. Two insurgents on a small motorcycle were approaching from an isolated dirt road, moving from one tree to another as if they were trying to avoid detection while getting closer to the KLE location. Osborn knew something was wrong and radioed the ground forces. 'Within seconds', she remembered, the American forces had engaged and neutralised the suspicious pair, and the mission continued without further incident, the ScanEagle escorting the forces back to base after the KLE was complete. Later that day, the American master gunner came down to the ScanEagle compound. 'He was ecstatic with the support I'd given his men on the ground,' Osborn said, 'and told me that my commentary had made their jobs so much easier.' He also told the ScanEagle crew that, without their hard work, the mission would not have been as successful. The two motorcycle riders had been armed, and it was likely they had planned a coordinated attack on the KLE VIPs, which would have been disastrous. 'It was the most stressful but also the most exciting mission I'd done to that point,' Osborn recalled, 'and one I will always remember.' This was just one example where the skilful employment of the ScanEagle drone in Afghanistan played a vital role in ensuring the safety of Coalition forces.

(Australian War Memorial P09971.001)

Up-armouring of tactical vehicles, improved body armour and radio-frequency jammers were all part of the solution. However, these measures were at the very end of the IED kill-chain, when ground forces were seeking to prevent an imminent attack or survive one. A better solution was to disrupt the chain earlier by discovering the devices as they were laid or, at least, the tell-tale signs of recent IED laying activity. Medium-altitude aerial surveillance was one possible way of doing this, and the Special Operations Task Group (SOTG) raised an operational urgent requirement (OUR) for airborne ISR with Joint Operations Command in late 2008.[6] The OUR specified downlinkable full-motion video capability to allow troops to see real-time video from laptop computers in the field. This type of drone capability was a need not anticipated during the development of the Defence Capability Plan published in 2009, but the National Security Committee directed it be fulfilled, nonetheless.[7] Why, then, did the ADF choose the Heron drone to address the increasing threat of IEDs to Australian forces?

Australian Army soldiers from the Special Operations Task Group patrolling in southern Afghanistan, 2010 (Chris Moore)

Two potential options were available to meet the OUR – manned aircraft or drones. The manned option was for contracted ISR aircraft based on the Beechcraft King Air. These were being introduced into service as the medium-altitude reconnaissance and surveillance system variant in support of American ground forces in Afghanistan at the time. This was the preferred option because it gave greater operational flexibility. However, as a contracted capability, this meant having civilians operating the sensors, which would be placing them directly in the kill-chain. Naturally, this was a situation that would need government consideration and approval. So, the matter was referred to the Attorney-General's Department for advice.

The IED threat in Afghanistan

IEDs (or improvised explosive devices) are particularly insidious weapons. They are not able to be monitored or controlled the same way conventional weapons used by state-based actors can be. IEDs can be made from commonly available components on a small scale in non-industrial – even domestic – settings. Insurgents commonly re-purpose conventional munitions, such as artillery and mortar shells, grenades and landmines left over from previous conflicts, adding trigger mechanisms to suit insurgent methods of operating. Ubiquitous palm oil containers often house the explosives. These improvised triggers can include simple pressure-plate switches made from old saw blades, tripwires linked to detonators or more sophisticated radio-controlled switches, often using garage door remotes and similar domestic devices. During the conflict in Afghanistan, IEDs became the insurgent weapon of choice.

The adverse effects of IEDs in Afghanistan were far greater than the tactical problems they caused for Coalition forces. They caused civilian casualties; they forced heavy military vehicles off some sections of road and into farmers' crops; they confined the movements of local populations. These effects worked directly against the effort to support local authorities and win hearts and minds. IEDs, therefore, were weapons of strategic influence.

IEDs had been part of the conflict in Afghanistan from the beginning, but their threat increased sufficiently by 2006 for the United States to form the Joint IED Defeat Organization. This provided greater effort in developing counter-IED tactics and equipment. Nonetheless, by 2008, insurgent successes against Coalition forces began to increase, and the Taliban gained considerable asymmetric advantage by using inexpensive weapons against the might of Coalition military technology.

(Mark Dowling)

Meanwhile, the RAAF had been exploring the use of drones. Despite having operated the de Havilland Queen Bee during the 1930s and some remote-controlled Meteor and Canberra aircraft at Woomera from the 1950s – all of which were variants of manned aircraft converted to drones – the RAAF had generally avoided aircraft without pilots in the cockpit and, therefore, had limited operational experience with drones. It had, however, recently taken part in some trials of the Global Hawk, Predator B and HERTI (high endurance rapid technology insertions) drones at Woomera.[8] Wing Commander Jeff 'Jack' Frost was the RAAF liaison officer for the HERTI and Mantis trials being conducted by BAE Systems and the United Kingdom's Ministry of Defence in secret at Woomera in 2008–09.[9] He had already been set the task of investigating whether drones might have a role with the ADF in IED detection, and he set up a project he named Project *Miles*, after Pika test pilot John Miles.[10] The HERTI, which had completed its first autonomous flight trials at Woomera in 2006, was one contender for the project.[11] British forces had used it in Afghanistan under Project *Morrigan* with cameras and software specifically designed to detect changes in patterns on the ground. However, the HERTI drone was not suitable for the ADF in Afghanistan because of the need for an electro-optical infra-red camera (EOIR) to meet the full-motion video requirement; the HERTI could not accommodate that.[12] Another potential option was the BAE Systems Mantis armed reconnaissance drone, but it only existed as a concept demonstrator and had not gone through trials and production.[13]

Royal Air Force-operated HERTI drone at an international air show (RAF)

While a manned option was preferred, it had its drawbacks. The likely contractor did not have a presence at Kandahar Airfield (KAF) and would probably not have been able to establish itself there in time. Also, their aircraft did not offer an electronic-warfare self-protection system, placing the crew at risk of being shot down. An electronic-warfare self-protection system would allow for the detection of attack by a surface-to-air missile and the release of flares to counter the threat. Civilian contractors would need to fly the aircraft, but ADF personnel would operate the onboard sensors.[14] However, when the Attorney-General's Department advised the Attorney-General may not approve the use of civilian contractors in the manned ISR option, the risk of meeting the OUR in a timely manner with that option became intolerable.[15]

Following public announcement of the termination of Boeing's contract to provide Israel Aerospace Industries (IAI) Malat I-View drones, Richard Variyan, international business director of Canadian geo-intelligence company MacDonald Dettwiler and Associates (MDA), engaged Robert Coorey of Canberra-based Geospatial Intelligence Pty Ltd to gauge Australian interest in a similar project being conducted by Canada. In October 2008, along with members of the Canadian Trade Commission, Coorey took a proposal to Australia's Minister for Defence Joel Fitzgibbon to use the IAI Heron to counter the IED threat in Afghanistan.[16] MDA had been awarded the Canadian contract to provide these medium-altitude, long-endurance (MALE) drones to operate from KAF and were poised to deliver the first one into service in December under Project *Noctua*.

Despite ministerial clearance to provide presentations to Joint Operations Command and other elements of Defence, Coorey and the trade commission received little ADF interest in the Heron proposal. The exception was Brigadier David Gillian, Director-General Intelligence at Headquarters Joint Operations Command. He and his team, including Captain David Scott, championed what became known as Project *Noctua* – Australia. Aside from representing MDA, Coorey's company took on the role of providing geo-intelligence support and training advice to the project. To show off a Heron, MDA brought one to the Avalon International Airshow at Geelong, Victoria over 10–15 March 2009 with Air Force Headquarters approval.[17]

One of the ADF officers approached for a meeting to inspect the Heron was Deputy Director–Air Combat Capability, Wing Commander David Riddel. In his mind, a manned option was still preferred, but Riddel took the meeting with MDA anyway, because he 'thought it would be rude to cancel.'[18] With the contractor-flown King Air option not likely to meet government approval and the Woomera trial drone options not yet viable, the Heron drone option offered by the Canadians seemed a good choice, noting time was running out to meet the OUR.

The RAAF subsequently cancelled Project *Miles*, and Wing Commander Frost and most of his small team were transferred to form a new project to meet the OUR. While it had begun by investigating manned ISR options, the project switched to drones.[19] The new project was led by Riddel, supported by Wing Commander Craig Meghan, and was established as an integrated project team (IPT) that combined the efforts of the RAAF, the Army and the Defence Materiel Organisation (DMO) – the organisation within the Department of Defence responsible for major acquisitions. The team of just five personnel included DMO representative Bev Kerr.[20] The HERTI team proved invaluable in advising the IPT. Particularly valuable to the new project was Flight Lieutenant Sarah-Jane Crane, a C-130J

Hercules captain and HERTI mission commander, who developed many of the Heron standard operating procedures. Frost was instrumental in drafting the initial concept of operations.[21] This document defines the roles and mission types a capability will perform and details the responsibilities of those who operate it, along with a range of safety and operational matters.

RAAF senior leadership realised, in addition to saving Australian lives in Afghanistan, there were benefits in taking up the unmanned option. Time had passed since the urgent need for airborne ISR was identified in 2008, and the OUR was potentially in danger of heading down the path of the ill-fated PJ129 program and becoming bogged down in the bureaucratic delays that can beset any major procurement.[22] However, the RAAF was in a position to make a rapid acquisition of the Heron as an '80% solution' and not wait for the 100% solution PJ129 sought. As a senior officer in Joint Operations Command said: 'If the capability acquired to satisfy the OUR turns out to be … the JP129 Phase 2 solution in due course, so much the better.' He reinforced this was very much a secondary outcome to meeting the Chief of Joint Operations' intent of getting an effective system into Afghanistan before the next fighting season.[23]

Further, the RAAF wanted to start down the path of using drones operationally, as was proving effective in other air forces worldwide. While the Australian Army had been the exclusive user of tactical drones on operations since their introduction into ADF service in 2000, the size and capabilities of MALE and HALE (high-altitude, long-endurance) drones placed them in a different league. With very long endurance and sophisticated sensor suites, these capabilities could provide ISR not only to Australian ground troops, but to commanders and other Coalition partners. This would make them theatre-wide operational assets of value to more than the immediate ground operations usually supported by small tactical drones.[24] Typically weighing more than some domestic light aircraft, the heavier drones need a runway and other airbase infrastructure. In short, they were not toys and would need to be considered like manned aircraft, with all their technical airworthiness and operating requirements. All of this pointed to any new medium to heavy drones in the ADF more naturally being a RAAF capability than an Army one.[25]

The IPT faced several constraints in seeking to acquire the new ISR drone capability. However, some of the normal acquisition considerations did not apply. These included the whole-of-life costs of owning the capability, such as long-term maintenance, spare parts supply chains and sustainability of the workforce over time. With the rapid changes in the technology used by ISR drones, it was likely any drone purchased outright would become obsolete within a relatively short time. So, commercial lease of a military off-the-shelf (MOTS) capability made sense, especially noting the likely short duration of the requirement and the urgency to introduce it. Riddel recognised the magnitude of the task when he later told a journalist: 'It's one thing to rent a truck and put it on the road, but it's a completely different task to get a complete aviation system into operational service within 90 days – and to do it in a war zone!'[26]

First Australian-leased Heron (A45-262) at the Israel Aerospace Industries factory, Tel Aviv, October 2009 - L to R: Robert Coorey (Geospatial Intelligence Pty Ltd), Major Jones, Menachem Schwachter (IAI) and Wing Commander David Riddel, October 2009 (Menachem Schwachter)

The ADF's Chiefs of Service Committee and the government's National Security Committee of Cabinet approved the project to acquire the Heron capability on 17 April 2009, only weeks after the meeting between Riddel and MDA at the Avalon Airshow. With the approval given to commence the project to acquire the Heron as a RAAF asset to meet the OUR, Riddel named the task Project *Nankeen* after an Australian native bird, the nankeen night heron *(Nycticorax caledonicus)*, which is also known as the rufous night heron. This nocturnal bird moves slowly, always looking down, to catch its prey. He did not ask permission for the project name and simply began applying it to the project's correspondence and briefs. He was never challenged. The project was so urgent that it was set a target of 90 days to introduce the drone into operations.[27]

Nankeen night heron on the wing (Grahame)

A rapid solution

As IPT leader Riddel put it: 'To get a major system into operations without ever even operating it in Australia, you've got to have an exemplar.'[28] The Canadian Department of National Defense (DND) had been operating the Heron drone in Afghanistan since late 2008 under its Project *Noctua*.[29] They did so with Canadian operating contractors MDA (Israeli company IAI would not have been allowed to operate in Afghanistan).[30] The Heron had also been in service with a wide range of military services and proved its value. The Indian Air Force began using Herons in 2003 and applied them to humanitarian aid and disaster relief operations in 2005 after the Indian Ocean tsunami. Turkey began operating Herons in 2005, as did the Israeli Air Force – calling them Machatz 1 drones.[31] In fact, two Herons had already been used in Australia in 2007 and 2008, when IAI demonstrated them to Border Protection Command in northern Australia for possible use in maritime surveillance and customs roles.[32] However, the ADF's intent was to acquire a drone capability with no planned retention or transition into service in mainland Australia and to be able to expand the scope of the operational capability if required in Afghanistan.[33] Choosing the Canadian model as the exemplar was made easier by Canada being one of the parties to the Five Eyes security alliance. The alliance allows for the sharing of signals intelligence between Australia, Canada, the United States, the United Kingdom and New Zealand.

Heron 169 with Australian civil registration VH-BJJ during demonstrations for maritime patrol, Weipa, Queensland, 2008 (Israel Aerospace Industries)

The Canadian contract model was designed so MDA provided the DND with a set number of flying hours per month. However, the DND was not able to use all those hours because of staffing shortages. So, piggybacking onto the Canadian model would be mutually advantageous.[34] The DND, therefore, pitched the proposal for the ADF to operate Herons collaboratively. While awaiting the arrival of the Australian Heron systems, the Australian cadre and first rotation crews would be able to augment the short-staffed Canadian crews to gain experience and confidence while being mentored during missions in support of ISAF. The Canadians were also very interested in the new elements of Heron operations proposed by the ADF, such as direct support to troops under attack and overwatch air support, that would take the drone beyond its initial IED detection role.[35]

Canadian-operated Heron CU-170254 in its hangar at Kandahar Airfield, Afghanistan
(© All rights reserved. Reproduced with the permission of DND/CAF (2023))

One factor that made the Heron the obvious choice was the constraints of airfield capacity in Afghanistan. To introduce an aircraft of a type not already operating there would have required considerable negotiation with all other airfield users.[36] In fact, there was simply no additional tarmac space at the most suitable operating base of KAF to introduce a new aircraft type and its additional infrastructure.[37] Another factor was that any contractor involved would have to be one accustomed and prepared to accept the risks associated with working in a war zone, yet not directly involved in the battlefield decision-making. The Canadian DND model met these two requirements.

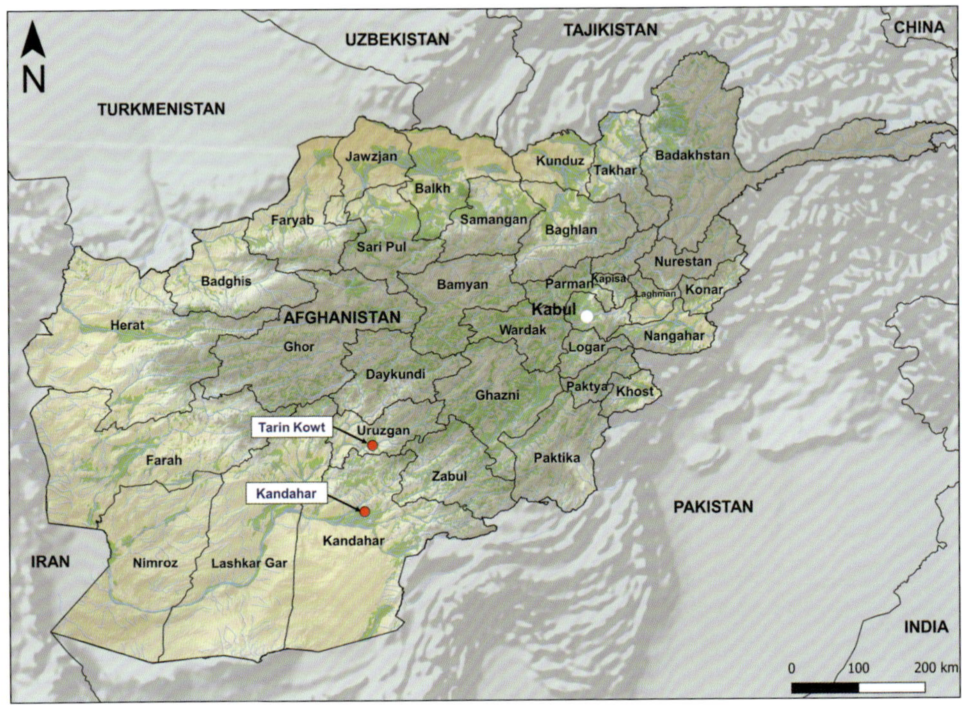

Afghanistan national boundaries and key locations (Defence)

Initially, the RAAF considered basing Heron operations at Forward Operating Base Ripley in Tarin Kot. The SOTG conducted most of its operations from there, and proximity to them seemed a sound arrangement. Under that option, the Herons would have been based at KAF but controlled from Tarin Kot, requiring mid-flight handover from MDA and probable major demands on radio bandwidth. If the HERTI drone option had gone ahead, that is where it would have been based.[38] However, the dirt runway was very rocky and not suitable for a light aircraft. So, the actual Heron airframes would have to take-off and land at KAF, with a mid-air handover to operators in Tarin Kot. Also, the logistics arrangements to accommodate contractors would have been very difficult and expensive. That plan did not last long, and the proposal changed to operating the Herons from KAF, with the added benefit that it was the location of the SOTG headquarters.[39] Nonetheless, some Heron equipment had been pre-positioned at Tarin Kot, and members of the Heron logistics team went from KAF to pack it into collapsible shipping containers for removal.[40]

Things began moving very quickly after the decision to use the Heron option was approved – so quickly, in fact, that the Deputy Chief of Air Force, Air Vice Marshal Geoff Brown, signed the letter drafted to invite MDA to take part in discussions for the multi-million-dollar service contract while at his front door in his slippers on the following Sunday morning.[41] Within days of that letter, the Australian IPT members travelled to Ottawa, Canada, to seek the advice of the Project *Noctua* team and contractor MDA in May 2009.[42] The team carried a letter of introduction from Australia's Chief of Air Force, Air Marshal Binskin, to Rear Admiral Davidson of the Canadian National Defense Headquarters that concluded by saying: 'I look forward to developing a mutually beneficial and productive relationship that will deliver important operational effects for forces from our countries deployed in Afghanistan.'[43]

MDA contractors preparing a Heron for flight, Kandahar Airfield, Afghanistan (Defence)

After three days of intense discussions, the IPT acted quickly in securing in-principle agreement from Australia's Deputy Chief of Air Force and Air Commander to share assets.[44] They did so overnight and stunned the Canadian DND by being able to announce in-principle agreement on the fourth morning. This left the DND in no doubt about how serious the RAAF was.[45] In an email to the commander of the cadre team waiting back in Australia, Riddel said, the 'Canadian military can't believe the speed of this!'[46] The Canadian experience with the Heron proved invaluable due to the very short lead time. The ADF was in the unusual position of needing to develop the concept of operations for the capability at the same time as negotiating its rapid acquisition,[47] and seeing how another Coalition partner was using the drone allowed for rapid progress in putting it into service. A critical element of the Canadian model was the use of MDA to supply and maintain the Heron.

As the contracted capability provider, MDA was the interface with Heron manufacturers and owners IAI. MDA liaised with IAI for operational support and higher-level technical and logistical support. While this arrangement avoided any need to purchase the Herons and to negotiate spares support contracts, IAI had to liaise with a wide range of similar sub-contractual providers and customers of their other products, so real-time engineering support was not always available.[48] A critical element of the arrangement was that the ADF did not seek to gain any engineering expertise in the Heron beyond that required for operational and technical governance. The *Nankeen* IPT negotiated a contract with MDA to lease Heron drones and to provide their maintenance.[49] Warrant Officer Charmaine Rule managed most of the financial arrangements for Project *Nankeen*. She raised the vast number of purchase orders required to make the project work.

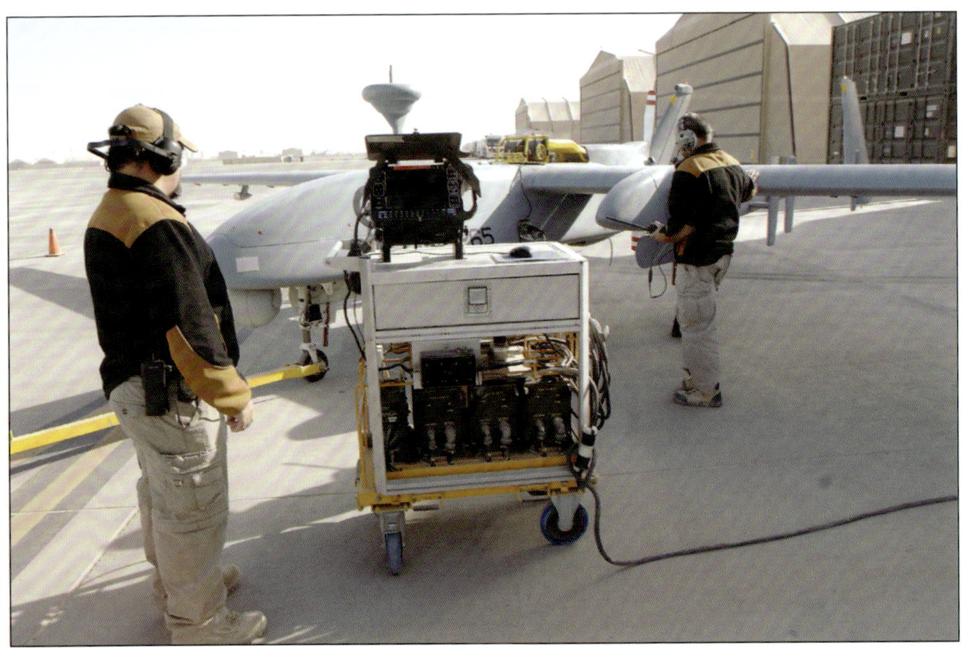

MDA staff carrying out maintenance on a Heron in at Kandahar Airfield, Afghanistan (Defence)

The operating arrangement for the Heron was somewhat unusual by Australian military aircraft acquisition models. Rather than leasing a set number of aircraft, the ADF leased a capability, expressed as a certain number of flying hours per month. The first Commanding Officer of No 5 Flight, Wing Commander Lyle Holt, explained that the contractor 'could provide one aircraft and put all his eggs in that one basket and if it goes down he is contractually liable for not providing the service, or he can provide 20 and totally take away that risk at his own financial cost, so that's his game to play.'[50] The lease initially called for 500 flying hours per month.[51]

Interestingly, the Canadian use of a contractor to engage with the drone supplier, and to carry out certain aspects of operating it, mirrored a similar arrangement made by Canada with Boeing to operate ScanEagle drones in Afghanistan from 2008.[52] In fact, the ADF had pioneered the arrangement with Boeing and the ScanEagle in 2006, and this has led to commentary that suggests Canada's lease arrangement followed Australia's lead and likely inspired the subsequent Canadian lease of Herons.[53] By 2010, the model was widespread, with Germany leasing three Heron systems from IAI operated under contract by Airbus in Afghanistan.[54]

ADF Heron cadre personnel posing beside the Heron drone during training at Canadian Forces Base Suffield, Canada, 2009 (Defence)

Heron training facility at Canadian Forces Base Suffield, Canada (Defence)

The *Nankeen* IPT also negotiated a memorandum of understanding (MOU) between the ADF and the Canadian DND regarding the cooperation between the two defence forces, including the financial, logistical, security, indemnity and intellectual property aspects. The MOU was signed by General Walter Natynczyk on behalf of the Canadian DND and Air Chief Marshal Angus Houston on behalf of the ADF – both in their capacities as chiefs of their defence forces – over July and August 2009.[55] The high-level document was followed by a detailed implementing arrangement that outlined the operational aspects of the cooperation between Australia and Canada.[56] This was important because it laid down the safety standards and operating protocols. It also recognised that MDA personnel at KAF were contracted to provide services to both the Canadian and Australian contingents. The arrangement had the immense benefit of allowing the ADF to deploy its much-needed capability without having to negotiate afresh for space and facilities at KAF. Wing Commander Holt noted: 'In essence, our insertion of a capability into Afghanistan was actually reasonably small. We weren't asking to build a new hangar for our aeroplanes.'[57] The Project *Nankeen* negotiations also led to the signing of a contract to train Australian personnel to fly and operate the Heron system. With an initial planned date of September 2009 to deploy the first Australian Heron, training of the key personnel began in May 2009.

First ADF-contracted Heron, A45-262, in the Israel Aerospace Industries test facility, Tel Aviv, December 2009 (Defence)

Those personnel completed their training in July and deployed to KAF to be embedded as part of the Canadian Heron team in August 2009.[58] They did so without an Australian Heron.[59] Minister for Defence John Faulkner nonetheless noted at the time, 'the ADF has rapidly established its Heron capability by drawing on the Canadians' operational knowledge, experience and facilities.'[60] This was so, in that the embedded ADF Heron team – while flying Canadian missions in support of ISAF – was able to develop its operational skills side-by-side with the more-experienced Canadian teams in preparation for the delivery of the first Australian Heron, publicly announced as being scheduled for December.[61] In fact, the RAAF's plan was to have them delivered in September, but manufacturers IAI could not construct them by then. Riddel, who was told this at a meeting with IAI in Israel, immediately flew to Turkey to discuss the possibility of borrowing Turkish-owned Herons. However, the country was still in a state of turmoil after the January 2009 attempted coup, and Riddel was unable to speak to military representatives.[62]

IAI completed the first Australian contracted Heron in early December 2009 and handed it over in Israel in the presence of the Australian and Canadian defence attachés. It began flying operations in January 2010 as part of an initial one-year lease.[63] Australian Heron A45-262 carried out taxi tests and its first flight on 2 January 2010. This marked the first flight of the modern A45 aircraft series and was the first flight of an ADF-registered MALE drone. On hearing the news, Chief of Air Force Mark Binskin sent a congratulatory message: 'Good job guys. Looking forward to seeing the results of all your efforts.'[64]

Heron A45-262 landing at Kandahar Airfield after its first flight in Afghanistan, 2 January 2010 (Defence)

The Heron system

The Heron drone system had been in operational service with several other defence forces since 2003 and was well regarded for its ISR capabilities. What was the Heron able to do that might have solved the ADF's urgent need for IED detection in Afghanistan?

The IAI Heron is a medium-altitude, long-endurance (MALE) remotely-piloted aerial system made by the Malat (UAV) division of Israel Aerospace Industries. That system comprised many elements aside from the airframe. The airframe itself can operate for up to 52 hours to a maximum altitude of 35,000 feet in ideal test conditions and with no payload. However, its effective continuous flight time is considerably less in the operational environment due to the weight of the payloads and the flight profiles of the missions flown. The effective flight duration is, therefore, about 22 hours. It weighs 1.2 tonnes and cruises at 100 knots (185 km/h). Typical mission speeds are slower at 60 to 80 knots (110 to 150 km/h). With a fuselage length of 8.5 metres and a wingspan of 16.6 metres, the Heron is an imposing drone. It is controlled in flight by the conventional control surfaces of ailerons, elevator and twin rudders, aided by wing flaps for take-off and landing. It is clearly built for function over aesthetic considerations.

The airframe has long narrow wings and a distinctive twin boom that mounts the elevator and twin tailfins. It is powered by a pusher-mounted two-blade propeller driven by a turbo-supercharged water-cooled flat-four internal-combustion engine. The engine is housed in the rear of the streamlined, if boxy, fuselage between the booms. The Heron uses a retractable tricycle undercarriage with the nose wheel in the front of the fuselage and the main wheels in dedicated pods on the wings. The starboard pod also houses the landing light. Aerials, sensors and other appendages hang off it all around. The Heron can carry a wide range of sensors – including a visible-light electro-optic camera, a thermographic infra-red camera, radio intelligence systems and a range of radar systems – up to a total weight of 470 kilograms.

The Heron navigates with inbuilt GPS and inertial navigation devices that can fly to a pre-programmed flight profile or by direct control from a pilot on the ground. Both autopilot and direct control can be used during a single flight. In each case, the drone uses a fully automated take-off and landing system (ATOL). The ATOL system uses DGPS (differential global positioning system) to position the Heron with accuracy below one metre, as opposed to the ten-metre accuracy of standard GPS. The ATOL system can also use a laser-defined approach path with the remote autoland positioning sensor (or RAPS). This system uses a tripod-mounted unit placed near the runway, which combines a laser radar and TV camera. It sends laser pulses to the Heron, echoed by the RAPS reflector mounted under the right wing, and provides video images to help during take-off and landing. The system is optional but can be set up at short notice of 30 minutes or so.

The Heron communicates with the aircrew who fly it and control its sensors through a ground data terminal (GDT). This uses C-band microwave radio communications in the 4 to 8 gigahertz frequency range to provide a continuous line-of-sight link of about 150 to 200 kilometres for flight control and relaying sensor information. It also carries very-high frequency (VHF) and ultra-high frequency (UHF) communication systems for contact with the ground for a variety of purposes. The payload can be controlled either in a pre-programmed autonomous mode or by direct control. The Heron has a failsafe system that automatically returns the drone to base and lands it in case of a communication failure with the GDT. It automatically attempts to re-establish contact with the GDT during the process. It is fitted with an IFF (identification, friend or foe) transponder to allow it to be identified by other aircraft and by battlespace managers and air traffic controllers.

IAI Heron

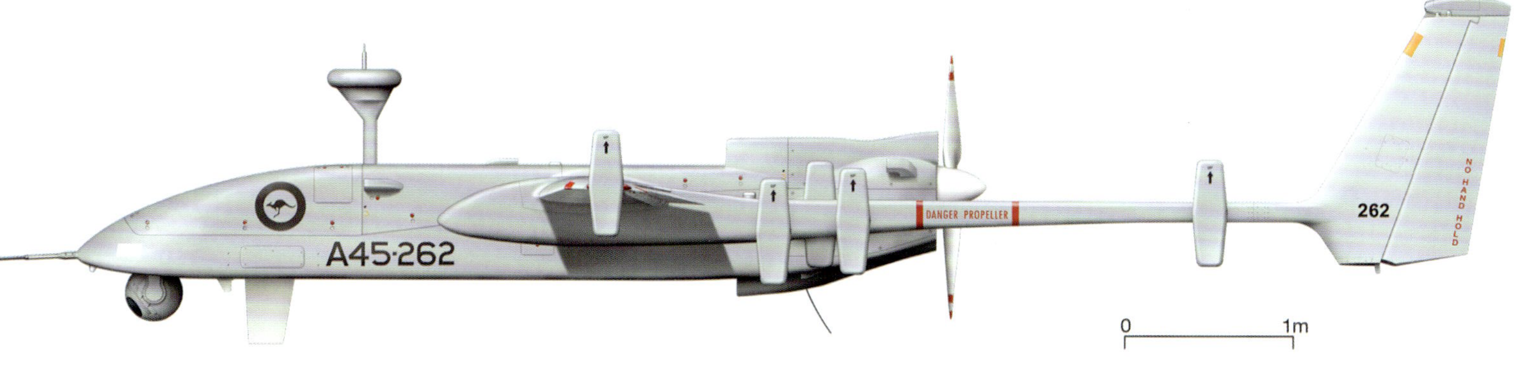

(Aero Illustrations)

Aircraft

- Designation: Heron (Machatz 1)
- Manufacturer: Israel Aerospace Industries
- Type: medium-altitude, long-endurance (MALE)
- Role: unmanned aerial surveillance and reconnaissance
- First flight: 1994
- Introduction to service: 2005

General characteristics

- Length: 8.5 m
- Wingspan: 16.6 m
- Max take-off weight: 1,270 kg
- Payload capacity: 470 kg
- Powerplant: 1 × Rotax 914 four-cylinder air and water cooled horizontally opposed piston engine, 86 kW (115 hp)
- Propellers: two-blade pusher propeller

Performance

- Maximum speed: 140 kn (260 km/h)
- Typical mission speed: 60–80 kn (110–150 km/h)
- Rate of climb: 490 ft/min
- Service ceiling: 35,000 ft
- Endurance: up to 52 hours max. (less depending on payload and operational requirements)

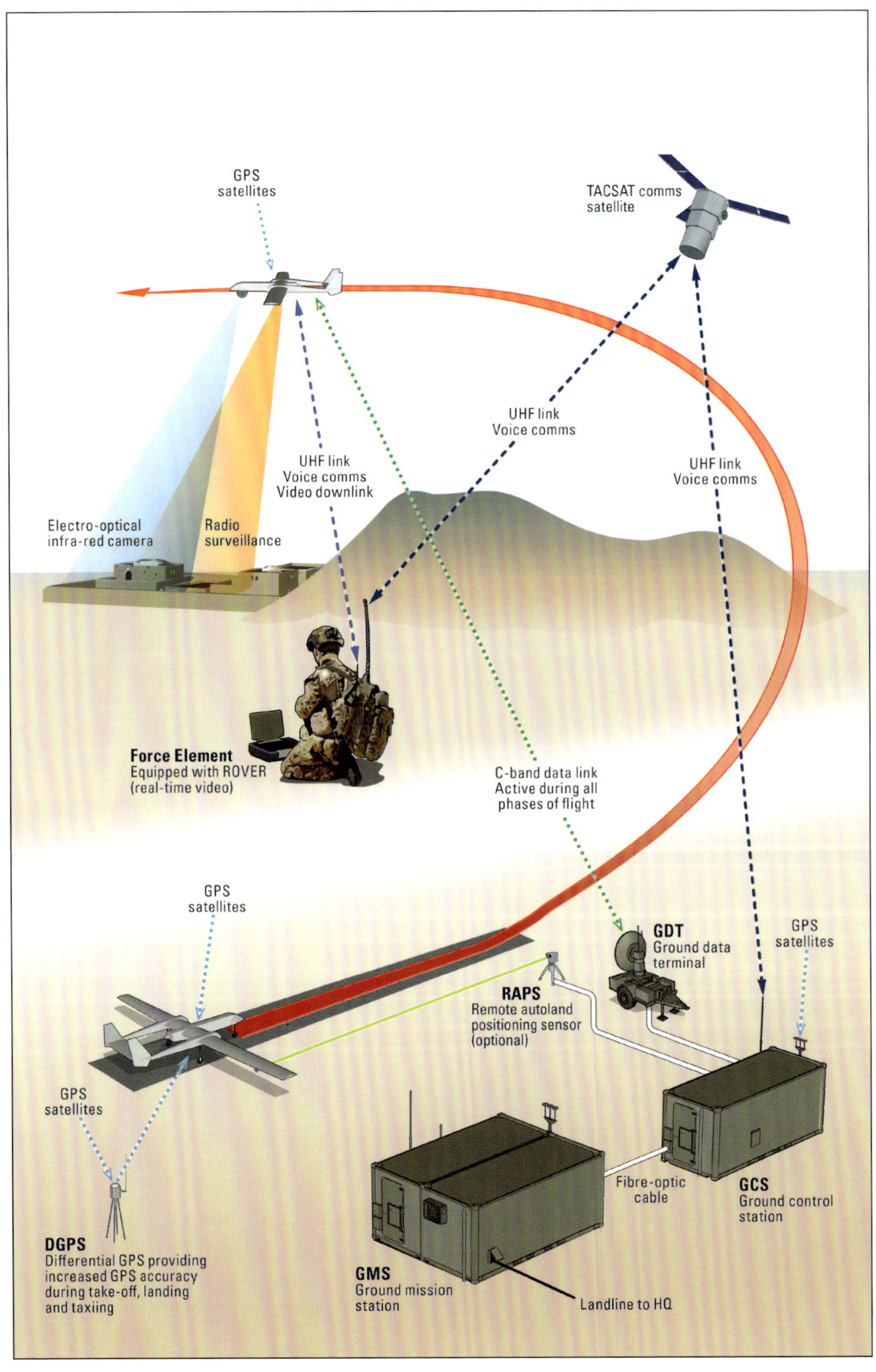

The Heron system in operation (Aero Illustrations)

Heron ground data terminal (GDT) trailer (David Riddel)

The GDT is a rugged trailer-mounted microwave radio transceiver. Usually painted to camouflage with its surroundings, it remains at the Heron's home airfield and is usually powered by a diesel generator. From the GDT, a fibre-optic cable runs to the nearby ground control station (GCS), where the aerial vehicle operator and payload operator sit at a pair of identical control panels to operate the drone and its sensors. The GCS is a metal box about the size of a small shipping container. To that point, those components – the airframe, the GDT and the GCS – are all made by Heron manufacturer IAI and form a complete system. However, to get the best ISR value from the system, the Canadian DND and the ADF added further elements.

The first major added component was the ground mission station (GMS) – connected by a fibre-optic cable to the GCS. Housed in a somewhat larger building adjacent to the GCS, this is where the intelligence staff operated. Other added components included the communications equipment, such as the tactical satellite radios for encrypted two-way voice communication between the GCS and troops in the field, and the air traffic and battlespace management systems. Landline communications to headquarters elements were also added.

Squadron Leader Michael Nygh of Rotation 4 at his station during a mission in the Heron ground mission station in Kandahar, Afghanistan, 2011 (Bill Guthrie)

To aid support to ground forces, the Heron also employs the remotely operated video-enhanced receiver (or ROVER) system. The ROVER III system allows those on the ground to view real-time full motion video from the Heron's EOIR camera on a laptop computer carried by a member of the patrol. The system uses a line-of-sight UHF transmitter in the Heron to send the video feed and locational data to the laptop.

ROVER III remotely operated video-enhanced receiver, as used to relay real-time video to ground forces by the Herons in Afghanistan (Defence)

The Heron's manufacturer – Israel Aerospace Industries

Having produced unmanned aircraft for more than 40 years, Israel Aerospace Industries (IAI) is a major international player in the ongoing global effort to develop better quality military drones. Established by the Israeli Government in 1953 as the Governmental Institute for Aviation (or Bedek Aviation Company), the organisation was created to maintain the Israel Defence Force's aircraft fleet. Over the following 20 years, IAI achieved accreditation as an authorised repair station by both Israel's Civilian Aviation Authorities and, from 1955, the United States Federal Aviation Administration. Then, in 1959, it transitioned from an aircraft servicing role to pursuing the design and manufacture of aircraft and land and sea systems. By the mid-1960s, IAI had developed its first sea-to-sea missile, the Gabriel, and produced its first indigenous aircraft, the Arava in 1969. It was in the 1970s, however, that the most noteworthy development (in the context of this book) occurred: the Israeli Air Force began operating IAI's first small drone, the Scout, in 1979. The Scout remained in service until the early 1990s. During that time, IAI fielded its first reconnaissance satellite, the Ofek 1, in 1988, tested its first in a family of anti-ballistic missiles, the Arrow 1, in 1990, and demonstrated the Barak in 1991 (a naval vessel defence system still in use today). In 1994, IAI's Heron MALE drone completed its first flight, and since that time, the aircraft has been delivered to more than 20 global customers, performing a range of mission types. IAI's technological development has continued apace. In the past 25 years, the company has produced airborne early warning and control systems, radar systems, high-speed patrol boats, communication satellites and business jets. In 2006, IAI completed the first successful flight of the Eitan, also known as the Heron TP, Israel's largest unmanned reconnaissance aircraft.[65]

The range of personnel needed to operate the deployed Heron system was considerable. They included pilots, payload operators, intelligence officers, imagery analysts, electronic warfare specialists, translators, and aircraft and computer technicians, along with administrative, operations and logistics support staff. In total, a typical Heron system used by the ADF required about 35 people. The ADF chose to staff it jointly, with personnel coming from all three services. Rotation 3 commander Wing Commander Robert Morris proudly noted in official reports, for the 'first time since commencing operations TU633.2.7 (HERON) is now Tri-Service having personnel elements of RAAF, Army and Navy.'[66]

Due to the sharing arrangement, the system configuration of the ADF Herons was that adopted by the Canadians – although there were some configuration changes later. They were fitted with an electro-optic long-range sensor system, known as the Multi-Sensors Optronic Stabilized Payload (MOSP).[67] The MOSP unit is the 'eyes' of the Heron. It contains an electro-optic camera for daytime use and a short-wave infra-red camera for night-time use, both with zoom capability. A gyroscope and a tracking system allow the cameras to remain focused on a fixed position, and it also has an infra-red laser pointer.[68] This pointer, however, is not capable of target designation for guiding weapons onto targets. The Heron also has a smaller camera mounted in one of the rear stabiliser fins dedicated to giving the pilot a set of eyes for landing and manoeuvring on the ground.

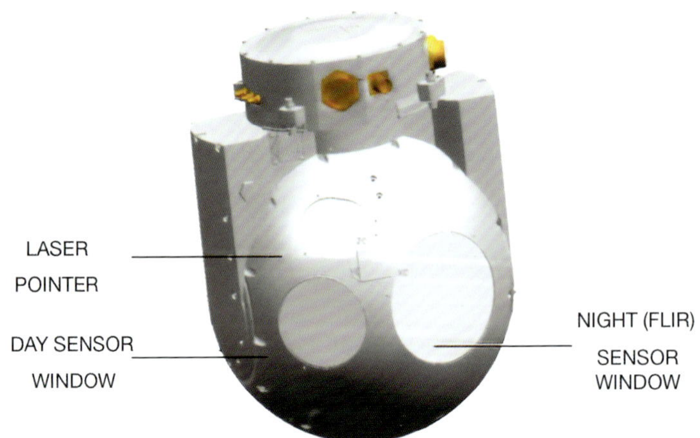

Multi-Sensors Optronic Stabilized Payload (MOSP) fitted to the nose of Heron drones (Israel Aerospace Industries)

The Heron also has 'ears' – its electronic warfare (EW) system that senses voice and data transmissions to track their origins, locations, quantities and types to provide information about insurgent activities, force size and structure. The information can be used to build what is known as an electronic order of battle. This EW capability of the Heron uses an array of VHF and UHF aerials outside the fuselage and subsystems inside the aircraft to collect and transmit the data.[69]

Software also plays an important part in the Heron system. Not the least important was the Kestrel Land moving target indicator software; this was not a standard software package that came with the Heron from the manufacturer. It was developed in Australia by Sentient Vision and KAZ Fujitsu Geospatial Intelligence in conjunction with the Defence Science and Technology Organisation.[70] Its use on the Heron was publicly announced in November 2010.[71] The software identifies motion by processing the imagery in real-time to detect changes in the video information as small as a few pixels – such as insurgents leaving vehicles or doorways – from very high altitude.[72] It was useful in detecting objects easily missed, such as camouflaged vehicles in rough terrain. The software automatically alerted image analysts of the detections, some of which may have been outside of their field of vision. It, therefore, reduced stress on long shifts and allowed for more comprehensive situational awareness.[73]

Geospatial imagery analyst Leading Aircraftwoman Poppy Longmate observing live vision from the Heron during Exercise *Pitch Black*, 2016 (Terry Hartin)

The software was originally developed to add metadata to recorded video for later analysis using the metadata for comparison, rather than the standard 'dumb' recordings that required advancing and rewinding to make the comparisons. This allowed for the identification of objects in the landscape that had changed over time (a day, a week, a season). The software, and the complex computer systems required to run it, again highlight the role of Australian industry in the development of sophisticated defence innovations and solutions. Riddel noted the complexity of the task: 'That effort has seen Air Force engage about ten different suppliers under about fifteen different contracts to develop the systems ourselves in house.'[74] The Heron was the first ADF ISR asset to have such capability, and through its development under Project *Nankeen*, it has gone on to be used on other ADF aircraft.

The Heron system in ADF hands was able to complement a range of other ISR assets in use by the Coalition in Afghanistan. These included the French Heron-derived Harfang and American Global Hawk unarmed ISR drones, American Reaper and Predator armed

ISR drones, as well as conventional ISR assets, such as MC-12 Liberty, P-3 Orion and U-2 surveillance aircraft.[75] One Heron liaison officer noted, however, 'ISR was the most sought-after asset, hands down, in the theatre. It is very difficult to get a hold of.'[76] So, having a dedicated MALE ISR asset to complement RAAF AP-3C Orion surveillance aircraft and Army ScanEagle tactical drones to serve Australian ground forces was a major step forward in the plan to give added protection against the IED threat that emerged from 2009 – a role that was to transform over the five years of the Heron's operational deployments.

Warrant Officer Darren Gray operating the electronic optic sensor in an AP-3C Orion aircraft during an Operation *Slipper* mission, 2012 (Bill Guthrie)

The rapid acquisition of the Heron as a MOTS system proved the ADF was sufficiently agile to be able to define an urgent operational need, identify a viable solution and have it in operational service in under a year. The ADF did so by learning from the experience of others. By adopting the Canadian model and inserting directly into the existing infrastructure, airspace and battlespace management, the ADF was able to reduce its acquisition timeframes and costs drastically. However, this meant taking what was given for the most part, without being able to specify critical components, such as the cameras (which were vastly inferior to those on the Reapers). Nonetheless, a Department of Defence press release announcing the start of Heron operations in Afghanistan in January 2010 noted: 'The UAV will help deliver high resolution, real-time intelligence, surveillance and reconnaissance (ISR) information to ADF commanders.'[77]

The Heron was a whole new class of aircraft for the ADF. As defence journalist Katherine Ziesing pointed out: 'To put it into perspective, some of the sensors on the Heron weigh more than double the ScanEagle as a whole.'[78] For the RAAF, which had not operated drones in living memory, this meant finding and training a workforce in new skills.

Chapter 3
BIRD TAMING

As sophisticated as the Heron was, it was the people who brought it to life and allowed it to be the important intelligence, surveillance and reconnaissance (ISR) asset it became. The Heron was indeed something new for the ADF – a drone similar in scale to some manned aircraft in the RAAF fleet at the time, including the PC-9A turboprop trainer and the Hawk 127 jet trainer. Unlike the lightweight drones used by the Australian Army, it had all the requirements of a standard aircraft, including the need to use hangars for storage and maintenance, hardstands and taxiways for manoeuvring and a runway to take off and land. It also came with all the risks of a standard aircraft; it had to be able to fly in controlled airspace alongside other air traffic, and a collision with another aircraft could be disastrous. In short, it needed professional aircrew to fly it and a maintenance regime of the same standard as any other aircraft.

While the ADF had a pool of well-trained people to exploit the sensors on the Heron – notably from within the RAAF AP-3C Orion and intelligence communities – it did not have a pool of aircrew experienced in flying medium-altitude, long-endurance (MALE) drones. It, therefore, had to train aircrew in a whole new skillset. Overall, more than 400 people were involved in operating the Heron in Australian hands. How did the ADF find the right people for the job, and how did they gain their highly specialised skills?

Standing up the capability

The RAAF applies its capabilities through entities called units. Each unit is assigned personnel and resources and given a set of required outcomes, known as the directed level of capability (DLOC). Each unit is assigned a commanding officer (CO), who is responsible for the welfare of the personnel and the best use of the assigned resources and expertise within the unit. Higher levels of command hold the CO accountable for the unit. Unlike during the Second World War, units no longer deploy as a whole to warlike operations. Instead, units are responsible for what is known as the 'raise, train, sustain' function of the capability on behalf of the Chief of Air Force, and they make the capability ready to be assigned to the Chief of Joint Operations for operational deployment. This arrangement ensures only the essential people with the right skills and equipment deploy and that they fit into the overall scheme of the operation. It also ensures a basis remains – away from the pressures of operations – to train new personnel and prepare them in turn for operations. Each new group assigned to replace the previous group deployed to operate a capability is known as a 'rotation', reflecting that the new group rotates into the theatre of operations as the previous group rotates out.

Rotation lengths vary across the ADF, eight months being typical for Army personnel. Aircrew need to return to Australia and maintain currency on their original aircraft with check flights, rather than the impost of full refresher training, so a typical Heron rotation was four-and-a-half months. In the usual Australian fashion, the word is shortened to 'roto'. During the first rotation, personnel devised a mascot similar to a Warner Brothers cartoon character called Tasmanian Devil and unofficially dubbed the Herons 'Little Devils'. The Tasmanian link gave the capability an Australian flavour. In the cartoons, the character is devious and ferocious and spends much of its time orbiting around its prey, which they felt reflected many of the Heron mission profiles.[1]

Heron detachment logo painted onto a ubiquitous anti-blast T-wall at Kandahar Airfield with one of the officers instrumental in acquiring the Heron capability, Wing Commander David Riddel, 2010 (David Riddel)

When assigned to Chief of Joint Operations, the personnel and equipment form a task element or task unit – depending on its size or role – of a higher-level task group within a joint task force. In many cases, task units comprise personnel from more than one ADF unit. The rapidly acquired Heron capability was assigned to Chief of Joint Operations as Task Unit 633.2.7 for deployment on Operation *Slipper* as part of Joint Task Force 633 in July 2009 and arrived at Kandahar Airfield (KAF) on 4 August.[2] However, in a most unusual situation, the Heron did not have a home unit. The speed of acquisition and deployment meant the RAAF had to catch up and establish a unit to foster the capability and knowledge back in Australia. The RAAF raised No 5 Flight on 18 January 2010 within No 82 Wing at RAAF Base Amberley in Queensland with a DLOC to establish the raise, train, sustain function of the deployed Heron capability.[3] The narrow initial DLOC pointed to the projected short-term nature of 5 Flight and the Heron capability. Much of the burden of establishing 5 Flight fell to Wing Commander Lyle Holt, its first CO. In fact, a subsequent CO said of Holt: 'He made this work almost singlehandedly … He was outstanding for 5 Flight.'[4]

Heron uniform patches (Defence)

A RAAF squadron normally employs more than 100 personnel and is organised into smaller elements known as flights. So, due to its small complement of 22 personnel, 5 Flight was given the lower designation of a flight.[5] The number assigned to a squadron or unit-level flight fits a pattern going back to the days of the Australian Flying Corps of the First World War and largely reflects the unit's role. From 1917, No 5 Squadron, AFC was a training unit embedded with the British Royal Flying Corps preparing pilots for operations on the Western Front. When re-formed during the Second World War, No 5 Squadron, RAAF was an army-cooperation squadron. It served in the Pacific Theatre, and its missions included aerial reconnaissance and artillery observation. The squadron reformed once more in 1964 and was equipped with helicopters, which it used in a range of conflicts in army support roles. So, '5' was a very suitable designation for the unit established to support ground forces using new technology. How, then, did the ADF select the personnel to operate the Heron?

No 5 Squadron RAAF Wirraway aircraft with crew being briefed by an Army officer during an army cooperation exercise, 1944 (Defence)

As most RAAF deployed capabilities also operate at home in Australia, most of the personnel chosen to operate them on deployments come from the home squadron or unit. The squadron has normally been training in their likely deployed roles and often had years of putting that training into practice on exercises. However, a different approach was needed, as the Heron did not fit that model. Instead, the RAAF gathered people qualified in other roles from across Australia and attached them to 5 Flight for Heron conversion training, before assigning them to Joint Operations Command to be deployed. From the outset, the staffing of the Heron was to be a joint responsibility. That is, it was to employ people from the three services of the ADF, especially in the aircrew roles. Noting the inherent risks of flying a drone on the scale of a light aircraft without an established operational airworthiness regime, the ADF insisted on only using qualified ADF pilots as Heron aerial vehicle operators (AVO). This contrasted with the Canadians, who used a mix of pilots and navigators.[6] While there was a predominance of fighter pilots, the AVOs came from a range of flying backgrounds. There were RAAF Hornet, Hawk, F-111, Orion, Hercules and other pilots, as well as Army Black Hawk pilots and Navy Seahawk pilots. Many were qualified flying instructors or qualified helicopter instructors, and some of the fast jet pilots were fighter combat instructors.[7] Lyle Holt explained there was a preference for fighter pilots due to the difficulty of flying a MALE drone in the dynamic air environment of Afghanistan (with the added need to talk to ground forces while talking to air traffic and battlespace managers).[8] Preference was given to those with close air support experience. One Canadian Heron AVO with extensive experience as a military and commercial pilot said learning to fly the Heron had its differences. He noted, due to not being on board the aircraft, it was difficult to maintain situational awareness. He also noted flying the Heron required a lot more communication with others involved in the mission.[9]

For the other member of the two-person aircrew team, the payload operators (PO), the RAAF selected people based on experience and airmanship. Most of the selected officers were RAAF air combat officers and air battle managers or Army helicopter pilots, while the enlisted POs were air electronics analysts and air surveillance operators. At least one Navy helicopter observer joined a rotation.[11] The POs were not trained as qualified Heron co-pilots but, as one 5 Flight trainer said: 'We like to think that we train them up as a co-pilot.'[12] Air vehicle operator and payload operator were not the preferred Australian titles for the two primary aircrew positions for the Heron, but the RAAF kept the terminology to avoid confusion with the Canadians and contractors.[13] Personnel for all roles were usually identified through an expression of interest process, but they had to be releasable from duties at their home unit.[14] They ranged in age from 19 to those in their fifties. In fact, one deployed member celebrated her 20th birthday on operations in Afghanistan.[15]

The unusual organisational structure of those who operated the Heron – being temporarily attached to 5 Flight for training only, then assigned to operations away from their actual home unit – led to yet another peculiar twist of military terminology. While those assigned to Task Unit 633.2.7 never considered themselves as members of 5 Flight – except for the few 5 Flight members who did deploy to fill late notice staffing gaps – they often referred to the task unit as the Heron detachment. Frequently shortened to the 'Heron det', this

What makes a good drone pilot?

Trying to capture the characteristics of any high-skill profession, including drone pilot, in a simple list is not easy and will inevitably be somewhat reductive. There are, however, some fundamental qualities that contribute to a good drone pilot.

They are detail oriented. Safely flying any aircraft requires the pilot to comply with its operating parameters; drones are no different. Adhering to the steps in pre-flight and post-flight checklists requires close attention to detail. Similarly, pilots must be meticulous about broader situational concerns, like managing airspace requirements, operating within government or operational constraints and fulfilling the needs of the mission. Close attention to detail allows drone pilots to avoid both seemingly minor, and major errors that can carry serious consequences.

They can read maps and 3D displays. Pilots must be comfortable engaging with analogue and digital mapping and other displays. This is necessary for understanding the mission parameters and maintaining airspace, which is essential to preventing collisions or airspace incursions. Although drones are unmanned, they operate concurrently with manned aircraft – a collision with one of these could kill other aircraft operators and, at very least, would cause damage to important equipment.

They remain calm under pressure. Drone pilots are required to manage numerous tasks while operating safely and achieving their stipulated mission. This creates cumulative pressures that require a steady hand and a calm head. These pressures intensify when pilots receive dynamic, critical tasks that may directly affect the safety of troops on the ground. In a rapidly changing battlespace, pilots must remain composed while coordinating their mission in evolving conditions and ensuring they continue to operate safely. For this reason, Heron pilots were typically military pilots of other aircraft who had experience with the complexities of managing airspace.[10]

Squadron Leader Luke Connell inspecting a Heron drone prior to flight (Terry Hartin)

implied they were a detached part of a larger unit. This was usually the case for, say, an air-to-air refuelling tanker detachment sent on operations from No 33 Squadron back in Australia, but it was not the case for the Herons. Some military terms are hard to shake, though, and most Heron personnel rarely thought of themselves as members of a task unit either – they were simply part of the Heron det. With a rich source of the right people for the task, how did the ADF go about training them?

An aerial vehicle operator and payload operator controlling a Heron drone on approach to the runway, Woomera (David Gibbs)

Training the personnel

The urgency to introduce the Heron into service drove matters at a considerable pace. The contract for training was signed on 1 May 2009, and the Australian project team travelled to Canada to negotiate operational aspects in Ottawa on 4 May.[16] Training for the cadre crews to be embedded with the Canadian Heron operators began in Canberra during the second week of May with the four-week classroom theory component for the AVOs, POs and electronic warfare (EW) specialists. From Canberra, the AVOs and POs travelled to Canadian Forces Base Suffield in Alberta, Canada. In June, they commenced the four-week practical training in flying the Heron and operating its sensors. The training in both locations was provided by the Heron's manufacturer, Israel Aerospace Industries (IAI), in collaboration with contractors MacDonald Dettwiler and Associates (MDA). The embedded cadre personnel and the commander of Rotation 1 deployed to KAF in Afghanistan after only a short return to say farewell to family in Australia and met the proposed deadline of 31 July 2009 for beginning the Australian Heron capability.[17]

Rotations 2 and 3 followed a similar path, but with theory training in Australia moved to RAAF Base Williamtown, New South Wales, before the practical training in Canada. Trainees on those early rotations remarked that the training provided by the contractors was a lot more relaxed and was very different from the way such training would have been given by an ADF training unit.[18] One PO felt the course was very deliberate and delivered 'in slow time', without the benefit of the operational context ADF trainers would have brought.[19]

A downside of the military off-the-shelf (MOTS) approach to rapid acquisition is it can come with an off-the-shelf training package not necessarily tailored to the end-user's needs; this was the case for the Heron. One AVO complained: 'The training was going into too much depth for a bunch of aviators,' after sitting through three lessons on the four-stroke cycle of an engine.[20] Another noted the training really was for first-time drone operators and remarked, it 'catered for people who have no idea about aviation.'[21] A member of the Canadian Heron team who underwent the same Israeli training found similar problems, noting: 'The idea is to take an eighteen-year-old kid that has never flown a plane before and … make that person an AVO.'[22] A critical failing with the training was it only extended as far as the equipment supplied by the manufacturer and did not consider the additional elements the Canadians and Australians had added, such as the ground mission station (GMS) and the range of communications equipment.[23] Wing Commander David Riddel identified this as a problem from the start: 'Whilst the contractor-provided training made the crew "safe solo", there was no operational conversion or tactics instruction, no mission rehearsal. … we did not have this luxury.' [24]

Heron Rotation 2 with their instructors at Canadian Forces Base Suffield, Canada, on their last day of training, 2009 (James Hutchins)

As the Canadian aircrew had also found, many of the Australian aircrew under training by IAI found language barriers and cultural issues impeded their learning.[25] Hebrew was the first language of the IAI instructors, and most were relatively young, having recently completed national service obligations. Most had joined the company to continue their employment in drone and simulator roles. One female Israeli instructor had extensive experience as an F-16 fighter simulator operator.[26] One AVO noted, the ADF personnel were 'quite accustomed to this well-practiced Air Force routine of training-the-trainers style and structure … and then you went to this translated from Hebrew or Israeli type training.'[27] The training was made more difficult by the fact IAI was also in the process of giving accreditation to the Canadian MDA contractors, for conducting the training themselves, during the training of the ADF personnel.[28] The inherent problems of training a trainer while live students were trying to learn were all too apparent. While this was not an ideal situation, the RAAF did learn from the process. The 'lessons learnt' process that follows any major ADF activity to record lessons for future activities recognised MOTS training packages will not always account for the range of previous flying experience and not be tailored to the ADF's operational requirements. It, therefore, recommended forming training documentation working groups from the very start for future MOTS acquisitions.[29]

Once in Canada, the flying training was carried out from a couple of demountable huts by the edge of the airstrip; weather conditions played their part. The huts were surrounded by snow at times, and trainees had to watch the weather for opportunities to fly. Sometimes a week could pass before the weather cleared. One AVO summed up the experience of most of them: 'Overall, we got on with it and enjoyed what we could.'[30]

Australian aircrew walking on sheet ice to enter the Heron training facility at Canadian Forces Base Suffield, October 2009 (Defence)

ADF personnel are expected to learn new skills quickly, and they are often one step ahead in their thoughts about how to apply those skills in new ways, so the training was quite frustrating for some. The practical flying training, which used the sensor pod to view live imagery, did not include operational scenarios.[31] However, the training did allow them to operate the Heron to an adequate level of competence. The same AVO said: 'I think we expected more of ourselves or wanted to feel a lot more comfortable with things than we did.' He added, he 'felt very underdone prior to going into theatre.'[32] This was a common concern, especially for those on the early rotations, before the ADF was truly familiar with MALE drone operations.

Training incidents did occur. While Rotation 3 was under training in Suffield, a series of problems culminated in the crash of Heron 255 on 16 July 2010.[33] The drone struck power lines running alongside Highway 884, narrowly missing a passing car. The crash caused a blackout of the base and nearby Crown Village of Ralston, as well as starting a grass fire and destroying the drone's million-dollar sensor pod.[34] Wreckage was strewn on the highway, and traffic was blocked after local authorities closed it. While the Israeli instructor was the authorised captain of the flight, the crash was blamed on the reduced situational awareness of the flight crew provided by the drone's landing and ground manoeuvring camera and by not climbing sufficiently after aborting the landing with the wing flaps still fully lowered. However, one report blamed navigation system failures.[35] As a result, the landing checklist was improved, and the landing abort function included raising the flaps automatically.[36] Nonetheless, Herons were grounded in Canada, and flying training for Rotation 3 ceased. While the POs had completed their training by that point, the AVOs were sent to Israel to complete their flight training, and Rotation 2 extended its deployment time in Afghanistan.[37]

Wreckage of Heron 255 after striking power lines near Canadian Forces Base Suffield, Canada, 16 July 2010 (Nigel Meadows)

The crash had a significant effect on Heron training. Losing the ability to undertake flight training in Canada meant the original intent of not flying the Heron in Australia had to be reconsidered, and demanding airworthiness regulatory approvals would be needed.[38] In the interim, Rotation 4 did all its flight training in Israel, while arrangements were made with IAI and MDA to commence training in Australia. This meant finding suitably qualified contractor staff members willing and available to travel to Australia over the Christmas period in 2009. This was not easy, and the need to train ADF Heron operators for an Australian-specific concept of operations added to the challenges.[39]

No 5 Flight had a 'gather, train, scatter' approach to training personnel for deployed rotations.[40] That is, the people were selected from their home units and brought together to train on the Heron system and sent back to their units after deploying.[41] For the early rotations, personnel were sent back to their home units for some months after completing initial training to await their deployment orders. For many on those early rotations, that was a gap of up to three months without any Heron experience.[42] However, this was shortened to just a few days for later rotations. Nonetheless, after deploying to KAF, refresher training followed that included two days of theory on the Heron and operating in the airspace of Afghanistan for the aircrew. Then there was refresher flying that included a minimum of five take-offs and five landings for the aircrew before they proceeded to operational flying. Meanwhile, the intelligence team members paired with their outgoing counterparts and began working on live missions in the GMS under strict supervision.[43]

Heron operating and training facility, Woomera (Defence)

Beginning with Rotation 5 in 2011, however, 'force preparation' training was conducted at RAAF Base Amberley, Queensland, and Woomera, South Australia. The standard force preparation training, as done by most previous Heron rotations, was conducted at Randwick Barracks, New South Wales, and was well suited to individuals and small groups. However, larger formed groups could conduct their own training at other locations, often involving mission rehearsals. The CO of 5 Flight in 2011, Wing Commander Holt, oversaw the Amberley force preparation course and was assisted by a range of specialist trainers under course coordinator Squadron Leader Nigel Meadows.[44] These included Israeli instructors from IAI and Canadian instructors from MDA who were undergoing certification to conduct the training.[45] The course included three weeks of theory training and three weeks of Heron simulator training at Amberley followed by further five weeks of actual flying at Woomera.[46]

The Woomera training was the first time many of the non-AVOs and POs about to deploy saw a Heron.[47] This sequential approach to flying training was significantly different from the normal ADF building block approach; that is, lectures on a topic are followed by simulator flights focused on that topic, then consolidated in actual flying. The next topic is then approached in the same manner. However, the location of the training assets, with the simulator in Amberley and the Heron in Woomera, caused a disjointed approach.[48]

No 5 Flight executive officer Squadron Leader John Jenkins giving a morning brief to Rotation 12 members during OP-UP, Woomera, 2013 (Aaron Curran)

The training for Rotation 5 was, however, also a major step forward in understanding how to prepare the Heron team members for their operational roles. As one AVO put it: 'In a very quick time, you have to smash together 35 people who have never worked together before.'[49] In fact, prior to Rotation 5, the intelligence and EW people deployed without training alongside the aircrew, and they met for the first time on deployment.[50] Consolidating at Woomera and completing their force preparation as a complete rotation allowed them to carry out mission-specific rehearsals and practice crew resource management (CRM).[51] CRM is an essential aviation skill that focuses on communication, leadership and decision-making within multi-member aircraft crews and is credited with improving aviation safety worldwide. For example, a PO may notice the undercarriage has not fully engaged on a landing approach and is authorised to speak up, even though flying the aircraft is not their responsibility.[52] While CRM is widely practiced in the ADF, fast jet pilots were less likely to be familiar with it than members of multi-crewed aircraft. The pre-deployment consolidation at Woomera also had workplace and social benefits. As one imagery analyst said: 'During that time, there is a bunch of missions that we get to do with the real aircraft and with the actual people you are going to be working with and deploy overseas with.'[53] This was important because, without being members of the same unit, already in close working relationships, each new rotation had to bond and begin to understand their individual differences and needs.[54]

Heron Rotation 12 ground mission station crew and instructors during a training mission at Woomera, 2013 (Aaron Curran)

Training for most of the intelligence team began in Amberley with the GMS introductory course before travelling to Woomera.[55] During the Motion Imagery Exploitation Course, the imagery analysts watched pre-recorded full motion imagery taken from the Heron and learnt how to analyse it and report on what they saw. Much of this course was delivered by industry partners Geospatial Intelligence and BAE Systems Australia.[56] The EW analysts learnt to interpret the types of voice and signal intelligence the Heron gathers. The intelligence officers, who also completed the ISRO (intelligence, surveillance and reconnaissance officer) course, interpreted those reports and learnt how to manage the specialised Heron intelligence cell.[57] Much of that time was spent in the simulator. Meanwhile, the maintenance personnel joined the team to become familiar with the Heron.

As the Heron was a rapid acquisition capability, the RAAF did not want to invest heavily in maintenance expertise for it. That would have entailed training dedicated technical staff and establishing a maintenance and logistics framework. That would have added months, if not years, to reaching full operating capability. So, the technical staff of 5 Flight and each rotation were engaged to provide a contract management and general airworthiness oversight role only. Nonetheless, they needed a broad technical understanding of the Heron system. The RAAF selected a handful of people to travel to Tel Aviv in Israel and take part in a two-week engineering overview course.[58] The course focused on the Heron airframe and the ground data terminal, including the datalink communication systems. They received firsthand training from the Heron design and manufacturing engineers themselves. They also went through the Heron factory and saw the entire assembly process. One technician noted: 'It's still a very basic airframe with nothing much to it – it is held together by fifty bolts.' He lamented, though: 'It's a little hard to handle as a technician, not being able to turn a spanner on a fairly simple platform.'[59]

MDA contractors preparing Heron A45-253 for flight, Woomera (Defence)

The training at Woomera meant bringing a Heron to Australia and gaining airworthiness approval to fly it. While there were initial teething problems with assembling, testing and flying the Heron at Woomera,[60] the benefits of practical training in Australia, rather than in Canada or Israel, were enormous. It also had the advantage of allowing a few extra flying hours for crews above those gained in the previous overseas training. This Australian training was termed the Operational Upgrade Course and took on an operational feel, becoming known as 'OP-UP'.[61] For each OP-UP, a team from the staff of 5 Flight travelled in advance and prepared for the trainers and students. They organised the hangar, set up the radio equipment and arranged accommodation with the local Transfield garrison support contractor.[62] Staff from MDA also had to unpack the Heron and assemble it each time, often doing a software upgrade to keep it current.[63]

Rotation 5 set the trend for OP-UP by devising scenario-based training missions that simulated likely missions in Afghanistan.[64] Some members of that rotation had prior foreign experience with drones, and their scenarios called for Heron team members to carry out role-play as insurgents on the ground.[65] The Woomera terrain is visually similar to southern Afghanistan, but without the mountainous areas, so it was highly suitable for the mission-specific rehearsals.[66] The weather was generally fine and stable, making it an ideal training location.[67] Over time, 5 Flight developed rehearsal missions that included pattern-of-life surveillance, convoy route reconnaissance, improvised explosive device (IED) identification and direct support to troops in contact. People took turns to take part in the role-play. It was hot and tiring work, especially in the summer with the added distraction of annoying flies. One 5 Flight trainer described his role in this very important aspect of the full-immersion training as, 'I get to play Taliban out in the sticks of Woomera.'[68]

No 5 Flight personnel preparing dummies for a search and rescue training mission during OP-UP training, Woomera, 2013 (Defence)

The scenario training was intensive for the AVOs, POs, imagery and intelligence analysts, computer systems technicians and others.[69] One trainer said: 'There are no punches pulled there,' adding, 'we want to make sure they can do the job because if you send people over who aren't full-bottle, you … are hurting other people.'[70] Another trainer said: 'We do not want to have someone who is not ready, or who we do not think is going to do an outstanding job.'[71] Failure rates on OP-UP were low, with only one per course on average over all the roles.[72] However, the trainers also knew the Heron was a new capability, and only operational experience would give the crews true confidence. The same trainer said his job was to give them a 'licence to learn', constantly reinforcing the flying priorities principal of ANCA – aviate, navigate, communicate, administrate.[73]

OP-UP went through steady refinement as 5 Flight trainers incorporated the lessons from each rotation. As the situation on the ground in Afghanistan changed, so did the training back in Australia.[74] This was one of the benefits of having a small and agile raise, train, sustain unit in Australia dedicated almost entirely to supporting deployed operations. A Canadian exchange officer with previous deployed Heron experience commented on the value of OP-UP, saying, the Canadians did not have an equivalent, and 'the idea of OP-UP is amazing.'[75] With the deployment rotations being four to five months long, and the training regime taking almost as long, new rotations passed through 5 Flight at a steady rate. One staff member likened the process to a sausage machine, with the regular succession of theory courses for the various roles, then the practical tutorials, followed by the live scenario training at Woomera seeming endless.[76]

Heron students and trainers during a scenario brief as part of OP-UP, Woomera, 2013 (Defence)

A refinement of the later OP-UP iterations was the introduction of joint terminal attack controllers (JTAC) into the training. They were the direct link between the Heron and ground troops in Afghanistan, directing where they needed the cameras to look while supporting troops in contact with the enemy or on patrol. Many JTACs did not get to see the Heron ground communications equipment until they were in Afghanistan.[77] No 5 Flight knew every Heron flying hour in Afghanistan should be dedicated to operations, providing ISR to ground forces, not being consumed by training. So, the ability to train rotations in Australia prior to deployment was crucial. In all, 15 Heron rotations supported Operation *Slipper*. Having been selected and trained, what was life like at Kandahar on deployment for those Heron rotation members?

Life on a Heron deployment

While there was a lot in common with other ADF deployments to the Middle East, the experience of those deployed with the Herons had many unusual aspects. Their living accommodation was within Camp Baker, the Australian logistics and support compound within the sprawling KAF in southern Afghanistan. The compound was named after Corporal Michael Baker of the Australian Army Aviation Corps who died during a Black Hawk helicopter training accident near Townsville in 1996. It provided the sleeping, showering, laundering and recreation areas for most of the Australians based at KAF, along with operations areas for some of the other ADF task units. Each Heron rotation integrated into the domestic life of the camp in different ways, some being more involved than others. As the operators flew the drone from the other side of the airfield, at a location they dubbed 'The Lair', they did not spend much of their working day in Camp Baker.[78] In fact, after a typical 14-hour shift, many crew members simply needed rest.

Typical view of the streetscapes at Kandahar Airfield, Afghanistan (Steve Campbell-Wright)

The Lair was the operational workplace for the Australian Herons and was located on the north side of KAF's single runway at an area known as Whiskey Ramp – one of many operating ramps with hangars and crew areas adjoining the runway and taxiways. It contained all the technical elements of the Heron system as well as a small briefing room, an office for the detachment commander and executive officer, an operations room, some storage spaces and a recreation room with outdoor barbecue area, table tennis area and darts area. The place acquired the name during the first rotation as their devil mascot's lair, or the place where it plotted, schemed and carried out its cunning plans. It made no difference that Tasmanian devils live in a den and not a lair.

Travel between the living accommodation at Camp Baker and The Lair was part of the daily grind. It could take from 15 to 30 minutes to drive there through the congested road traffic of the airfield. With only a limited number of vehicles, they devised a 'wheels plan' to make sure everyone was there in time for their shift.[79] In fact, many rotation members thought the separation of their workplace and living accommodation was good because it allowed them to switch between working and resting modes. Some expressed sympathy for the members of the Force Support Unit that ran Camp Baker because those soldiers woke up and went to sleep in their working environment.

Inside the crew room at 'The Lair', Kandahar Airfield, Afghanistan (Sean McClure)

Sport played a large part in the recreational activities of the deployed Heron personnel, as it always has for Australian service personnel. KAF had five large gymnasiums, including one run by the British forces with an indoor soccer pitch and basketball court. Camp Baker had a beach volleyball court beside grass nurtured and maintained by ADF members on successive deployments. Heron personnel often played as a team against other elements in the camp.[80] There was also a small gymnasium, a recreation room, a smoko hut and a barbecue area, but it was no holiday camp. The threat of indirect rocket fire from insurgents outside the camp was real,[81] and the sleeping accommodation was 'hardened' – that is, reinforced to give some protection against explosions. One imagery analyst later recalled, on arrival in Kandahar by C-17 transport: 'We went into briefings on what happens around the airfield, what life is like at Camp Baker and Kandahar – how to deal with rocket attacks, all the different alarms that will go off … that was pretty full on.'[82] One technician said of his experience: 'You jump off the Hercules, and at that time, you are straight to the load'(that is, you put a full magazine of ammunition onto your rifle or pistol). He, in his turn, noted the demeanour of the next rotation as they arrived: 'You can see it in their eyes, they are all new and wide-eyed.'[83]

Gates to Camp Baker, the Australian support and logistics hubs at Kandahar Airfield, Afghanistan (Steve Campbell-Wright)

The threat became very real for some members of Rotation 11 when an insurgent-fired rocket detonated on the aircraft ramp near the Heron hangar. One technician described the situation: 'A big chunk of rocket casing hit the ground outside our hangar and danced on through the hangar – just missed one of the MDA techs, probably about fifteen metres from where he was standing in front of the Heron.' He noted the rocket warning alarms went off after that. 'I got a nice little bit of take-home shrapnel,' he said, adding laconically, 'that was an interesting day.'[84] Flight Sergeant Andrew Earl, a PO on three rotations, later recalled an occasion when a rocket hit the hardened sleeping accommodation. From his room, it sounded like a thump followed by a large handful of gravel being thrown on the roof. The rocket had gone through the roof, and shrapnel had peppered the bedroom. Again, the alarms went off after the attack. Ironically, that was for the best because the room's inhabitant was outside smoking a cigar at the time of the attack and would have rushed into his room if the warning had gone off before the rocket hit.[85]

Typical late afternoon scene at Kandahar Airfield, Afghanistan (Steve Campbell-Wright)

Women on operations in Afghanistan

Women in the ADF have played a vital role in Australia's operations in Afghanistan since 2001, spanning trades from postal staff to combat medics, armoured vehicle drivers, helicopter pilots and, of course, drone pilots. Serving on operations in Afghanistan, women provided a unique and vital capability to Australia's mission. Cultural values in the region typically dictate women should not interact with men outside their family group and this meant Australian forces often had little to no interaction with Afghan women. The result was a significant gap in local cooperation and intelligence opportunities. Female soldiers were deliberately deployed and integrated into patrols to balance all-male teams with extremely valuable results. Patrols achieved far greater engagement with women in villages, engagement which brought precious intelligence that helped Australia in developing stronger community links, central to the 'winning hearts and minds' aspect of counter-insurgency operations.[87] Women in Coalition forces were essential to the creation and employment of female search teams, female engagement teams and also female human intelligence exploitation teams – all vital aspects of the Coalition's successes with local communities.[88] Simultaneously, of course, female soldiers, sailors, and aviators fulfilled a wide range of essential roles on Australian and multi-national bases in Afghanistan. The Australian Army deployed women to Afghanistan as ScanEagle and Shadow pilots and operators from 2007 and 2012 respectively.[89]

A female engagement team from Mentoring Task Force Three speaking with women in the Karrmisan Valley, Afghanistan, 2011 (Defence)

Gravel lined many of the roads and paths to stop them becoming mud during the winters, and dust from road users was a feature of all the other months. It obscured the horizon on most days, and seeing the sun pass the horizon at sunset was rare for the 20,000 or so people at KAF. Nonetheless, it was possible to see the desert and mountains at times, particularly from the western side of the airfield after the perimeter road was finally paved. Driving around the runway threshold from Camp Baker to The Lair for a shift, therefore, afforded a good view for those on later rotations.[86]

There were five dining facilities at KAF. Each dining facility, or DFAC in American terminology (pronounced dee-fac), had acquired a unique name. There were Cambridge, Far East, Luxembourg, Niagara and North Line DFACs. Heron staff often ate in different ones to try to have some variety. North Line DFAC was on the north side of the runway close to The Lair. A 5am omelette with the lot was a favourite start to the working day for one AVO, while one technician complained: 'The food is the same old bland stuff' every day.[90] KAF also had a few BX stores. Short for 'Base Exchange', these stores were retail shops set up by the Americans, Dutch and French, somewhat like a small department or discount store. They sell items and supplies from their home countries on almost all deployed airbases and army camps, where they are more commonly known as PX (Post Exchange). A unique feature of KAF was the Boardwalk, which one rotation executive officer (XO) said was surreal. He described it as 'a 400-metre running track, almost one hectare in size I think, but surrounded by fast food joints and stuff like that.'[91] A covered timber boardwalk formed a promenade connecting a series of demountable shops featuring well-known Western fast-food shops such as Green Beans Coffee, Pizza Hut, KFC and TGI Fridays. Nearby, there was a tent market run by local merchants who sold a wide range of souvenirs and local crafts.

The Boardwalk at Kandahar Airfield, a raised timber promenade surrounded by shops with a running track and other improvements in the centre (South Carolina Air National Guard)

One Heron pilot, later recalling his deployment, said it was relentless and very tiring, but they got into a good routine.[92] An intelligence analyst recalled he started work before lunch each day and concluded his shift at 10pm. His nights of pattern-of-life surveillance were usually quiet, watching 'to make sure there was no one doing dodgy stuff during the evening.'[93] One PO recalled the Heron team members were 'at work for fourteen hours a day, pretty much every day.'[94] The standard battle rhythm was nine days straight of flying then one no-fly day or perhaps a day with only a single Heron operating after dual operations began.[95] Days with only a single Heron operating allowed for a staggered tenth day off for individuals, while allowing continued support to ground forces.[96] Despite one ADF liaison officer saying the deployment was 'quite literally just sleep, eat, work, gym, sleep' over and over again, he also noted: 'You get so caught up in the fight that it is like you just insert yourself in there, and all of a sudden, you have just lost four months.'[97]

A stall in the tent market at Kandahar Airfield, Afghanistan (Steve Campbell-Wright)

The midway point of any long deployment can be an unusual time for many. Some count the days and identify their 'hump day' – the day that marks the top of the climb to the midway point, after which 'it's all downhill.' It is a time when people are more aware of their situation and not just focused on their work. One technician noted around his rotation's midway point: 'It was the first time I had seen people's personalities start to rub.'[98] Deployments of six months and longer attract an entitlement to ROCL (remote out-of-county leave), which gives personnel a break partway through their deployment to reunite with family in Australia or another country for two weeks. The Heron rotations did not have this entitlement due to the shorter length of their deployments; the one exception was Rotation 13, which was extended by about two months.[99]

Part of camp life was to invite fellow military members to see the Heron in operation. In August 2010 alone, the task unit hosted eighty visitors from the ADF and Coalition forces.[100] It was not unusual for visitors to be allowed to operate the sensors while the Heron was in transit to or from the task zone, and those with the right clearances could sit in the GMS and watch a mission in action.[101] This was all part of giving fellow sailors, soldiers and aviators an understanding of the capability and importance of MALE drones as they were entering Australian service for the first time (as well as building camp rapport). This extended to a series of short exchanges between the Heron crews in Kandahar and the Army Shadow drone crews in Tarin Kot, further north in Uruzgan Provence. Personnel from each drone type saw what the other did with their systems and took back new knowledge to help improve their own operations.[102] The Heron crews also paid regular visits to the Special Operations Task Group (SOTG) in Tarin Kot to build the connections between the two teams as rotations went through for each.[103]

Chief of Air Force Air Marshal Geoff Brown addressing Australian troops during a visit to Multi National Base Tarin Kot, Afghanistan, March 2012 (Mick Davis)

As some of the initial champions of introducing the Heron into RAAF service, it was only fitting that air marshals Mark Binskin and Geoff Brown paid visits to the task unit during their operational liaison visits to the Middle East. During his visit on 12 November 2010, Air Marshal Binskin presented the task unit with a cricket set on behalf of His Excellency Mr Michael Brice, husband of the Governor-General.[104] An Australian parliamentary delegation that came to KAF in May 2011 also focused on the Heron in their itinerary.[105] Occasionally, there was time to visit Coalition drone forces at KAF. A highlight was to visit the British or American Reaper squadrons, where they met the

Shadow missions over Afghanistan

A typical Shadow drone mission in Afghanistan launched from Multi-National Base Tarin Kot (MNB-TK) at any time of the day or night, though best efforts were made to avoid midday launches during summer. In those scorching ambient temperatures, commanding the Shadow to climb to its operating altitude could put serious strain on the engine. The drone, or 'bird', was run through pre-flight checks by the Shadow Group's Navy maintainers, both on and off the launcher. Once the maintainers radioed through to the launch and recovery crew that the drone was ready, the air vehicle operator took the bird through its launch sequence on the system's FGCS, the light and mobile forward ground control station. Every Shadow operator could tell you the precise series of revs a Shadow RQ-7B engine makes on the launcher when testing its spark plugs; that's how closely operators came to know the system they were flying. After launch, and hand-over to the FGCS, the bird would transit to begin its mission. For most of the Shadow Group deployments, this included distant overwatch of various road convoys or perhaps ongoing surveillance of a stretch of road considered likely to be targeted by insurgents. Inside the mission control station, the mission commander and the analysts sat together, monitoring the mission and directing the operators as necessary to get the best imagery. A staple task throughout much of 2013 was flying overnight deterrence missions – loud, low-altitude loiters to warn-off any insurgents thinking of launching a rocket at MNB-TK. This was not always successful. One morning, while still dark, the sortie observed three rockets being fired at the base, the makeshift projectile launchers glowing white on the infra-red screen. As the morning continued, another bird was prepared and launched, before the first was brought down to ground and safely caught in the arrestor gear, and so the next mission began.

(Australian War Memorial P10950.489)

operators and swapped notes about recent sorties.[106] Wing Commander Matt Bowers, who led Rotation 14, enjoyed showing visitors the Heron system. He said, it was 'a good opportunity to showcase the capability, but more importantly for me, it was the talents of the people that we had, because that's what made the capability work.'[107]

Chief of Air Force Air Marshal Mark Binskin manoeuvring a Heron from the ground control station during a visit to Kandahar Airfield, Afghanistan, November 2010 (Neil Ruskin)

On the rare full day with no rostered flying, many of the Heron rotations organised barbecues to get together as a whole team and to host Coalition colleagues. With enough time to plan, they could arrange for meat and salad packs to be flown in from Al Minhad Air Base on one of the regular sustainment flights. The XO of one rotation said they were 'some of the best fillet steaks I've ever had.' While these were casual occasions, they were still in a warzone, and he noted how strange it was to be socialising in shorts and T-shirts but carrying weapons.[108] Rotation 10 was on deployment on Australia Day in 2013 and celebrated in typical Aussie style. It centred on the volleyball court – the only green grass in the camp – where they held a barbecue and played ping-pong, their Steyr rifles stacked underneath.[109]

Some rotations were deployed over Christmas. One technician remarked: 'It has actually been one of the most memorable and enjoyable Christmases I have had – you are in the middle of Afghanistan, and it is cold.' He added: 'We ended up decorating the vans with decorations and tinsel. Some of the girls had brought over stuff in their trunks for Christmas.'[110] Rotation 10 was deployed over Christmas 2012, and the warrant officer in charge of maintenance arranged for a friend in Townsville, Queensland, to bake a large Christmas cake, which he had shipped to Afghanistan. Flying did not stop just because it was Christmas Day, so the crew, all dressed in Santa hats, cut the cake in the hangar in front of the Herons.[111] They also set up a Christmas tree with lights in the hallway and presents beneath.[112]

An ADF member playing football in Camp Baker, Kandahar Airfield, with a Steyr rifle slung over her shoulder (Steve Campbell-Wright)

The members of the task unit marked Anzac Day and Remembrance Day each year in the way they might usually have done at home, by taking part in a short commemorative ceremony by the Australians at KAF that included a minute's silence for the fallen. They also celebrated significant occasions as they occurred during their deployment. Rotation 3 held a barbecue to celebrate reaching 2,500 Australian Heron flying hours; they enjoyed a cake made by the cooks of the Cambridge Mess at KAF.[113] Rotation 13 clocked up the milestone of 20,000 hours of operational Heron flying during their time; they marked the event with a cake decorated with a model Heron on top.

One AVO summed up his experience of the social life of his deployment: 'The accommodation is great, food is fantastic, and you get great people to work with.'[114] They made sure everyone's birthday was celebrated, usually with a cake in the crew room, or doughnuts from Tim Hortons, procured from the boardwalk.[115] In October 2010, one

PO became a father for the first time while on deployment, with his wife giving birth to twins back in Australia. The Heron team arranged for flowers and a gift basket to be sent to her.[116] The strong sense of generosity often extended to supporting those less fortunate back home. One rotation ran a Relay for Life event that raised almost $8,000 from KAF Coalition and other personnel.[117] By adding up their accumulated jogging and cycling distances, another rotation ran the equivalent of the distance from Amberley to Kandahar – some 10,600 kilometres – to raise money for Legacy. Their trivia nights raised money for the Royal Flying Doctor Service.[118]

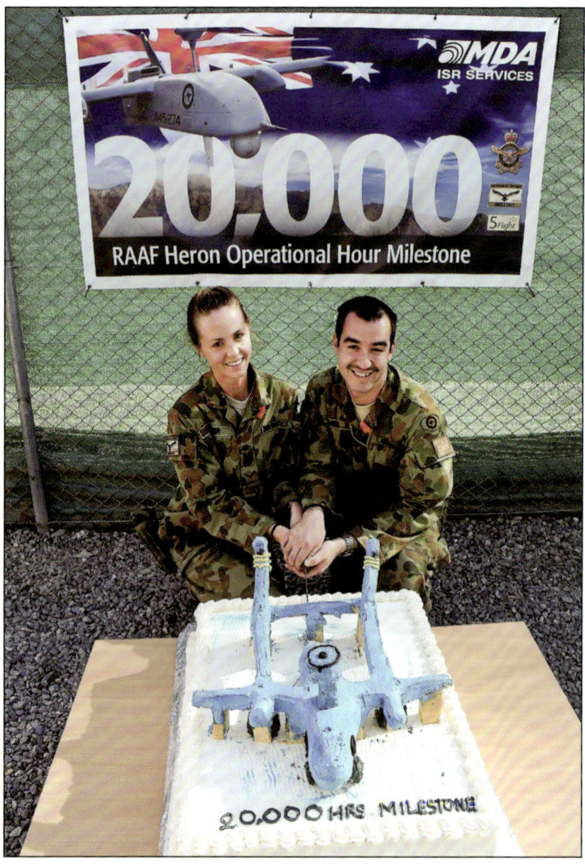

Members of the Heron detachment marking 20,000 flying hours with a celebratory cake, Kandahar Airfield, Afghanistan, 2013 (Chris Moore)

Some rotations raised money by a very unconventional method. In an unprecedented move for RAAF members, they sought permission to grow beards in return for substantial donations to the Returned and Services League. While not normally allowed in the RAAF at the time, the commander of JTF633 gave his approval, providing the beards met the Navy standard. The 'fine' for growing a beard was $250, and participants sought sponsors to match or exceed the fine. One rotation raised well over $10,000 for Legacy. Apparently, it did not go down well with the Army personnel at Camp Baker, but the cause was too good to disallow the beards.[119]

Flight Lieutenant Ryan Ginty (left) and Flight Lieutenant Joel Mortimer from Heron Rotation-14 pedalling through the heat during the 'Dawn Until Dusk' challenge for Legacy, Kandahar Airfield, Afghanistan, 2014 (Kelly Freebody)

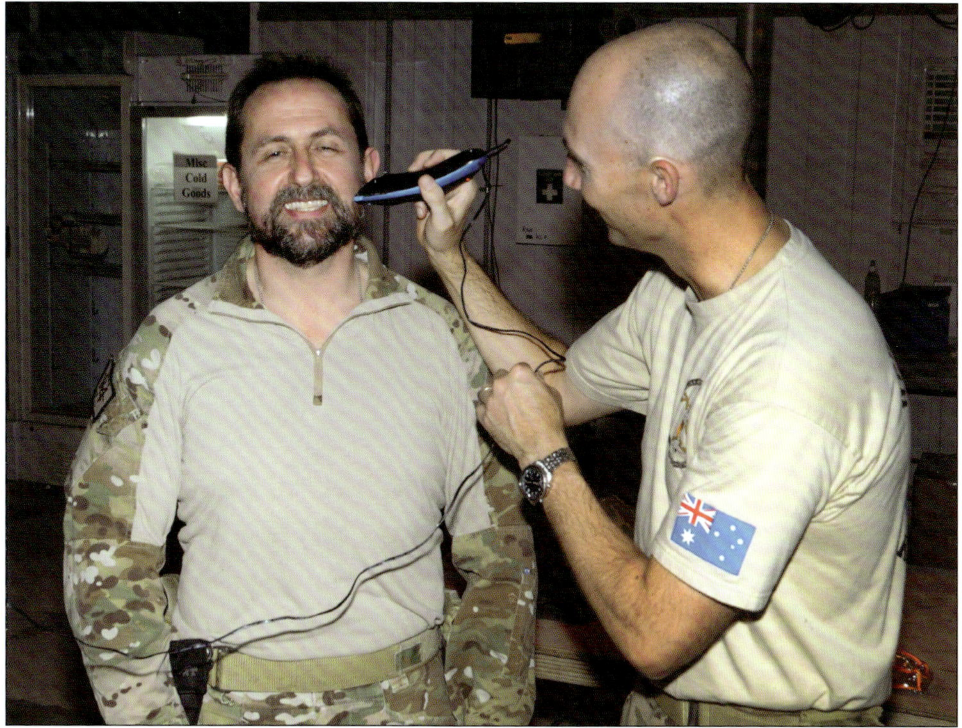

Heron Rotation 14 commander Wing Commander Matt Bowers (right) taking the clippers to executive officer Squadron Leader John Jenkins during a Legacy fundraiser, Kandahar Airfield, Afghanistan, 2014 (Kelly Freebody)

Communication with family back home in Australia for the early rotations was good by the standards of the time. Welfare phones were provided to call home. Due to the limited bandwidth for non-operational communications, call durations were limited, and the phones were monitored for breaches of OPSEC – as operational security is commonly known. Later rotations had the benefit of Skype and FaceTime.[120] The ADF went to considerable lengths to ensure contact with home was available, perhaps more so than other nations. It knows the value of connectedness with home and the support it can bring, and it invests heavily in providing communication infrastructure wherever it can. A Canadian exchange officer with one Heron rotation enthused: 'Camp Baker is very nice – it has Wi-Fi,' adding: 'Camp Baker is the only place I know of that has Wi-Fi everywhere in the area.'[121] Importantly, care parcels from home with resupplies of personal items and treats came through the deployed mail system.

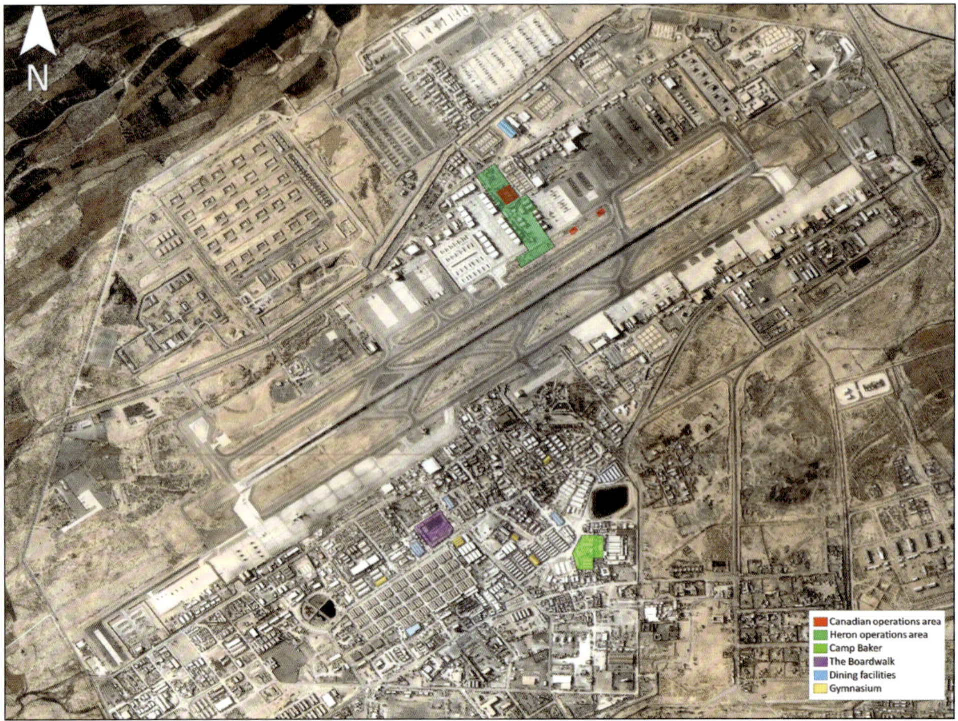

Kandahar Airfield runway, working areas and domestic areas (Defence)

Rotation handovers and support

The changeover point of rotations is known administratively as a 'relief in place' (RIP). This is when the arriving rotation spends time integrating itself into the deployed environment and conducting a handover-takeover – known as a HOTO – with the departing rotation. This typically two or three-week period is a time of intense activity for all concerned. To reduce the stress, the later Heron rotations had staggered RIPs that divided the new rotation of about 35 personnel in half, with Chalk Alpha arriving two weeks before Chalk Bravo.[122]

The ADF administrative and logistical support personnel in the Middle East conduct the reception, staging, on-forwarding and integration (RSO&I) regime to ensure the new personnel are prepared for life on the deployment and the threats it offers. This entails issuing passes, weapons, body armour and specialised equipment. New arrivals also get the latest threat assessment and medical briefs. Those same local support staff prepare the old rotation for their return to Australia. The initial phases of RSO&I – reception, staging and on-forwarding – were conducted at Al Minhad Air Base in the United Arab Emirates. The integration phase takes place when personnel arrive at their final deployment location in the Middle East Area of Operations. Over the integration phase, new personnel pair with their outgoing counterparts to gain as much operational knowledge as they can to learn the work cycle and to build on what they have learnt back in Australia. Those who had deployed on previous rotations were keen to learn what had evolved since their last rotation.

For some Heron RIPs, living accommodation was tight. Most rooms had four double bunks that were only occupied by one person each, often keeping some of their personal equipment on the other bunk. Each bunk was separated by a curtain or hanging blanket to give a measure of privacy. Rooms normally accommodated crews that worked on the same shift times to minimise disruptions. However, during accommodation shortages, new rotations sometimes double bunked with the old. The cramped conditions placed stress on the teams, as those going on shift could easily wake others at all hours.[123]

Heron Rotation 12 commander Wing Commander Steven Parsons handing over the task unit pennant during a brief handover-takeover ceremony at Kandahar Airfield, Afghanistan, 2013 (Justin Brown)

A HOTO is also the most vulnerable time for the capability itself,[124] as new operators refine their technical and professional mastery and apply it to the operational situation. This was a particular risk for the early Heron rotations because people arriving had only just completed initial training to fly the aircraft and did not have many relevant flying hours logged. One CO of 5 Flight noted most arrived with only 12 hours of flying time.[125] As the new crews gained their experience on the job, the capability could go through a see-saw effect. One way of helping to combat this was the lecture packs of lessons learnt by the outgoing rotation and provided to the incoming one.[126] In typical ADF language, one AVO described the process as 'passing on all the good gouge' – the hard-won information that could not be found through the official training.[127]

One intelligence analyst noted HOTOs are 'always an interesting dynamic', saying: 'A new bunch then gets in there and has a totally different mindset towards the way things should be done.'[128] Fresh from their training, this was understandable, and the weeks of handing over were valuable in allowing them to appreciate the practical realities of using the Heron system in the operational environment. On the other hand, one AVO said taking on the new knowledge was like drinking from a firehose, adding he was 'still not very comfortable' after the two-week HOTO.[129] The Canadian Department of National Defense approach to the rotation of its Heron personnel was quite different. Each member of the rotation deployed for seven months, but the rotations were staggered at the three-month point. This meant every new person was sitting with someone who had at least three months' experience.[130]

Aerial vehicle operator Squadron Leader Keith Dybing (left) and electronics technician Mark MacDonald from MDA conducting the pre-acceptance inspection of a Heron at Kandahar Airfield, Afghanistan, 2011 (Defence)

The contracted MDA staff members in Kandahar were an essential part of deploying the Heron. They provided the drones in accordance with the ADF flying schedule. They made sure the drones were in a serviceable state and ready to fly through a thorough maintenance regime; the turbocharger and other critical components were changed every 300 hours, and the engine at 500 hours.[131] MDA staff members towed them to the taxiway, and the ADF Heron crew took over for start-up. After landing, MDA staff accepted them as they taxied off the runway, shut them down and towed them back to the hangar. One task unit commander said: 'They were fantastic, always there when you needed them.'[132] An AVO noted, they were 'fully involved in the fight, and they understand the importance of their task,' adding: 'They would bend over backwards to make sure that we had platforms available.'[133] This was only possible through the close relationships that evolved between MDA and the Heron task unit staff, particularly the maintenance and logistics staff. One technician said, as almost half of the MDA staff members during his rotation were in fact ex-military Australians working for the Canadian contractor, the arrangement 'had a nice Australian flavour.'[134] One had even deployed as an Australian soldier with the ScanEagle drones, and to give the team an Anzac flavour, there were ex-New Zealand military member as well.[135]

The goodwill between the contractors and the ADF Heron team was the result of an immense amount of coordination and cooperation, with one AVO noting, the warrant officer engineer was the 'key important conduit between contractor and ADF.'[136] They also acted as the maintenance liaison officer (MATLO) for the ADF Herons. Local fortnightly meetings at KAF reviewed in-service support and technical aspects, while regular conference calls to the home locations of the various elements reported on contract performance, supply matters and approvals for configuration changes. This often involved coordinating meetings over multiple time zones – Afghanistan, Canada west coast, Israel, and Australia east coast and central.[137] Many people had to work outside of their normal working hours to attend these teleconferences. A Heron task unit commander summed up the relationship by saying: 'If they could help us and it was within their physical capacity to do so, they would. It was certainly a collegiate approach.'[138] A good example was when the post-flight inspection of a Heron in August 2010 determined it needed an engine change. MDA staff changed it overnight, allowing the Heron to resume tasks the following day without interruption.[139]

Some of the challenges of operating the Heron were outside the control of the task unit and the contractors in Afghanistan. Due to the nature of the lease, with IAI leasing the Herons to MDA to provide them to the ADF, any requests for modifications or deep technical support had to pass through MDA. While this was a necessary way to do business within the rapid acquisition model, one senior technician noted: 'It is quite a painful red-tape process and does cause some delays,' commenting: 'If we owned the platform, it would be a totally different story.'[140]

MDA contract staff lived in their own accommodation at KAF. Their role in providing maintenance and flight preparation during non-flying hours meant they worked to a completely different schedule from the uniformed ADF members.[141] They were deployed for eight-week rotations with scheduled rest periods at the end of each of their rotations. Initially, they did their force preparation training in Australia, having travelled from Canada, before then travelling to the Middle East. There, they took part in RSO&I without the weapons training component. This arrangement reduced their effective time at KAF each time they deployed. Eventually, an arrangement was made with Joint Operations Command to give them abridged training entirely at Al Minhad Air Base, regaining many days of support to operations.[142]

MDA and ADF personnel pushing Heron A45-262 into the hangar after a flight, Kandahar Airfield, Afghanistan, 2011 (Defence)

The ADF communications electronics technicians were also critical to the Heron capability. Drones rely very heavily on communications, and as Wing Commander Frost asked of the rotation he commanded: 'If you can't talk to the aircraft or provide the information to the right people at the right time, why are you out there?' He was full of praise for the technicians: 'They worked ungodly hours, they would be in there at three in the morning getting the systems all up and running … so you would walk in, do your checklists, and go flying.'[143]

The smooth running of each deployed task unit relies on those in the support roles, such as the administration, logistics and operations staffs, as well as the computer and communications technology personnel. Using typical RAAF acronyms, one AVO said of his rotation: 'Both the ADMINO and the LOGO were fantastic, excellent!'[145] One senior technician went as far as to say the MATLO, the administration officer and logistics officer 'are the gel to make sure the little detachment is functioning.'[146] The MATLO role was always filled by the technical warrant officer, and one said he was 'the jack of all trades' because so many secondary roles fell to him – ground vehicle manager, ground

The maintenance effort

Unlike the maintenance of manned aircraft, maintaining military drones requires managing an entire and complex system that not only includes the aircraft, but also the ground control station and the associated communications equipment. Each has its own specific maintenance requirements, resulting in a mammoth ongoing maintenance schedule. This is further complicated by the greater reliance of drones on computer technology, radio transmission and associated fields, making the maintenance effort for these platforms a significant one.[144] During the Herons' mission in support of Operation *Slipper* in Afghanistan, these inherent maintenance challenges were compounded further by its operating environment. Flying out of Kandahar Airfield, the scorching Afghanistan summer heat poses a particular challenge to the engine and flight systems of a drone, as does the region's icy winters. Moreover, the high number of flying hours due to continual operational demand for the Herons' valuable ISR feeds imposed a heavy load on the platform, which inevitably necessitated a rigorous schedule for maintaining each drone's baseline readiness. Operational tactics and the platform's systems, including, most vitally, its sensors, also continued to evolve. These developments brought further ongoing burdens for technical maintenance that had to ensure the Herons were performing at their highest possible operational capacity for extended periods of time to best support the Australian soldiers on the ground who were relying upon the drone's products.

(Defence)

work-health safety advisor, airfield management representative and a range of other minor roles.[147] As the senior enlisted airman, he also looked after any first-line welfare and discipline issues that arose.

During their handover as MATLOs from Rotations 3 to 4, Warrant Officers Barry McCrabb and Trevor Dix averted potential disaster. They were walking along the runway ramp near the Heron hangar and were watching a Canadian Chinook helicopter carrying out power checks in the hover prior to departing on a mission. McCrabb noticed an oil leak from one of the helicopter's two engines, but the pair was unable to signal the helicopter to land. They reported the leak to a nearby Canadian technician, who contacted the operations cell, which radioed the helicopter crew. The helicopter had landed at a nearby forward operating base, and the flight engineer immediately confirmed the leak and shut down the aircraft. The Canadians recognised McCrabb and Dix for their significant contribution to flight safety with a 'For Professionalism' award, stating: 'The early detection of this leak not only prevented an in-flight emergency in an operational theatre but also prevented the unnecessary exposure to risk for the passengers and crew.'[148]

Stressful times

Tragedy struck the task unit on 30 May 2011 when Lieutenant Marcus Case was killed in a helicopter accident. While the 27-year-old Army officer had previously served overseas in Malaysia and Timor-Leste and had been part of the ADF's Queensland flood relief operation in 2011, it was his first deployment to the Middle East. He had served as an infantryman, a commando and a helicopter pilot, at which he excelled. Case was the youngest of six children and a keen sportsman. His family said he was 'born to fly' and had concentrated his efforts on becoming an army combat aviator.[149] Despite being a trained helicopter pilot awaiting conversion to an operational type, Marcus was deployed as a PO.[150] The 2014 inquiry into his death found Lieutenant Case was riding on the ramp of an Australian Army Chinook helicopter during a familiarisation flight. The helicopter entered an episode of uncontrollable 'porpoising', and despite using a restraint strap, Case was thrown out of the helicopter and left hanging. He was killed when the Chinook crash-landed on him. He was the 26th Australian soldier to die during the Afghanistan conflict.[151]

On first hearing of the crash, the Rotation 5 task unit commander, Wing Commander Jonathon 'Muff' McMullan, ordered the crew to land the Heron flying that day in support of SOTG pattern-of-life surveillance. All task unit members were called to The Lair – even those in their beds at the time – and all internet and phone communications were disabled. They assembled and waited for many hours, not knowing why they had been called, except there had been an incident. McMullan finally arrived and had the grim and unenviable task of telling the 30-plus team they had lost one of their own. Case was well-respected and popular, and his loss was hard felt. McMullan bore much of the brunt of the tragedy; as the Heron task unit commander, it happened on his watch. He had authorised Marcus Case to take part in the flight, and he identified the body after his death.[152]

Lieutenant Marcus Case

A member of the Sydney-based 6th Aviation Regiment, Lieutenant Marcus Sean Case was 27 when he deployed to Afghanistan on Operation *Slipper* in 2011 as a Heron UAV Operator. He had previously deployed to Malaysia as an infantry soldier with Rifle Company Butterworth in 2005, to Timor-Leste with the 1st Commando Regiment on Operation *Astute* in 2007, and to Queensland on Operation *Queensland Flood Assist* earlier in 2011.[153] On 30 May 2011, Case was completing a familiarisation flight on *Brahman 12*, an Australian tandem-rotor Chinook CH-47D helicopter on a mission to recover a broken-down American aircraft. There were six personnel on board, Case included, as they headed north at 200 km/h from Kandahar Airfield in Afghanistan's south. Along with the crew's gunner, Case was riding on the open rear ramp when a gust of wind hit the Chinook, causing the helicopter to oscillate wildly. As the chopper tilted nose up, the crewman managed to grab the fuselage. Case flew out the Chinook's open rear hatch, the force extending his safety strap so he was left dangling more than four metres outside of the aircraft, and he swung there as the pilots desperately attempted to regain control of the aircraft. When they failed, the Chinook crashed and caught fire. The five other personnel survived, but Marcus Case was tragically killed instantly in the crash.[154] He remains the only Australian Defence Force drone operator to die on operational service.

(Defence)

The team knew Case would have wanted the task unit to continue their important role of protecting the lives of Australians on the ground and that flying should re-commence as soon as possible. The task unit commander authorised the next scheduled mission to go ahead as planned at four o'clock the following morning and for all to report to the medical facility in the meantime. Those flying that mission were individually medically cleared to fly. The 11 aircrew – who had spent months together training to fly the Heron – mounted a piquet on Case's body in the morgue. They did so, armed with their weapons, 24 hours a day in two or four-hour shifts for four days – singly during the day and in pairs at night.[155] Heron flying was cancelled on the day of his ramp ceremony, when the whole rotation attended as eight of Case's aircrew colleagues bore his coffin to the C-130 Hercules to start the journey home.[156] The ramp ceremony – a form of military funeral by those who remain in the warzone while the coffin returns to the family in Australia – was attended by hundreds of Australian, American and other Coalition troops. Fellow Army pilot Lieutenant Adrian Wilson accompanied Case's body home to Australia.[157] As an enduring testament to Lieutenant Case, the nose cowling of Heron A45-274 was painted with a tribute. In August 2015, IAI presented the nose cowling to the Australian War Memorial at a brief ceremony in Canberra. It is the only Heron component retained by the ADF after Heron flying ceased.

Lieutenant Marcus Case's coffin approaching the ramp of the C-130 Hercules transport aircraft during the ramp ceremony to farewell his body from the Middle East, June 2011 (Defence)

Heron nose cowling painted in tribute to Lieutenant Marcus Case (Jonathan McMullan)

Those on Heron rotations were involved in stressful missions at times. In June 2010, an IED struck two members of the Mentoring Task Force and their bomb detector dog. Sapper Jacob Moreland was killed in the blast, as was border collie Herbie, and Sapper Darren Smith later succumbed to his injuries. The Heron was called in to provide overwatch support and came on station soon after the casualties were extracted. The AVO 'in the box' at the time said, it was a 'very sobering moment, and I think that was the first exposure I had had to Australians killed in action.' He added, the situation was 'quite surreal … we could see groups of Afghans looking from not too far away and kids playing next to the group.'[158] Deaths or injuries to Australians led to communication lockdowns at the Kandahar base, which had the flow-on effect that those who were safe could not let their families at home know, causing stress on both sides.[159]

Sergeant Iain McGrath standing with the artwork he and a colleague painted following the death of Lieutenant Marcus Case in 2011 (Janine Fabre)

Tragically, on 21 June 2010, during operations in Shah Wali Kot in Uruzgan Province, three members of the Special Operations Task Group (SOTG) died and seven were seriously injured when the United States Army UH-60 Black Hawk helicopter they were flying in crashed at night. The commandos who died – Privates Scott Palmer, Timothy Aplin and Benjamin Chuck – were reportedly on their last scheduled mission of their deployment.[160] A helicopter crewman was also killed, and another suffered serious injuries. The Black Hawk, one of four assigned to the attack, rolled several times and caught fire. A Heron was supporting that airborne assault and provided overwatch of the crash site and recovery operations.[161] The Heron's time on station was over eight hours that night, so most of the crews carried out a shift and were exposed to the scene. A PO with more than 1,300 hours of flying time on the Heron over three rotations said it was a sombre time, and 'nothing else affected the whole team like this did.'[162]

Special Operations Task Group soldiers preparing to be extracted by a US Army Black Hawk helicopter alongside their Afghan National Security Force partners after completing clearance of a cave system in Uruzgan Province, Afghanistan, 2012 (Defence)

In another incident, a Heron was providing overwatch to an SOTG patrol positioned in a valley. The patrol was running low on water and unable to gain access to local wells due to Taliban activity in the area. It was very hot, and the patrol had already been there for a few days. They were becoming tired. Through the overwatch radio communication, the AVO said: 'You hear these noises in the background – the click, click, click noises – and they say "contact, wait out" ... your heartrate elevates a bit, but you are still trying to do your task.' The Heron had to respond quickly to the instructions of those on the ground – the troops in contact – to scan for the threat. With the altitude of the drone and the range of the camera, the AVO said it was like 'looking through a straw.' They faced the difficult task of precision scanning in the surrounding area without being able to see how the patrol was coping. He said: 'It just really sticks in your mind,' especially noting, at the end of his shift only minutes later: 'It was time to handover to the other guy and go back and play PlayStation and have a coffee.'[163]

That AVO was typical of many who deployed to operate the Heron when, on a second rotation, he was working with American forces in a dynamic targeting support role against Taliban spotters. He said: 'I remember seeing at least two or three strikes carried out on these guys, which I know were successful. We saw it all happen in full motion video.'[164] The role extended to battle damage assessment at times, and the AVO later noted: 'We even saw the recovery of the body and then taking it down to the township for burial.'[165]

A tough job

On one mission, there were some spotters that were having a rat at some of our guys from the hill. They decided to take these guys out with an Apache, and it wasn't pretty. They achieved their aim in that regard, and then our guys had to stay on target whilst they determined what they were going to do for disposal of the bodies. What I found was how professional all my junior ranks were with how they treated that with the utmost respect. I never saw any of them talking condescendingly or disparagingly against what happened. They realised that people had actually died, and despite the fact that these people were probably not nice people, they might have been under circumstances not under their control. You know the 'here is a gun, go up on that hill or we will shoot your family' type stuff. They were always very professional in their approach to that, so that was really rewarding for me.

Wing Commander 'Jack' Frost, Rotation 7 Task Unit Commander

The constant stress of potential rocket attacks also has a cumulative effect over a four to five-month deployment. As an indication of their heightened alertness, the XO on one rotation later recounted there was one member of his team who could whistle the start of the rocket alarm, and he had to tell him not to, because 'there would be people hitting the ground left, right and centre.'[166]

The ADF was very aware stresses might affect members of all the Heron rotations, and psychological briefs were part of the pre-deployment training. There were also psychologists available at KAF and other bases. One AVO who had supported 'some pretty serious missions' said: 'I didn't see anything I wasn't prepared for.'[167] Cohesion among the Heron teams was important in combatting stresses. One task unit commander noted: 'You could see the ups and downs,' and 'then their friends would come around them, and they would pick back up again.'[168] They also made a point to debrief after significant stressful actions to see how everyone was coping. Importantly, everyone deployed with the Herons understood the rules of engagement covering their actions, procedures and decision making. This gave them an ethical basis for their work and allowed them to act as members of the profession of arms in the service of Australia and not as individuals forced to act in accordance with their own conscience alone. After the eventual completion of Heron operations, a Defence report recognised there was a psychological impact caused by the crews working in the hothouse environment of the Heron operations area, separated from the domestic environment of Camp Baker. The report identified facilities to let crews debrief informally in a social setting will be important in future warlike drone deployments.[169]

Outdoor breakout area behind The Lair at Kandahar Airfield decorated for the Christmas season, 2010 (Sean McClure)

Post-traumatic stress disorder (PTSD) is a potential hazard of service in military forces worldwide, particularly among those close to the combat action. The 2015 Australian Senate report into the use of drones by the ADF stated: 'It is worth noting studies from the US military which have indicated some "drone pilots" have suffered elevated levels of mental health disorders.'[170] The report failed to recognise it is not only the pilots who are susceptible to PTSD. All involved in the operations of the Heron can be affected. A former Royal Air Force drone operator pointed to one major stressor being, during pattern-of-life surveillance, intelligence operators live day in and day out with those they are covertly observing, and they feel it if an attack needs to be made on them.[171] This can be exacerbated by the same crews who contributed to the pattern-of-life surveillance needing to carry out the subsequent battle damage assessment and seeing the effect of the strike at a human level.[172] Mental health issues may take some time to appear. In McMullan's case, it did not hit until three months after his return from Afghanistan.[173] One PO with considerable experience on armed drones with Coalition forces found, while he was trained to see the signs of PTSD in others, it crept up on him without him realising.[174]

An Australian medical study showed the rates of identifiable self-reporting of PTSD symptoms is low in the ADF, especially by aircrew, who are often afraid of being grounded. However, reporting in anonymous military surveys is much higher.[175] So, there is a potential well of undiagnosed and untreated PTSD in the serving and veteran communities. One Heron rotation commander when later speaking of one of his fellow officers said, he is 'a guy who came back and [has] never been the same.'[176]

Not all have suffered from their experience, and some have reported post-traumatic growth – that is, coming out a more-resilient person with a greater understanding of themselves. One Heron aircrew member, reflecting on his two deployments to Afghanistan, said: 'If it wasn't for the bad people, it would be a nice place to be.'[177] The ADF philosophy is each rotation or each individual assigned to operations sees it as their duty to make the deployment better for those who follow; the Heron detachment was no different.[178] Many were proud of the part they played and were happy to return to Australia knowing their good work would be taken over and improved by the next rotation.

Chapter 4
ON THE WING

The people selected for the Heron deployments were well chosen and appropriately, if only just adequately, trained to operate the new technology the Heron system represented for them. They learnt on the job and brought their prior aviation and military experience to the fore as they applied their new-found Heron knowledge to the technology and grappled with a new way of flying and an improved way of protecting ground forces in Afghanistan. How difficult was it to operate the Heron, and what challenges did its operators face in their role of providing a real-time intelligence, surveillance and reconnaissance (ISR) and electronic warfare (EW) capability?

Concept of operations

During the normal acquisition process for any new ADF capability, the way it will be used is an early and important consideration. This concept of operations (CONOPS) informs so many aspects of the capability – from the options it allows the government, to the whole-of-life costs of operation. However, the rapid acquisition of the Heron meant the CONOPS was being developed as the capability was being introduced. Herons were already flying in Afghanistan in the hands of other nations, but their CONOPS did not necessarily align with the effects the ADF wanted to achieve. As Wing Commander Lyle Holt put it: 'We are new at this game so we are learning what we can do. The approach we are taking is we will try anything we need to protect the guys on the ground.'[1] Operating without a clear CONOPS is risky, and the RAAF was well aware of that.

To help mitigate this risk, the first two Heron rotations – those that really developed the initial CONOPS – used fighter aircrew to lead the aviation and mission efforts.[2] These aviators, from Air Combat Group, were not as heavily tasked as aircrew from some other groups within the RAAF and were more readily available to assist in the introduction of the Heron into operational service. Other nations were using their Herons in a predominately ISR observation role without any real-time effect in active ground operations; the ADF wanted a more active role from its Herons.[3] This is where the fighter aircrew came to the fore, and as Wing Commander David Riddel explained: 'We have a team of highly trained people who know how to conduct unarmed offensive air support operations to contribute to the SOTG [Special Operations Task Group] effort.'[4]

Nonetheless, embedding ADF Heron crews with the Canadians in Afghanistan in the first instance was sensible during the formative phase. Riddel noted the early embedded crews were the right people for the job, and they were able to establish the tactics, techniques and procedures to be used in the Australian CONOPS very quickly. This set the Australian Heron teams up very well for operating on their own.[5]

On 13 January 2010, the first Australian-leased Heron achieved initial operating capability and began operations in Afghanistan.[6] The Australian Government announcement at the start of Heron operations highlighted the added safety the Heron afforded Australians on the ground, stating: 'Heron uses leading edge technology to boost force protection by providing ground commanders with live situational awareness.'[7]

AP-3C Orion on the flightline at Al Minhad Air Base, United Arab Emirates, prior to a mission in the Middle East Area of Operations (Andrew Heatherington)

The Heron, with its long endurance and high operating altitude, fitted into a much-needed role between the ISR provided by the Army's low-altitude tactical ScanEagle drones and that provided by the RAAF's theatre-wide AP-3C Orion surveillance aircraft. The Heron had longer loiter time and greater range than the ScanEagle and was more agile than the Orion. It could get 'down in the weeds' and do so in a tight location for hours at a time. As journalist Patrick Walters reported: 'The hope is that the all-round day-night capability of the Heron will reduce the incidence of roadside bomb attacks by insurgents, given the aircraft's endurance and ability to scout out patrol routes used by ground forces.'[8] These were high hopes indeed for a new capability in Australian hands, and Air Marshal Binskin reinforced its importance publicly, declaring: 'We are operating Heron as a National asset in Afghanistan.'[9] What, then, was it like to use the Heron? One initial indication at least was that, after the first one-year lease, the Australian Government extended the lease for another year from January 2011.[10]

Newly delivered Australian Heron A45-262 being removed, section by section, from its transport container at Kandahar Airfield by MDA technicians, December 2009 (Andrew Eddie)

Operating the Heron system

The Heron system comprises several elements, all of which go together to achieve the capability effect. Each element was operated by specialists who worked in concert throughout the mission. The aircrew component of a Heron rotation typically comprised six crews of an aerial vehicle operator (AVO) and a payload operator (PO) each.[11] For many rotations, these crew members remained as a pair, but not always. They sat in the ground control station (GCS), often referred to as 'the box', where they operated the Heron drone itself and its sensors. They communicated with the ground forces in the field.[12] The aircrew typically operated for two to three-hour blocks before handing over to the next crew.

One of the Heron flight crews, payload operator Squadron Leader Matt Basedow (right) and aerial vehicle operator Flight Lieutenant Steve Edwards at the controls during Exercise *Diamond Storm*, 2017 (Andrew Eddie)

Some aspects of the drone were the same as flying conventional military aircraft. The AVO left the GCS to carry out pre-flight walk-around checks of the aircraft and to sign for it.[13] However, the mindsets of the AVOs varied with their roles as pilots of their conventional aircraft. Those from large multi-crew aircraft backgrounds were accustomed to doing things in a deliberate and steady manner. However, one AVO who normally flew P-3C Orions said the fast jet pilots 'are just those highly charged individuals who are really pushing what you can do with the airframe, so I think that really set the tone for us.'[14] The fast jet pilots were also used to providing close air support to ground forces, and they were instrumental from the first rotation in establishing how best to meet their needs.[15] As with any aircraft, crew duty times for all crew members were strictly adhered to. As they reached duty limits, they were stood down, even if it meant they did not get to see a mission to its conclusion. One rotation executive officer (XO) explained: 'I know the adrenalin level is way high, and you want to see the things through to the end, but I have a duty of care to those people on the ground.'[16]

Some aspects of flying the Heron were counterintuitive for the AVOs. For example, to increase the cruise speed, rather than increase the throttle (as in a standard aircraft), the AVO had to pitch the nose of the drone down first. Naturally, that will make the drone fly faster, but it will also start to drop altitude. Without further input from the AVO, the autopilot senses the drop in altitude and increases the throttle to correct it, thus increasing the speed of the drone.[18] While there was a joystick, it was used primarily for the cameras, and much of the flying was controlled through menu tabs in the software; these could be configured to suit different operators.[19] Tabs were selected using a track-ball beside the joystick. It was like using a personal computer flight simulator game from the 1990s. The control system of the Heron was a legacy of the era in which it was created, noting it first flew in 1994. Many AVOs quipped that its flight controls were designed by an engineer and not a pilot. However, one AVO said: 'You thought it was a crazy piece of equipment and wondered how we could ever trust it, but as time went by, we soon saw that it worked quite well.'[20]

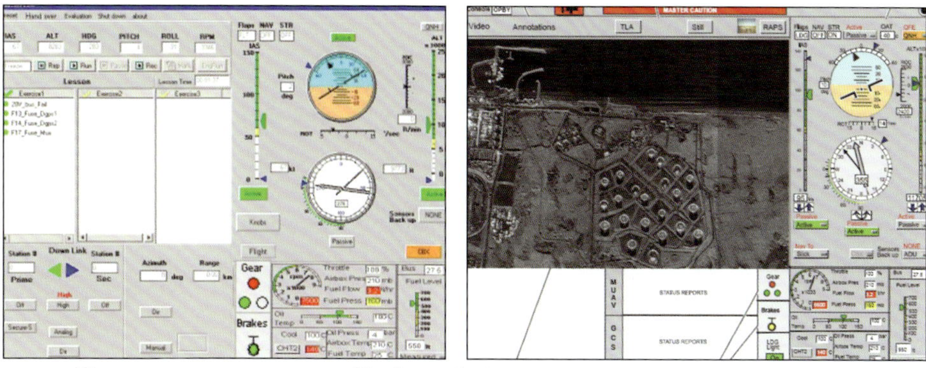

Heron main operating screens used by the aerial vehicle operator and payload operator (Defence)

Trust in the drone and its flight control system was important. Wing Commander David Riddel – who oversaw the introduction of the Heron into ADF service – made the point that the Heron is not like a low altitude tactical drone, in that it is an aircraft 'operated by

Heron ground control station

Like many military drones to date, the Heron is piloted by two personnel sitting side-by-side in a ground control station (GCS) that looks like a shipping container. GCS configurations may differ slightly from platform to platform, but the basic constituent pieces remain the same. The systems must allow the pilot to control the drone safely within the regulations for that area of operation while maintaining positive airspace control. They must simultaneously enable the co-pilot, as the payload operator, to obtain the imagery required to fulfil the mission. Within the tight confines of the GCS, each operator sits before their own dual operating screens and a personal keyboard, as well as sharing two central displays. Each side of the GCS has its own purpose: the pilot, or aerial vehicle operator's, side is for controlling the Heron's flight path and monitoring the drone's altitude, attitude and airspace, while the PO manipulates the Heron's sensors to capture imagery and video for the mission. Both operators wear headsets to enable communication with others. The Heron's GCS facilitates manual and autonomous flight of the drone, allowing the pilot to fly the Heron using the menu-driven options or to enter the mission into the computer as a series of waypoints the drone then follows, although the ADF rarely used this mode. Crucially, the Heron is equipped with an automatic take-off and landing system.[17] Like the cockpit in a manned aircraft, the Heron's GCS is the nexus of the drone's operations, and everything within it is designed for the safest and most effective flight.

(Defence)

trained and qualified aircrew, utilising aviation risk management processes … developed for manned aircraft.'[21] He reinforced the Heron flies 'at medium and high altitudes, sharing the airspace with other piloted aircraft, and we must comply with the same airspace control orders as manned aircraft.'[22] To fly in the congested airspace over Afghanistan, the aircrew had to be fully assured the Heron was where it was meant to be and was responding to their commands.

ADF-leased Heron A45-262 on the taxiway at the busy Kandahar Airfield, Afghanistan, July 2010 (Raymond Vance)

Adding to the challenges of flying the unconventional aircraft was that Kandahar Airfield (KAF) was then the world's busiest single runway airport. There were 370 aircraft stationed there, and a further 150 had transit rights through the airport. Aircraft movements, that is take-offs and landings, peaked at 800 per day, which is an average of 33 per hour or just over 2 every minute. The Heron was probably the smallest, at a little over 1 tonne, while the Antonov 124 was the heaviest at 450 tonnes.[23]

With so many aircraft movements, the airspace, runway and taxiways were very congested. It was so busy that the runway built up rubber very quickly and covered the centreline. Maintenance teams de-rubberised the runway every month, which further obliterated the centreline and taxiway marker lines. Approaching KAF meant flying through very busy controlled airspace – mixing with fighters, helicopters, transports, civilian airliners and other drones – for the last 30 miles of the landing approach at the high speed of 120 knots (220 km/h) then slowing to about 60 knots (110 km/h) for slotting into final approach with the other aircraft. Once in the sequence, the AVO engaged the auto-landing function and monitored the landing. One AVO explained he 'thought it would be a lot more surreal than it was, but very quickly you get into the headspace that you are flying an aeroplane still.' He added: 'You are sitting on the ground, but I still very much thought as if I was flying, which I found to be good.'[24] Another AVO, Fight Lieutenant Jayson Nichols, said: 'Sometimes you can get swept up with the mission so you have to remind yourself you're actually on the ground.'[25]

The PO sat beside the AVO and operated the payload. The PO also supported the AVO in flying the Heron, and one PO described his role as the 'non-flying co-pilot.'[26] This meant performing actions such as giving challenge responses to flight checklist items and supporting time-critical decision making.[27] When very busy, the PO might also communicate with air traffic control and carry out other non-flying aspects of the mission. Like the AVO, they needed excellent air sense and the ability to keep calm under pressure.

Members of Rotation 4 during a pre-mission brief, Kandahar Airfield, Afghanistan, 2011 (Bill Guthrie)

The payload – the electro-optic infra-red (EOIR) camera for most missions – was operated from a duplicate control panel and screens adjacent to those for the flight controls. This was a similar configuration to a side-by-side cockpit layout in a conventional aircraft, but with the captain on the right. Front and centre for the PO was a screen used to display either the full-motion video feed live from the Heron or the route maps. The crew could send the video feed to joint terminal attack controllers (JTAC) on the ground via the ROVER (remotely operated video-enhanced receiver) system to allow them to see the video feed from the Heron in real time.[28] JTACs could request where the camera was aimed to suit their requirements. However, there were some constraints in the system.[29] The video feed could only be sent via an unencrypted UHF transmission, which could potentially be intercepted by anyone within range and line-of-sight. So, the link was often turned on at the latest possible time to avoid compromising security.

Integration of the communication systems in the GCS was difficult to achieve, and the working area became cluttered with an ad hoc array of laptops and radios. These needed to communicate with air traffic control, battlespace managers, ground forces and higher headquarters. This was not a typical cockpit environment for aircrew and made for an uncomfortable communications human–machine interface.[30] The Heron's Israeli-provided hardware and software not being compatible with any of the ADF or NATO computers and communications networks – with the exception of CENTRIXS–ISAF (Combined Enterprise Regional Information Exchange System–International Security Assistance Force), which all

Heron sensors

The Heron is designed for a wide range of operations using different sensors that can be configured depending on the mission. Sensors include electro-optical and infra-red cameras and synthetic aperture radar; other payloads include a laser pointer.

Infra-red. This sensor detects and measures an environment's infra-red (or heat-based) radiation to create an image. Everything above 5 degrees Kelvin (or minus-268 degrees Celsius) emits a degree of infra-red radiation, so this sensor is adept at distinguishing living and non-living forms, though this is made more complex in very cold or very hot environments. The sensor is susceptible to the vagaries of weather and is usually rendered ineffective by thick cloud layers.

Synthetic Aperture Radar. The imagery provided by SAR is completely different from that provided by visible and infra-red sensors. It generates directed pulses of radar-frequency energy, and SAR 'reads' the high-resolution returns reflected by various terrain surfaces. The differences between these surfaces' physical and electrical characteristics render the imagery. In generating the energy pulses that reflect to it, SAR supplies its own source of illumination and is therefore useful for conducting 24-hour operations. It provides a vital all-weather sensor not inhibited by the cloud cover that would obscure an electro-optical camera and confuse an infra-red sensor.

These sensors, among others, were a crucial part of the Herons' missions in Afghanistan. Skilled Payload Operators reacted to changing situations on the ground to determine the best way of capturing the imagery required to fulfil their mission.

(Defence)

nations at KAF were able to use.[31] The standard Heron cockpit configuration, therefore, needed two additional monitors, two tactical satellite radios and two mouses, as well as the added complication of the six additional intelligence personnel on the communications network.[32]

When asked about how to turn the data gained from the Heron into usable intelligence, Chief of Air Force Air Marshal Mark Binskin said: 'That's the art.'[33] He pointed to the real-time nature of that analytical art and the need to provide the intelligence to those on the ground in a timely fashion.[34] That analytical work was performed by the team of intelligence personnel including ISR officers (ISRO), air intelligence analysts (AIA), geospatial imagery analysists (GIA) and EW specialists. They operated in the ground mission station (GMS) close by the GCS, where they performed signals intelligence and imagery intelligence roles including full-motion video imagery analysis, ISR effect analysis, post-mission reporting and intelligence mapping.[35]

Heron task unit intelligence personnel at work in the ground mission station at Kandahar Airfield, Afghanistan, 2014 (Janine Fabre)

To get the most value from the intelligence teams, they arrived at the GMS towards the end of the Heron's climb and transit to the mission location, just in time to set up. Their work began with a brief on the day's mission by the ISRO. While the AVO was the mission commander, the ISRO was the mission coordinator. They determined what profiles to fly on each mission to achieve the best ISR collection. As the head of the intelligence team, the ISRO was an integral part of the mission crew and was able to increase the value of the intelligence information for both the aircrew and the ground forces.[36]

Each intelligence team for a single mission comprised up to seven members. The GIAs operated in pairs. One was the 'screener', continuously monitoring the video imagery and calling out what they saw. The other was the 'reporter', who recorded the observations and transmitted them for analysis by the AIAs and ISRO.[37] During the early rotations, the EW specialists scanned radio transmissions to carry out 'gisting'. That is, they were listening for any insurgent radio discussion about the ground forces they were providing overwatch for. However, as confidence in the Heron's EW capability increased, they progressed to developing advanced electronic order of battle mapping.[38] The EW teams used interpreters for language and cultural advice. These specialists were engaged through the United States military system.[39] They provided the context for what the EW operators were hearing. An EW team could identify a network of insurgent spotters and managers. They could then pass that information to higher headquarters for targeting and use in later operations.[40]

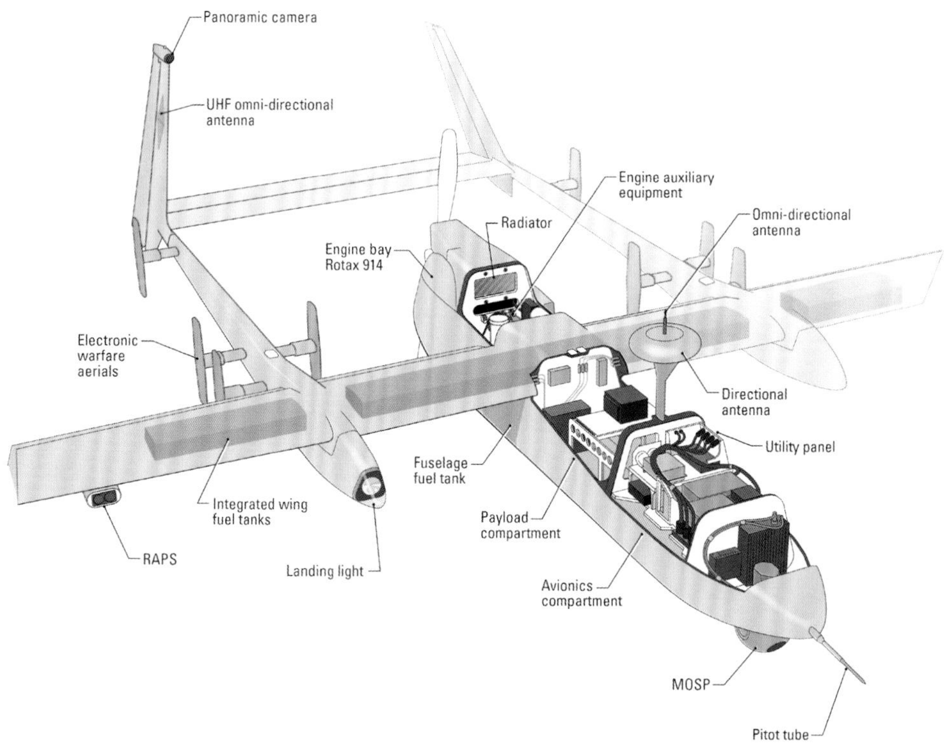

Internal layout of the Heron (Aero Illustrations)

A rotation XO, when referring to the EW role of the Heron, said: 'That's what we do best.' He bragged that operators of manned EW aircraft paid visits to the Heron team to see how they operated.[41] He gave credit to the Heron and its sensors for being very capable, especially in the press-to-talk radio bands. However, he gave greater credit to the operators, saying 'we have pretty much an entire P-3 crew sitting on the ground doing all of the analysis and pushing the information … to the customer'.[42] EW missions were limited to 12 hours, even though the drone might have been flying for up to 20 or so hours. This was due to the interpreters only being able to work a 12-hour shift. Many shifts were shorter because the nature of the work required intense concentration, listening very hard for hours at a time. One ISRO noted he took part in 120 missions during his rotation.[43]

The intelligence teams used crew resource management (CRM), normally only used by aircrew, to enable rapid decision making within the team and to increase the awareness of the intelligence cycle for the aircrew. In fact, the whole intelligence crew was considered a critical and integral part of the mission team, especially during tactical direct support missions.[44] They helped to enable rapid decision-making by ground commanders. They were fully integrated into the missions and were aware of many aspects not normally seen by image analysts in other roles. One AVO, an experienced P-3C Orion pilot, said to have a junior enlisted person 'talking to the pilot captain in another room and making sure I remembered something is quite different.' However, these CRM practices led to better aviation safety outcomes.

Another important aspect of operating the Herons was the liaison officers. These were embedded with headquarters elements and some ground units. They were critical in the planning and execution phases of missions to ensure commanders received the best advice on how to use the Heron to good effect.[45]

Operating challenges

Some challenges stand in the way of a successful Heron mission. Cloud cover or a sandstorm can affect the quality of the imagery, although the EW surveillance is not significantly affected. During much of August 2010, the prevailing dust reduced visibility and degraded support to SOTG missions.[46] In some cases, the weather was so poor that the drone could not even take off, and dodging cloud on the transition phase of missions was a frequent occurrence during the winter months.[47] Cloud increased the risk of ice forming on the wings; the Heron did not have a weather avoidance system, either through weather radar or meteorological support services.[48] Around 200 hours of flying time could be lost per month during the winters, as was the case in February 2011, when 220 hours were lost.[49] The single runway at KAF also meant the Heron missions had to coincide with favourable crosswind conditions. Even so, as one AVO put it: 'If we could fly, we would.' Other drone assets in Afghanistan made the decision not to fly or delayed their launches based on weather conditions or forecasts more often than the Herons. That AVO claimed there was an prevailing attitude of: 'I think we can give it a shot.'[50] The commander of the task unit during Rotation 14, Wing Commander Matt Bowers, put it more eloquently: 'We tried very hard within reasonable levels of risk to accommodate the needs of the guys on the ground because that's what we were there for.'[51]

During Rotation 14, a Heron was close to KAF on return from a mission, only to be told to hold by air traffic control. A sudden thunderstorm generated in its holding area, and the aircrew had to dodge rain and lightning for almost half an hour. One technician noted: 'The storms just roll in so quickly over there, and they manifest from nothing.'[52] The other Australian Heron flying that day was caught in the same storm as it also returned from its mission. Both sustained hail damage, one with 52 dents. The two Herons were grounded as MacDonald Dettwiler and Associates (MDA) carried out difficult repairs to the carbon fibre sections of the wings and replaced the damaged radiators. Missions continued for the next week or so with the one remaining serviceable Heron.

Afghanistan's topography created rapidly variable weather conditions (US Air Force)

Management of airspace while flying the Heron was a problem at times. Rather than talking on the radio to air traffic controllers as they would in Australia, aircrew of all types of aircraft flying in and out of KAF communicated through 'mIRC chat'. Short for internet relay chat, this is a secure form of communication on a computer screen (similar to social media chat). The system is effective, in that it highlights relevant information for a particular aircraft on the screen; this then alerts the aircrew. However, if there is a typo of the call-sign in the chat, the line of text will not highlight, and the aircrew may not see a call for them before it scrolls off the screen to make way for the following chat. The text was small, and an '8' might look like a '6' by the end of an eight-hour shift.[53] The Heron aircrew factored these problems into their visual flying scan routine. However, typos in the altitude and heading assigned by air traffic control and typos in acknowledging, led, in the words of one AVO, 'to us busting airspace several times.'[54] The ADF and the wider aviation community take occurrences such as deviating from assigned airspace very seriously and report them using aviation safety occurrence reports (ASOR). The ASOR system allows reporting, investigation and publication of all types of aviation incidents to prevent them occurring in future. The Heron operators submitted several.

Occasionally, the mIRC chat system went down altogether, so the Heron aircrew had to communicate through air liaison officers, adding an extra layer of complexity and risk. One early rotation called a self-imposed no-fly day to address the communication issues, with the rotation's aviation safety officer saying: 'Our little icon going across the line on the screen might seem very benign, but if I put Heron into a manned aircraft and caused it go down …'[55] No-fly days like these are a sign of an aviation organisation's maturity, placing safety above all else. In the case of the Heron, it was a sign that drones demand the same level of safety vigilance and, despite popular misconceptions, drones are not toys.

Australian ground data terminal (GDT) near the runway at Kandahar Airfield, Afghanistan (Sean McClure)

The ground data terminal (GDT) requires continuous line-of-sight to the drone to maintain contact.[56] So, at short distances, the drone can fly quite low. However, as the range increases, the altitude of the drone must also increase to maintain contact over the horizon. This is more critical when there is high terrain close to the GDT. Operations out of KAF into the neighbouring Helmand Provence therefore had to be at 21,000 feet instead of the preferable 7,000 feet or lower due to the communication shadow cast by a large hill to the north-west of KAF. This degraded the imagery from the EOIR camera. Also, loss of the datalink between the Heron and the GDT or the satellite was possible, but thankfully rare for the Australian operators.[57]

An AVO – himself a fast-jet fighter combat instructor – stated: 'The most difficult thing about Heron is driving this thing on the ground … it's the most stressful thing you will ever do … all the other AVOs will tell you the same.'[58] The drone has a large turning circle, with a radius of more than 20 metres. Visual acuity from the drone is also very difficult on the ground. It is not possible to use the downward-looking MOSP (Multi-Sensors Optronic Stabilized Payload) pod cameras, so the Heron is fitted with a panoramic camera on top of the right tail fin. Once on the ground, the Heron's auto-landing function hands control back to the AVO, and they have to taxi it off the runway. Aiming for taxiway entries was very difficult at KAF, especially with the runway markings in poor condition. In March 2010, the German Army crashed a Heron into the side of a C-160 Transall transport aircraft while taxiing in northern Afghanistan, and there were regular reports of American armed drones ending up in ditches beside the runway at KAF.[59] This was rare for Australian Herons, but it did happen.[60] An AVO described the stress of the situation: 'You might have an F-16 up your clacker and an air trafficker yelling at you to get off the runway.'[61] Low angle light, such as during sunset, obscured the AVO's vision from the cameras and made it difficult to see the taxiway entries. If the AVO missed the first taxiway, they had to head for the next one. The same AVO noted: 'You can hear the jets going around behind you and it was stressful.'[62] The situation was even worse after dark.

MDA contractors towing Australian-leased Heron A45-262 past Coalition and chartered aircraft at the busy Kandahar Airfield, Afghanistan, 2011 (Bill Guthrie)

There were some minor issues with operating the Heron. For example, the low speed of the drone could made it difficult to re-task in sufficient time, and the need to maintain de-confliction with other aircraft – and indeed artillery fires – in the crowded sky over an area did not always allow the drone to fly where it would have best effect.[63] Occasionally, there were problems with the drone itself. A mission-critical component might fail, which could downgrade the intelligence product or even force the drone to return home. One such problem occurred in September 2010, when four missions were cut short due to fuel pressure problems with Heron A45-262. This was ultimately resolved, but it did cause frustration at the time.[64] More often, however, crews could reprioritise and swap the task to the other drone after dual ops started.[65] The Herons suffered two days of no flying during October 2010, when mice chewed through the fibre optic cables that connected the some of the critical ground mission communication lines.[66] The later rotations were fortunate to have three ground control stations, so they had a spare in case of critical failures in the ground components of the flight control system.[67]

Issuing many of the flight control orders to the Heron was done by holding down a key on the computer keyboard and moving a trackball installed in the desk of the control station. For example, to climb or descend to a new altitude, the AVO held the key and rolled the trackball until the desired altitude showed on a slider bar on the screen then released the button to lock in that altitude. The autopilot raised or lowered the nose and flew the drone to that height. However, the keys used to stick sometimes, and the command was not locked in. Any further movement of the trackball would set a new altitude. The aircrew knew of this problem and noticed it very quickly, tapping the key to unstick it.[68] These 'sticky trackball events' led to more than 20 reported incidents in 2011 alone. After a program of regular cleaning of the trackballs and a strict policy preventing food and beverage in the GCS, each trackball was eventually replaced with a standard optical computer mouse.

With a natural focus on the safety of the control systems and sensors for the drone, the underlying computer systems for processing the information received did not have a lot of spare capacity. An AVO claimed, 'they were maxed out.'[69] That is, they could do the job, but they were operating at full capacity. He was full of praise for the ADF communication technicians who looked after the computers. 'They kept that whole thing running, day in and day out, and they worked so unbelievably hard because, if those servers dropped, we were done.'[70] One Heron task unit commander said it took a lot of effort on the part of the communications electronics technicians to keep the GMS technology running. He saw them working one night, then 'saw the same faces working there at midnight the next night … I almost had to order some of these guys to go off and get their heads down.'[71]

Communications and information systems controller Leading Aircraftman Joshua Schoeneck maintaining the computer systems to operate the Heron, Kandahar Airfield, Afghanistan, 2014 (Janine Fabre)

Airfield lockdown procedures, due to the threat of rocket attack, could also play havoc with the flying program, with an aircrew member noting the lockdowns always seemed to come at the wrong time. In one case, the flight crew had readied the drone for the day's flying and were awaiting the intelligence team members to arrive. It was about 6am, and the lockdown alarm sounded. They were obligated to launch the drone without the intelligence team but managed to get approval for the Army personnel in Camp Baker to drive the team to the GMS in armoured Bushmaster tactical vehicles.[72]

Operational problems

In the classic Swiss cheese slice model of a series of small errors leading to a serious failure, all the holes aligned when Rotation 2 crashed Heron A45-265 on final approach to KAF on 4 June 2010. The software design allowed AVOs to issue a command to the drone that was only able to be executed during a later phase of flight. Inbuilt safety checks in the software were not comprehensive and did not necessarily identify inappropriate commands and prevent them from being stored for later execution. For example, it was possible to flick the engine cut switch during flight, but this command would not take effect until the auto-landing phase was operating.[73]

Another hole in the stack of Swiss cheese slices was that, while selecting the landing gear, it was possible to accidentally and unknowingly flick the engine cut switch. Training did not prepare the aircrew for such a possibility, and that is what happened on the day of the crash.[74] He set the drone up for final approach to the runway, and as soon as he selected auto-landing through the on-screen menu, the engine cut out automatically. The Heron can land without power like a glider, but it was set up for a powered approach, and the glide slope was wrong.[75] The AVO immediately carried out the emergency landing sequence, but the drone was too low.[76] The operations officer in the neighbouring GMS looked up at the screen streaming the vision from the cameras, and she was heard to say: 'That doesn't look so good.' She was looking at the Heron sitting at an odd angle in a paddock with antennas dangling off it.[77]

The crew on duty acted quickly to quarantine anything that would help with the investigation and plan the recovery of the drone. Meanwhile, the camera was still operating, and they watched as Afghan goat herders approached and souvenired components. Members of the Royal Air Force provided force protection for the rapid 40-minute recovery – the Heron aviation safety officer noting: 'They were very polite, I'm surprised they didn't offer us a cup of tea.'[78] The recovery team managed to secure the return of the souvenired antennas, but the taillight was not found, the safety officer guessing it might have been put to good use as a desk lamp in a local village.[79]

The Heron airframe proved its reliability and resilience that day, with it ultimately being repaired in Israel and returned to service after five months.[80] Meanwhile, the one remaining Australian Heron (A45-262) had to complete the flying program of up to 20 hours per day on its own, leaving little time for maintenance, so the Heron task unit negotiated a local arrangement with their Canadian counterparts at KAF to share their combined pool of

Herons.[81] As they were all leased and maintained through MDA and were identical, they could all achieve the same operational effect. The first use of the pooling agreement was on 16 October 2010, when A45-262 was taken offline for major servicing of the engine and flight controls, and Canadian Heron 170254 was re-badged to fly as A45-254.[82]

Canadian Heron 170254 in Afghanistan, which also flew as A45-254 after rebadging (© All rights reserved. Reproduced with the permission of DND/CAF (2023))

Later in 2010, one of the Herons needed repairs after the nose wheel failed to extend for landing on 28 September. The AVO and PO completed the exhaustive emergency checklist, including many high-G manoeuvres to induce the landing gear to move. They were assisted by a senior Canadian AVO and test pilot called in to advise advanced methods of overcoming the problem. They finally attempted to land the Heron without the nosewheel after 19.1 hours in the air. Luckily, the drone sustained only minor damage to some of the aerials. This emergency shut down the busy KAF runway, but the Heron was cleared rapidly, and the runway was open again in 17 minutes.[83] The drone itself was flying again within 36 hours thanks to the efforts of the MDA contractors.[84] This incident was followed by another on 30 October, when the landing gear failed to extend on the first attempt. After several attempts, it did extend for a successful landing.[85] MDA grounded its fleet of Herons worldwide for a day on 1 November to receive advice from Israel Aerospace Industries (IAI) because these were not isolated incidents, other Herons having suffered the same problem.[86]

In another serious incident, Heron A45-262 began leaking oil during a long mission on 2 May 2011. This later proved to be caused by a pinched rubber seal on the oil return tube from number 4 engine cylinder. The crew regularly logged the drop in oil pressure to watch for signs to cancel the mission and fly the drone back to base. The pressure became critically low when the Heron was about 20 minutes from KAF, and the crew headed the drone straight for the airfield, running out of oil pressure three miles short of the runway. AVO Flight Lieutenant Jonathon 'Harro' Harrington had been overseeing the AVO during the flight as part of the rotation handover, and he took over the controls. He managed to get the drone to the runway at KAF for an emergency landing with the engine on fire. Those in the GCS could clearly see flames in the video feed from the panoramic camera mounted on one of the tail fins as the drone made its final approach to the runway. With oil pressure at zero and the engine temperature beyond limits, Harro had no choice but to cut the engine at a height of 100 feet, right on the threshold of the runway. The nosewheel collapsed with the hard landing.[87] Fire crews put out the fire and towed the Heron off the busy runway. Harrington had been the last RAAF pilot to carry out a dump-and-burn on an F-111, so his deployment mates gave him the dubious honour of being the only person to have also done so on a Heron.[88]

MDA technicians inspect Heron A45-262 after its successful return to Kandahar Airfield, Afghanistan, with an engine fire, 2 May 2011 (MDA)

Despite the systemic factors leading to these incidents, the RAAF realised shortfalls in training leading up to deployments were a contributing factor. One later rotation commander said, the 'Air Force had very accurately identified that … graduating with 12 hours on this aircraft, and being trained by an Israeli whose second language is English … didn't accord with any military standard of training anyone in the Air Force had ever done.'[89] The difference between the training cockpit, of standard Heron configuration, and the one used by the task unit, with its additional communications equipment, did not help.[90] The Directorate of Defence Aviation and Air Force Safety carried out an audit in the field on Heron operations and, by the time people were being selected for Rotation 5 in early 2011, the commander of Air Combat Group, Air Commodore Mel Hupfeld, decided to increase the amount of fighter pilots in the AVO role. His reasoning was they had proved their ability to acquire new skills quickly and had demonstrated superior situational awareness in the air and on communications systems. So, Rotation 5 had a full complement of six fighter pilots assigned.[91]

The aim was to restore the reputation of the Heron and to ensure the best possible support to the SOTG in particular.[92] Of the 41 Australians to die on operations in Afghanistan, ten died during the tenure of Rotation 2. One rotation member said: 'This was the most harrowing part of my time in Afghanistan,' adding that the casualty count doubled over his time.[93] Half of those had been killed by improvised explosive devices (IED), and the main reason why the Herons were deployed was to prevent IED deaths.

Changes, upgrades and trials

The first significant change to Heron operations was the erection of a second ground data terminal (GDT). This GDT was ground and air tested on 7 August 2010 and proved to be fully reliable, with no loss of communications or video link, throughout the test.[94] It provided redundancy that gave greater surety to operations. The Heron task unit began by operating two drones to generate one daily mission, or 'line of effort', as it is often called. However, the withdrawal of most Canadian forces from Afghanistan in July 2011 – with their Herons having flown more than 15,000 operational hours – left the Australian Heron task unit as the sole support requirement for contractor MDA.[95] This led to the possibility of 'dual ops' – or using three drones to generate two lines of effort.[96]

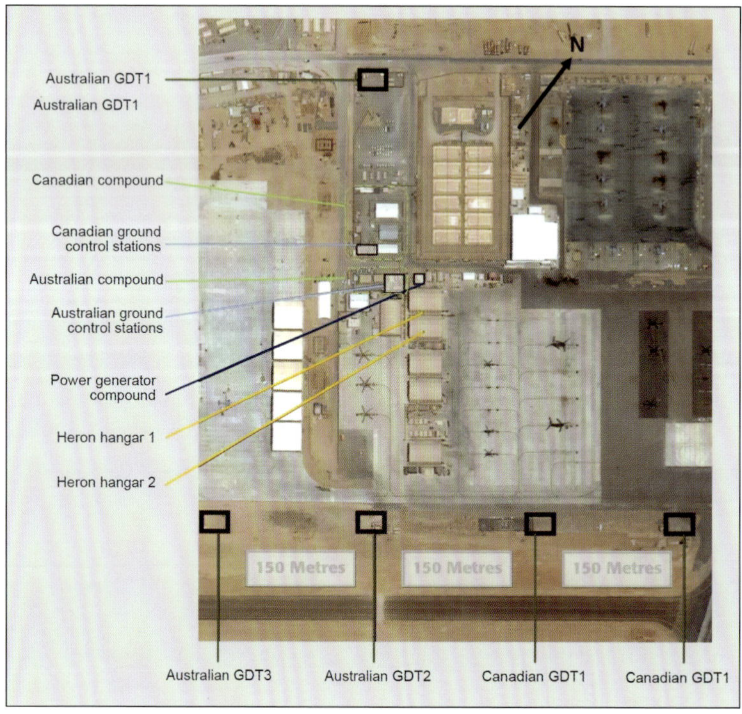

Australian and Canadian Heron operations area on Kandahar Airfield, Afghanistan (Defence)

Previously, MDA had taken from the joint pool of airframes (under an agreement signed in August 2010) to satisfy the flying program of both nations. However, under modern conflict conventions, nations must make their combatants and principal arms identifiable. Exterior clothing of combatants bears the flag of their nation, while aircraft bear an identifying national marking. Since the First World War, most nations have used a roundel or similar device. The Australian roundel has a kangaroo in its centre, while the Canadian roundel has a maple leaf. The Herons in Afghanistan displayed the Australian roundel in black against the grey drone exterior, and the Canadian roundel was white against the grey, each designed to give a subdued appearance. MDA personnel applied new stick-on roundels whenever the operator of a Heron airframe changed. Maple leaves are symmetrical, and the same sticker was applied to both sides of the drone. However, despite the kangaroo normally facing to its right to be heraldically correct, it needs to face forwards on aircraft in a visually important heraldic anomaly. The MDA contractors were not aware of this and reportedly sometimes provided a Heron ready for an Australian mission with one of the kangaroos flying backwards.

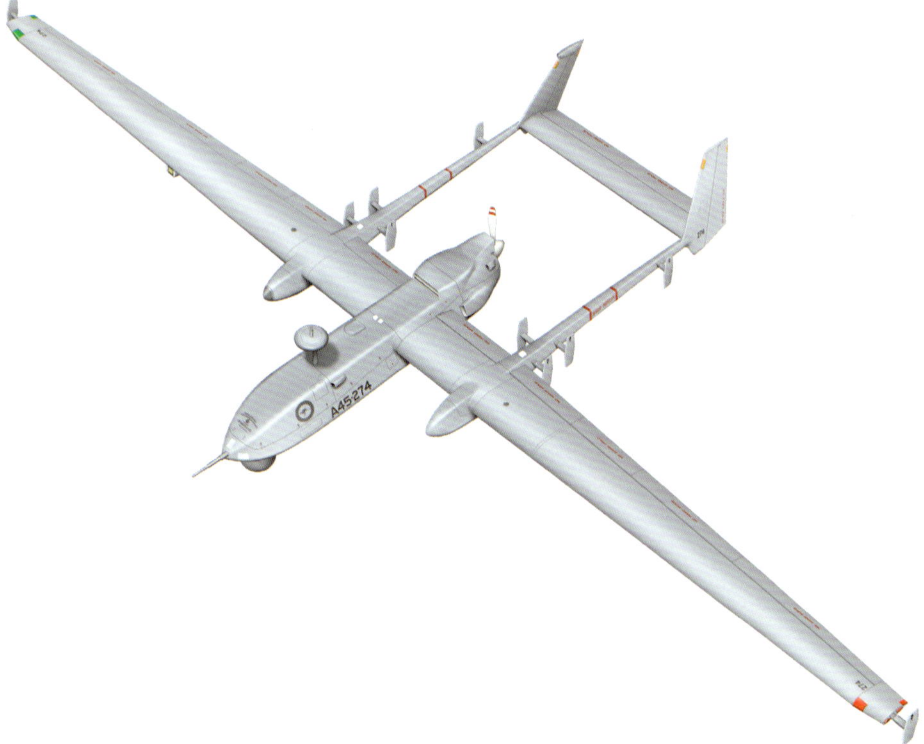

The long wings of the Heron provide a high aspect ratio that reduces the power required from the engine, thereby allowing long flight times (Aero Illustrations)

Dual ops proved a more difficult undertaking than first assumed. When Wing Commander Frost arrived in November 2011, the task unit had been trying to establish dual ops for some months. It placed strain on many of the support requirements, including an increased need for fuel resupply, computer and communications equipment, aerial masts, logistics support and another complete set of temperature-controlled facilities for the GCS and GMS.[97] Originally planned to commence in January 2012, through a massive effort during the cold 2011–12 winter, it was up and running on 4 April 2012.[98] Dual ops provided greater flexibility and a vast increase in the protection offered those on the ground. A Heron commander gave the example that, if a patrol was heading through a valley, one Heron could watch as they entered, while the other could search the path ahead of them to the other end of the valley. Alternatively, they could carry out two different missions over separate areas.[99] Another advantage was, with staggered flying times, it was possible to give 24-hour coverage if needed. The monthly flying hours increased under the contract from 500 to 650.[100]

Also in 2011, significant experimentation was being conducted at Woomera with the Heron available there. In July, Heron A45-253 flew test flights to validate the airborne UHF transmitter receiver relay (AUTRY) system. The AUTRY equipment was subsequently fitted to Heron A45-262 at KAF in the following September. With the system on board and the Heron flying at high altitude, the relay allowed encrypted radio communications between hand-held radios on the ground over an area encompassing ranges well in excess of those required to cover the entire Australian area of operations in southern Afghanistan. This relay capability removed the need for ground forces to use satellite communication phones, an added complexity and weight not welcomed on the battlefield. The AUTRY system was made by Australian company RF Industries in collaboration with the Defence Science and Technology Organisation (DSTO). The system went on to be sold to the United States Army and was used on its Aerosonde drones.[101]

Heron A45-253 undergoing AUTRY systems integration testing at the Woomera Test Range by RAAF, Army, DSTO, DMO and contractor staff, July 2011 (Scott Woodward)

A highly significant aspect of the RAAF's experience with the Heron was that it acted at times as a flying 'battle lab', to use Wing Commander Riddel's turn of phrase.[102] That is, rather than the normal process of testing capability enhancements in Australia, then deploying them, the drone became a flying testbed for some leading-edge technology. This involved the support of the DSTO, Capability Development Group and contractor MDA, along with Heron owner and provider IAI. In 2011, DSTO scientists deployed to Afghanistan to conduct a trial of a synthetic aperture radar (SAR) pod they had trialled at Woomera.[103] This secret classified trial – under the code name of Project *Athena* – was not even made apparent to the members of Rotation 10 unless they were directly involved.[104] Normal Heron flying operations stopped for about six weeks while the project fitted an ELM-2055DX pod and conducted SAR experiments.

Defence personnel and contractors at Woomera during Project *Athena* laying fake roadside IEDs for detection by the synthetic aperture radar (Israel Aerospace Industries)

A SAR pod was a standard civilian option for the Heron from the manufacturer, but Australia's highly advanced method of processing the data was classified secret by the Department of Defence. A separate computer system to run the pod was installed, and a SAR operator sat in the GCS with the aircrew.[105] The project allowed them to test the effectiveness of SAR in Afghanistan using standard electro-optic imagery for comparison. As challenging as the SAR test missions were for the technical crew, they were not popular with the aircrew because it meant flying in long straight legs for hours at a time.[106] One AVO remarked: 'If you didn't fly them exactly according to what the computer wanted ... then it just wouldn't work.'[107]

Heron Project *Athena* uniform patch

SAR is widely used in civilian geological survey applications, but the aim in fitting it to the Heron was for coherent change detection. As an intelligence gathering process, coherent change detection compares a series of time-lapsed radar images to highlight minor changes in terrain. The trial aimed to determine its effectiveness in detecting IEDs by discovering recent changes in road surfaces.[108] After the trial was completed, the SAR went straight into service on the Heron. Using it operationally and devising the best way to gain maximum value from it fell to Rotation 10.[109] Heron PO Flight Sergeant Sean McClure, on his third rotation, recalled it was a significant undertaking and not the way introducing a new capability would have been done at home in Australia. McClure was one of the operators working with the SAR pod, and he felt the trial and subsequent operational use of the pod showed real promise in detecting IEDs, but there were challenges in using it effectively. It required the drone to fly the exact same path several times a day to show a meaningful amount of change in road surfaces. Flying so precisely was not always possible in poor weather, and keeping up the rate of passes was not always possible when there were many other tasks to perform on a mission. The SAR was removed during Rotation 11 as the task unit's missions evolved.[110]

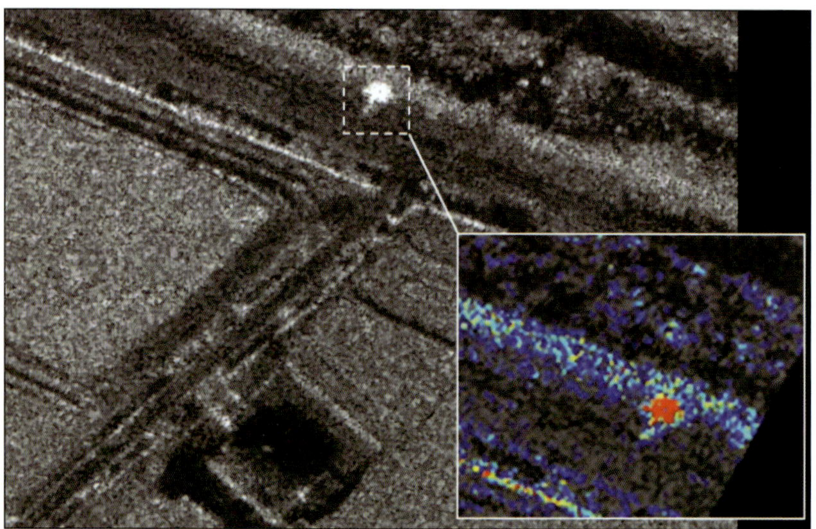

Image produced with synthetic aperture radar (Defence)

Heron missions

Flying with the call-sign 'Bluey', typical Heron missions fell into four categories: pattern-of-life surveillance, overwatch of friendly ground forces, direct support of ground operations, and specific requests from ground commanders.[111]

Pattern-of-life surveillance establishes the normal pattern of activities in an area to note departures from that. Overwatch provides a friendly 'eye in the sky' to help alert patrols to unseen dangers. Direct support involves the Heron in actual combat operations by providing real-time critical information in the thick of an engagement. Specific requests varied considerably and often involved observing a target designated for attack at a later stage. Direct support tasks were much more frequent during the fighting season.[112]

Many of the routine overwatch and pattern-of-life tasks were carried out for the ADF's Mentoring Task Force (MTF) – part of the multinational Task Force Uruzgan, later renamed Combined Team Uruzgan.[113] The MTF was a combined arms battle group of various combat elements of the Army and predominantly based on regular infantry regiments. Typical of MTF support tasks were watching for suspicious activity in localities of interest or around forward operating bases, accompanying road convoys, and surveillance of a bridge or building prior to a patrol clearing it.[114] Departures from the norm could be sentries posted outside a community meeting, weapons being handed over or an unusually large number of motorcycles amassing.[115] In March 2012, an MTF patrol was conducting a clearance mission in the Langar Valley with support from a Heron. The drone located three probable spotters on high ground, and the team devised a route for the patrol to avoid the possibility of encountering IEDs.[116]

Soldiers from the Mentoring Task Force and the Afghan National Army jointly patrolling in the Mirabad Valley Region, Afghanistan, 2010 (Mick Davis)

On another occasion, one of the POs was on a shift at night, tasked to carry out surveillance on a vehicle check point manned by Afghan National Security Forces (ANSF) personnel. The checkpoint had been hit frequently by rocket-propelled grenades, and the Heron team was sent to watch for the Taliban insurgents responsible. The team noticed a group of about 40 people who split into small groups to head off and take up firing positions. They saw the insurgents fire their rocket-propelled grenades and recorded the events and locations on video. With no direct communications with ANSF personnel, they were unable to give them any warning, and with no armaments on the Heron, they were unable to respond with force. However, the insurgents were tracked the next day, so the Heron team knew they had had a positive effect.[117]

Most direct support tasks were for the Australian SOTG element, which was known as Task Force 66. In Afghanistan, the SOTG divided its operational ground troops into two main elements. Force Element Alpha (FE Alpha) was made up of soldiers from the Special Air Service Regiment, and FE Bravo from the 2nd Commando Regiment. There were two other elements that made up the SOTG as needed – FE Charlie, comprising members of the reserve 1st Commando Regiment, and FE Echo, made up of members of the Incident Response Regiment, later renamed the Special Operations Engineer Regiment.[118] FE Charlie was assigned to tours over the winters. These elements performed counterinsurgency and counter-terrorism operations, and they were supported by a smaller element, the Fusion and Targeting Cell.[119] The Heron task unit communicated with SOTG planning personnel through an Australian Army ISR liaison officer based in Tarin Kot. Air support for the SOTG was often provided by Task Forces Brawler and Gunfighter of the United States Army, as well as the ADF Rotary Wing Group. Generally, the Heron teams were not briefed on the full extent of the SOTG missions and were only given enough information to be able to play their part.[120]

Soldiers from the Special Operations Task Group landing at Gizab, Uruzgan Province, Afghanistan, in a US Army Black Hawk helicopter to reinforce a community-led operation against the Taliban, 2010 (Aaron Oldaker)

FE Bravo mostly conducted disruptive operations to target narcotics production and distribution networks.[121] The Heron's role was to carry out surveillance on a village for a week, up to 20 hours a day, to establish the pattern-of-life. This was repetitious and sometimes boring work, but it was important. FE Bravo then descended on the village en masse and carried out a sweep, looking for what they called 'squirters' (insurgents trying to flee the sweep). At other times, they positioned themselves in an area for up to a week to disrupt illicit activity and draw fire. Their mission tasking packs were detailed and lengthy. The Heron supported FE Bravo with overwatch, warning about potential ambushes and the locations of squirters by communicating with the Special Operations Command Centre, often through a JTAC embedded in the command centre or on the ground. These were slow and deliberate operations. The surveillance phase often took weeks, and the conduct phase took days to carry out.[122]

Australian Army soldiers from the Special Operations Task Group preparing to board CH-47 Chinook helicopters during a night-time operation in Uruzgan Province, Afghanistan (Paul Berry)

By contrast, support to FE Alpha's conduct phase was usually over within six hours. FE Alpha was tasked to seek out insurgent commanders and other high-value people, such as IED facilitators. It was a counter-leadership role, and they called these people 'objectives'.[123] Pattern-of-life surveillance was very important in ensuring the objective had remained in their known location. On occasion, the objectives emerged as a result of FE Bravo stirring things up through their persistence in an area.[124] When the intelligence picture gave the right trigger, FE Alpha responded rapidly and rushed to the location in Black Hawk or Chinook helicopters for surprise snatch and grab operations. Their operations were run with surgical precision, and as one PO said: 'They were always good to work for – their tasking packs would be short and sharp.'[125] The Heron ensured the helicopter landing areas and routes were clear and provided overwatch. The same PO added: 'They would be pretty hands-on … driving you around because they were after a certain effect … to get the one guy.'[126] Though, one Heron commander made the point: 'We didn't see a lot of what they were doing … our job was to watch for other people.' He added: 'We would spend a lot of time looking for spotters in the hills … we found a lot.'[127]

Days in support of FE Alpha could be very busy. For example, in early 2012, a single Heron supported the helicopter insertion of an FE Alpha patrol in search of a reported weapons cache in the vicinity of Deh Rafshan in Uruzgan Province. The drone flew on to the Garmab Valley in support of another patrol that resulted in the capture of an insurgent objective who was a known Taliban commander and IED layer. It then flew to support MTF in the vicinity of the town of Sowzi on its way back to KAF. A week later, the Heron was supporting an FE Alpha cordon-and-search activity in the vicinity of the town of Deh Ravod in Uruzgan. The Heron team alerted the patrol to a squirter fleeing the search. He was killed in the subsequent engagement and later identified as an objective, a local Taliban commander and IED emplacement expert. Two days later, the Heron team discovered spotters on high ground near an FE Alpha patrol in the vicinity of Tangay, north of Kandahar. FE Alpha was able to call in support from an air weapons team that despatched two Apache AH-64 attack helicopters to engage the spotters, resulting in two insurgents being killed.[128]

Barrels of morphine solution and a drug press found during drug lab raids in Helmand Province by Afghan National Security Force and Special Operations Task Group soldiers on 26 September 2011 (Defence)

Key high-value targets for the SOTG were the makeshift drug laboratories sought by the Drug Enforcement Agency, particularly in Helmand Province. One Heron PO said: 'We would be transiting across there, which is a long way to go, and you could normally pick out the drug labs when they were cooking from twenty miles away.'[129] This was due to their heat signature being highly visible on the infra-red camera. An AVO remarked on the success of one of their missions: 'We were chasing one or two and ended up finding in the order of ten.'[130] They marked them all and let the SOTG deal with them while the Heron provided overwatch.

The Herons became a highly valued asset for the SOTG. A PO recalled FEs Alpha and Bravo 'would squabble amongst themselves over who got Heron', especially before dual ops began. He noticed a tendency for FE Alpha to 'pull rank' over Bravo on occasion.[131] Part of the value the Heron offered was, as one AVO boasted: 'We were never late for a tasking.'[132] They achieved this on his rotation by always trying to be on task 45 minutes before the requested time. This gave them time to make up for any delays due to airspace congestion or serviceability problems.[133] Heron tasking needed to be very flexible and react to events as they unfolded, especially to a call for 'eyes-on ASAP'. The normal intelligence gathering tasks had to be queued and prioritised before the Heron was re-tasked and flown to the new location. De-confliction with other airspace users was crucial in such cases and provided challenges for many agencies.[134]

The value of protecting lives was demonstrated early in the deployment of Herons to Afghanistan when a drone carried out surveillance on a Taliban facility earmarked for a deliberate air strike in the very near future. The Heron operators noticed women and children in the area and reported this back through the intelligence chain. The strike was called off as a result.[135]

The Heron capability, and No 5 Flight as a result, transferred from Air Combat Group to Surveillance and Response Group in April 2013, reflecting the capability was well established and considered to be a normal part of deployed ISR operations.[137] This was influenced by the fact that Air Combat Group had been called on to provide strike capability to Operation *Okra* in Iraq and did not have the capacity to support both Hornet and Heron operations.

In October 2013, the Australian Government announced it would begin drawing down military commitments in Afghanistan; most Australian troops returned home by the end of that year, including the SOTG in Tarin Kot. About 400 Australians remained in Afghanistan, mostly in headquarters and training roles in Kabul and Kandahar.[138]

However, in December 2013, Minister for Defence David Johnston announced the Heron capability would remain in Afghanistan as an ongoing commitment to the International Security Assistance Force (ISAF) and heralded the use of Australian Herons beyond Uruzgan as part of the ongoing training and specialist contributions by Australia to Afghanistan.[139] Rotation 13 was flagged to be the last Heron rotation, encompassing the change in the Heron role from supporting the SOTG to supporting Coalition forces under NATO's Regional Command South (RC South); it no longer acted as an Australian

Capturing a Taliban surface-to-air missile cell

FE Alpha from the Special Operations Task Group set the Herons the task of watching a grassy paddock in Southern Afghanistan. Day after day – 24 hours a day – they carried out surveillance of the seemingly vacant piece of ground as nothing happened. This was mind-numbingly repetitious work. However, if FE Alpha had called for it, the paddock must have been important. It was challenging for the Heron operators to keep their morale up on such a long surveillance, fearing they might be wasting their time. After five days, something happened around midnight. A man walked into the paddock, slowed slightly then lowered on one knee to pick up a long cylindrical object before continuing to walk through the paddock. The Heron team reported this to FE Alpha, which immediately started their assigned Black Hawk helicopters and prepared for action. The Heron tracked the man while the FE Alpha team made its way to the scene. He walked up a narrow goat track for a few kilometres then leant down and dropped the object before continuing to walk. Using their infra-red camera, the Heron watched the object and the man as he walked away. Another man approached the object and picked it up. FE Alpha landed in two Black Hawks and captured both men and the object, an SA-7 Grail. These Soviet-made MANPADS (man-portable air-defence system) are surface-to-air missiles capable of bringing down aircraft at low altitude. Based on the DNA and fingerprints on the weapon, the SOTG was later able to identify and capture many other members of the Taliban weapons supply cell.[136]

national asset.[140] The NATO commander, General Paul LaCamera, therefore, had the authority to employ Australian Herons against his tasking lines of effort. In effect, with most remaining NATO forces in Afghanistan being from the United States, the Australian Heron task unit began working directly for the American military forces.[141] Their missions were typically in support of Task Force Griffin of the United States Army's 12th Combat Aviation Brigade and the 4th Brigade Combat Team, known as Task Force Mountain Warrior.[142] Due to their tenacity in making it on station despite challenging weather en route, the Americans dubbed Rotation 13 the 'Honey Badger' in reference to its reputation for being fearless and relentless.[143]

Soldiers from the US 4th Brigade Combat Team interviewing village elder Mah Mah Azim during a patrol (US Dept of Defense)

The return date for Rotation 13 was not clear initially and was then extended. Then, Rotation 14 deployed, went through a full tour and was also extended. Finally, Rotation 15 deployed behind it and was the last. While the members of Rotation 16 were selected, and they began the theory component of their training, their training ceased.[144] The transfer of the Heron capability to NATO's RC South proved a success, and the Australian Government continued the extensions as a way of making a meaningful contribution to the NATO effort while maintaining a small and safe profile.[145]

Those three final rotations performed very different work from their predecessors. Without Australian troops to support, these rotations focused on ground defence operations around Kandahar. They did some ISR support for American forces as they trained members of the ANSF in the surrounding provinces, as well as the closing down of forward operating bases (FOB) when troop numbers reduced. After a period of pattern-of-life surveillance, the Herons provided overwatch for the personnel as their convoy returned to Kandahar. They also watched for spotters in the hills around the FOBs. Most of Rotation 15's work centred around Kandahar, with the Herons often providing overwatch for patrols heading to FOBs west and north of Kandahar. The rotations also worked closely with the Dynamic Targeting Cell (DTC) in building intelligence pictures on insurgent objectives.[146] The work was tiring and relentless, with the task unit working a pattern of nine days straight before having one day off.[147] However, an XO explained: 'My guys were more than happy to always be at work because there was nothing else to do other than go to the gym.'[148] One aircrew member described a typical day as: 'The aviators would get up at 3 or 3:30 [am], and the car would be on the road by about a quarter past 4, be at work at 4:30, get the platform ready and airborne, so it would be on station around 6 o'clock.'[149] Transit times to the surveillance location were short or almost non-existent, with the Heron being on station immediately after completing the climb overhead. There, the team could locate the subject of the mission, often the road convoy they were assigned to escort or a route reconnaissance.[150]

Afghan National Army soldiers posing with Taliban explosive ordnance and medical supplies seized during a clearance operation, Afghanistan (Defence)

The Herons were providing real-life support in the training of Afghan National Security Forces (ANSF) troops by the Americans. The change in operating mode, however, meant direct communication with ground forces became a problem. Unlike when working with ADF troops, they only occasionally had near-direct communication with those on the ground. The secure Battlefield Airborne Communications Node (BACN) system – colloquially pronounced 'bacon' – was in place in Afghanistan, and it used dedicated loitering aircraft as relays with the benefit that the ground and air systems did not need to be compatible. The system, operated by the United States Air Force, employed EQ-4B Global Hawk drones and conventional E-11A Bombardier aircraft. However, it was not used to achieve full direct communication with ANSF ground forces.[151] One aircrew member called their work 'nanny-cam' – they were able to watch events unfold but not able to do anything about what was happening on the ground. The same aircrew member, a fast jet pilot on other deployments, said: 'That was horrendous … we saw vehicles that were blown up.'[152]

NATO forces did occasionally call-in air strikes to support the ANSF using armed drones, such as the United States Air Force's MQ-1 Predators and MQ-9 Reapers. The Herons crews did not take part in the decision to use a weapon from these armed drones, but they did give those operators additional imagery to allow them to make a targeting determination.[153] This strengthened the targeting decision and helped to avoid collateral damage. Despite the lack of armaments, quick thinking and ingenuity by the Heron operators could make the difference between life and death. On one occasion during Rotation 14, AVO Squadron Leader Cameron Lyne and PO Flight Sergeant Andrew Earl observed an insurgent attack being prepared on an ANSF vehicle checkpoint from behind a nearby berm. They had no communications with the ANSF personnel, so they requested the lowest airspace they could get and dived the Heron to fly just above the insurgent group, cycling the throttle to make as much noise as they could with the aircraft.[154] Their actions had the desired effect. The EW operators heard the insurgents discussing that they had been discovered and deciding to call off the ambush and flee – one report suggested they thought they were about to be bombed.[155] As Air Marshal Mark Binskin once noted: 'You can have a "show of force" and that may well break the engagement. It does with some situations involving small terrorist or militia type groups.'[156] Earl later recalled: 'That was a shining moment, where we actually stopped an attack, rather than enabled bombs.'[157]

Voters queuing at a polling centre in Afghanistan during the 2014 presidential election (USAID)

Working for a new command chain had meant establishing new relationships and proving the value of the Heron to a new set of customers. In particular, the value of the EW capability was highlighted, as it was able to inform the DTC about insurgent networks and their ways of operating. For example, the Heron was able to locate and identify teams of spotters on ridges and determined, even though they appeared only to be lookouts, they were often coordinating the fight.[158] One aircrew member said the EW sensors were very valuable in this work, as the spotters and insurgent leaders used press-to-talk radios that were easy to identify.[159] The EW work led to the Heron finding the insurgents more readily with the cameras and, therefore, was able to give accurate and timely information to inform decisions by the DTC. As a result, the relationship between the Heron task unit and RC South was very good.[160]

A key task assigned to the Herons in 2014 was oversight of the Afghan presidential election in April. The weather forecast for the days each side of voting day was poor, and the United States Air Force decided not to fly its drones. The Herons conducted surveillance on many polling places in the lead up to voting and for 12 hours on the voting day itself before the bad weather finally arrived. The American commanding general asked for the Heron to take a photo of the blue sky on the day to show to his Air Force colleagues.[161]

Australian Air Component Commander Group Captain Tony McCormack standing alongside members of Heron Rotation 13 after the completion of 20,000 flying hours in Afghanistan, 2013 (Chris Moore)

The last year of Australian deployed Heron operations in 2014 was a period of considerable uncertainty, noting the final three rotations each thought they would be the last. This led to some interesting challenges. The whole team, including the contractors, needed to continue operating; however, they also had to plan for the withdrawal, whether it was

Meritorious Unit Citation – Number 5 Flight

Meritorious Unit Citations are awarded by the Governor-General through the Australian Honours and Awards System to units for sustained outstanding service in warlike operations. Governor-General Sir Peter Cosgrove presented the warrant of the citation at a ceremony at RAAF Base Amberley on 12 September 2016. Members of the unit wear the insignia of the citation in the form of a gold-framed ribbon pinned to the right breast of their uniform.

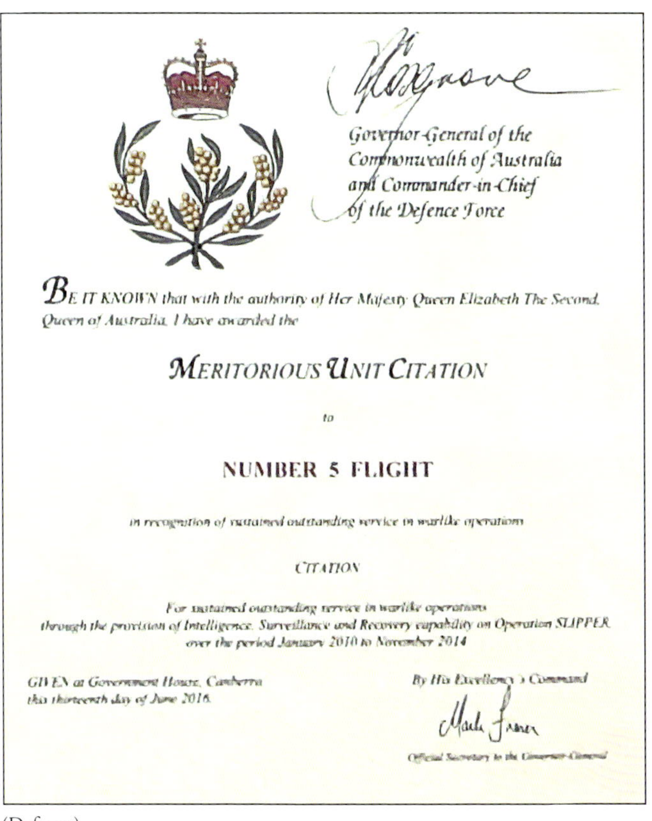

Governor-General of the Commonwealth of Australia and Commander-in-Chief of the Defence Force

BE IT KNOWN that with the authority of Her Majesty Queen Elizabeth The Second, Queen of Australia, I have awarded the

MERITORIOUS UNIT CITATION

to

NUMBER 5 FLIGHT

in recognition of sustained outstanding service in warlike operations

CITATION

For sustained outstanding service in warlike operations
through the provision of Intelligence, Surveillance and Recovery capability on Operation SLIPPER
over the period January 2010 to November 2014

GIVEN at Government House, Canberra
this thirteenth day of June 2016

By His Excellency's Command

Official Secretary to the Governor-General

(Defence)

going to occur during their rotation or not.[162] Adding to the stress, the reduced Coalition presence on KAF allowed security problems to develop, with increased reports of thefts and trespassing. The usually open gates at Camp Baker were locked, and incidents of 'green-on-blue' attacks increased. At any time of day, the whole of KAF could go into 'Op Buccaneer' – the base response to an intruder alert. Heron rotation members sat piquet on the entrances to their buildings until the 'all clear' was sounded. There were also suicide bomber attacks on the entry points to the airfield, with one killing three security guards at the gate near The Lair.[163]

Wing Commander Phillip Parsons, commander of Heron Rotation 15, in front of the rotation's painted concrete T-wall, Kandahar Airfield, Afghanistan, November 2015 (Janine Fabre)

Back in Australia, due to uncertainty about whether they would deploy at all, Rotations 14 and 15 were mostly staffed with aircrew members who were to be on at least their second Heron deployment; this considerably reduced the training and work-up time and effort. However, it was the first Heron deployment for some of the other team members. By contrast, a couple of members of Rotation 14 even extended their deployment to cover Rotation 15, spending almost a year away.[164]

The final Heron mission in support of Operation *Slipper* in Afghanistan was flown on 30 November 2014.[165] It coincided with the conclusion of NATO's ISAF 'transition' mission and the commencement of its 'transformation' *Resolute Support* Mission that handed over the responsibility for national security to Afghan forces. Over the five years, Australian Herons had flown 2,331 operational missions, clocking up some 27,100 flying hours and achieving a mission success rate of 97%.[166] Almost 500 personnel from the ADF – aviators, sailors and soldiers – along with foreign exchange personnel, scientists and contractors, deployed to operate and support the Heron.[167]

In the 2016 Queen's Birthday honours, No 5 Flight was awarded the Meritorious Unit Citation for 'sustained outstanding service in warlike operations through the provision of intelligence, surveillance and reconnaissance capability on Operation *Slipper*, over the period January 2010 to November 2014.' Governor-General Sir Peter Cosgrove presented the warrant of the citation at a ceremony at RAAF Base Amberley on 12 September 2016, attended by many of the almost 500 personnel who had served with the Heron.[168] In his speech, the Governor-General noted the War in Afghanistan was 'one of the most difficult, dangerous and hostile conflicts ever to confront Australia's military,' adding the award recognised 'the critical role these Australian Defence Force members played in the successful planning and execution of missions in support of Australian, Coalition and Afghan National Army operations on the ground in Afghanistan.'[169]

It is interesting to note the Herons operated in support of Operation *Slipper* as Task Unit 633.2.7, not as 5 Flight. Nonetheless, the citation was awarded in the name of No 5 Flight, but all personnel who served with Task Unit 633.2.7 or 5 Flight are entitled to wear the insignia of the citation. They do so with pride.

Chapter 5
HOMEWARD BOUND

The original intent of not operating the Heron at all on Australian soil had been overturned by the need to train operators in Woomera after training ceased in Canada in 2010. This had the unplanned consequence of allowing for Heron operations to continue in Australia after the late 2014 withdrawal from Afghanistan, if desired. While not part of the initial plan, it presented an excellent opportunity to retain drone operating skills and to support the projected introduction of other large drones into service in the ADF, notably the MQ-4C Triton maritime surveillance drone and the armed MQ-9B SkyGuardian.[1] Therefore, No 5 Flight changed from being a sunset unit with the sole purpose of providing the raise, train, sustain function for deployed Herons to being an enduring RAAF flying unit.

In October 2014, the Minister for Defence announced the RAAF would retain a limited Heron capability in Australia after the end of its mission in Afghanistan the following month.[2] About 75 drone aerial vehicle operators (AVO) and another 75 payload operators (PO) had been trained on the Heron.[3] This was a substantial investment in knowledge and skills and was too good to waste, along with the considerable development in intelligence skills. No 5 Flight, therefore, was to operate two Herons to support the integration of drones into the Australian environment, with the added aim of supporting the retention and development of tactics and procedures for overland ISR (intelligence, surveillance and reconnaissance) gained during the four years in Afghanistan.[4] Part of the plan was to assist the normalisation of military drones in Australia, particularly among other aviation operators.[5] What, then, did continuing to fly the Heron in Australia achieve?

Heron A45-262 taking off at RAAF Base Amberley, Queensland, April 2016 (Brenton Kwaterski)

Heron operations in Australia

While it might have seemed simple enough to bring home one Heron system to complement the one already operating in Woomera, making the opportunity of operating Herons in Australia into a reality took time. Aside from the need for a recommendation from the Chief of Air Force and formal ministerial approval, contract negotiations had to be carried out between MacDonald Dettwiler and Associates (MDA), the Defence Materiel Organisation and the RAAF.[6] Noting those challenges, it is a credit to all involved that the Australian flying program was able to commence in June 2015. The two Herons – A45-253 and A45-262 – were granted an unmanned aircraft system operating permit by the Chief of Air Force, Air Marshal Geoff Brown, on 11 June. The permit only allowed them to fly over sparsely populated areas, with brief transits over populated areas for operational imperatives, and the laser pointer was not allowed to be used until a risk assessment was performed.[7] The Herons flew until June 2017, logging a total of 710 hours.[8] They operated out of Woomera and also flew at RAAF Bases Amberley and Tindal, as well as Rockhampton Airport. Herons were not a new sight for the Australian public, albeit not in the sky. The original Woomera-based airframe made trips to take part in air shows around the country. A45-253 was displayed at the Avalon Air Show in Victoria in 2011, 2013 and 2015, and at the RAAF Centenary of Military Aviation air show at Point Cook, Victoria, in 2014.

Members of the general public visiting the Heron display during the Centenary of Military Aviation air show at RAAF Base Point Cook, March 2014 (Aaron Curran)

One very important aim of flying the Heron in Australia was to normalise drone operations within the civilian air operating environment.[9] This will be critical in paving the way for the Triton, which will become a regular feature of Australian airspace as it takes off and lands, likely daily, from RAAF Base Tindal and possibly other locations in the future. Fostering acceptance by the general public is also important, particularly in allaying any fears about drones flying near passenger jets. Commercial aviation is founded on safety, and considerable effort is made to avoid unnecessary risk. So, any attempt to mix crewed and uncrewed aircraft in proximity will be very difficult to achieve from cultural and regulatory standpoints.

The Amberley based No 5 Flight retained its pre-deployment training facilities at Woomera; this allowed currency training for Heron flight crews. The Heron's first foray from the safety of the restricted military airspace of Woomera was to Rockhampton in Queensland. The two Herons were freighted and assembled there in July 2015 to take part in exercises *Talisman Sabre* and *Hamel.*[10] This meant operating out of Rockhampton Airport, which also hosted daily commercial passenger flights.[11] They were based there with Hawk jet trainers and Black Hawk helicopters and operated with a wide range of transiting military aircraft, such as Hercules, Orions and Globemasters.[12]

From Rockhampton, the Herons flew to the Shoalwater Bay Training Area for sorties of up to ten hours for almost a month and were cleared to operate through civilian airspace by Airservices Australia controllers. A key element of the cooperation between Airservices Australia and the RAAF was the Herons were to be integrated into the airspace, rather than carefully accommodated. This required considerable planning and coordination. The memorandum of agreement outlined local procedures with the Rockhampton air traffic control tower and airfield emergency services and agreement on separation, which was the same as for all instrument flying aircraft in the area. The RAAF gave assurance that there were multiple levels of redundancy in the airborne and ground control systems.[13]

The Herons operated under the call-sign of 'Unmanned Bluey', and an enthusiastic plane spotter was thrilled to hear the AVO give his pre-take-off call to air traffic control, including the statement: 'Persons on board – zero.'[14] Significantly, the deployment to Rockhampton showed unsegregated integration of drones and manned aircraft in civilian airspace was possible and safe.[15]

Heron A45-253, operated by No 5 Flight, returning to Rockhampton Airport, Queensland, and operating in the same airspace as a commercial airliner, June 2015 (Defence)

During September and October 2015, 5 Flight returned to Woomera to take part in Exercise *Iron Moon* in support of Special Operations Command.[16] The next significant period of Heron flying was at RAAF Base Amberley in April 2016. Two Herons (A45-253 and A45-262) were packed into their transport containers and sent via contracted road freight from Woomera to Amberley. However, A45-253 arrived in damaged condition due to the fuselage mounting trolley coming loose on the rough roads. Nonetheless, the remaining Heron proved it could fly in congested military airspace, mixing in the circuit with C-17 Globemasters and F/A-18F Super Hornets over a period of ten days.[17] This showed it could be integrated into the airspace, rather than simply accommodated.

Heron A45-253 in its road transport container after suffering transit damage on the rough roads from Woomera, South Australia to Amberley, Queensland, April 2016 (Defence)

In recognition of the outstanding achievements of 5 Flight, the Chief of Air Force granted the staff members of 5 Flight a gold-level group citation in 2015. The citation stated: 'Through your superior drive, esprit de corps, flexibility and devotion to duty, you have been able to collectively achieve operational outcomes in direct support of Heron Unmanned Aerial System operations in Afghanistan.' It went on to note the capability offered to the International Security Assistance Force Regional Command South and the efforts involved in selecting and training personnel for the short-notice final rotations.[18]

Two RAAF F/A-18 Hornets following Heron A45-253 along the taxiway at RAAF Base Tindal to commence their missions during Exercise *Diamond Storm*, June 2017 (Andrew Eddie)

The Herons deployed again to RAAF Base Tindal in the Northern Territory in July and August 2016.[19] They took part in Exercise *Pitch Black*, where members of foreign forces – including the German and Singapore Air Forces – were able to see how the RAAF operated its Herons and share their own experiences.[20] During 2015–17, key 5 Flight executives held meetings with drone operators from other countries and travelled to the United Kingdom, Germany, Israel and the United States to foster relationships with manufacturers and operators of similar technologies. Throughout that time, 5 Flight also retained two Canadian exchange officers on the strength of the unit in an arrangement that continued the cooperation that started the RAAF's operational engagement with the Heron.

Ground staff towing No 5 Flight Heron A45-262 from to the taxiway in preparation for take-off during Exercise *Pitch Black*, 2016 (Terry Hartin)

Early in 2017, the RAAF announced it intended to cease flying the Heron in the coming June, giving sufficient notice for the MDA contractors to plan their return to Canada.[21] The final series of flights was conducted in June 2017 as part of Exercise *Diamond Storm*, where the Heron provided ISR support during 17 sorties for the RAAF's inaugural Air Warfare

Instructor Course.[22] During the exercise, held at Tindal, the Heron flew its last mission for the RAAF on 23 June 2017. The MDA contract was concluded on 31 July, and the drones and supporting equipment were removed from Woomera and Amberley after two and half years of post-deployed operations in Australia.

Heron A45-253 receiving a traditional 'crossed swords' spray of water by RAAF Tindal firefighters after the final mission for the RAAF on 23 June 2017 during Exercise *Diamond Storm* (Andrew Eddie)

The RAAF had planned to lease the two Australian-based Herons for six years to bridge the gap until the Tritons and SkyGuardians arrived. This was to include the renovation of facilities at RAAF Base Amberley, but the lease was renegotiated to end in 2017.[23] The Heron was designed to be operated in Israel, so it was well suited to operations in Afghanistan. It was not as well suited to flying in more humid locations like Queensland.[24] Lease costs also mounted while waiting for the Triton and other new drone acquisitions to arrive.[25] Further, by then, the Heron was very much a legacy system and too far removed from the high-altitude, long-endurance (HALE) drones to follow. Without armaments, it was not necessarily a good steppingstone to the next generation of drones.

The RAAF formally disbanded No 5 Flight on 30 November 2017.[26] By the end of operations, the ADF had trained 150 drone aircrew and 300 intelligence operators well versed in drone operations.[27] To maintain and build on that knowledge, the RAAF began embedding ex-Heron personnel and others with the United States Air Force 432nd Wing to allow Australians to fly MQ-9A Reaper drones at Creech Air Force Base in Nevada.[28] The RAAF also embedded personnel with the Royal Air Force in the United Kingdom to operate Reapers.[29] With years of operational drone experience and some valuable ventures into civilian airspace integration, what lessons had the ADF learnt from operating the Heron, and how has the ADF's experience with the Heron set it up for drone operations into the future?

The legacy of Heron

Australia's military aviation forces have a long, if not always welcomed, practice of sporadically introducing new technology directly into theatres of operations without first establishing a training capability at home. Sunderland flying boats at the beginning of the Second World War are the most famous example, and examples since then include Meteor jet fighters during the Korean War and Caribou transport aircraft during the Vietnam War – in addition to almost all aircraft types used during the First World War. In each case, there were lessons to be learnt. So, within weeks of the last Heron flight, the ADF called for a 'lessons learnt' workshop. This was held over two days in July 2017 to identify what could be learnt from the ADF's experience with the Heron to help inform the future acquisition and employment of large drones.[30]

Very early in the Heron's operational term, Air Marshal Binskin had identified: 'Ground forces nowadays are very reluctant to move unless they've got some sort of overwatch coverage from an ISR platform, … and I don't blame them.'[31] Flight Lieutenant Nelle Sheridan, who had deployed as a PO in 2014, went as far as saying: 'A lot of commanders wouldn't let their guys go outside the wire without the ISR the Heron provided.'[32] However, Binskin warned: 'It's not good enough to have it there, it needs to be fully integrated into the scheme of manoeuvre of the ground forces.'[33] While this was generally the case, the Heron was not fully integrated into the wider deployed Australian or Coalition intelligence information systems.[34] This was due to it being introduced as a short-term standalone capability to meet an urgent operational need, the limitations of the deployed networks, and the lack of interoperability of the various computer networks.[35] The communications with ground forces were likewise limited. Apart from the lack of encryption already noted, joint terminal attack controllers (JTAC) needed a clear line of sight to the Heron to be able to see video. Therefore, the Heron had to be overhead, and de-confliction with other aircraft was a problem. JTACs also had to use a second SATCOM radio to be able to talk to the Heron operators, adding extra stress on the battlefield.[36]

The engine noise of the Heron could be a problem at times. An ADF liaison officer responsible for coordinating Australian fixed-wing assets in support of ground forces said: 'If noise wasn't a concern, which was rare, then it was okay.' However, in areas such as the Baluchi Valley, 'you can hear it from everywhere.' The valley was quiet, without a lot of wind, and the sound of the engine carried and could be heard from a long way away. He added: 'Any ISR is good compared to nothing, unless there is a lot of noise.'[37] Further, the EOIR sensor was not up to the standard of the Predator or Reaper. It was good, but it could have been better.[38] The liaison officer gave an example of these shortcomings. While trying to confirm the whereabouts of an individual they wanted to capture and detain, they were using a Heron and a United States Air Force Reaper, both in the stack – the layers of controlled air battlespace – at the same time and at about the same range. Both drones were looking at the same piece of ground. The Reaper, with its 22-inch sensor, was able to identify the individual by his clothing and his distinctive limp. However, the Heron, with only a 14-inch sensor, did not have the resolution to identify there was a person there at all. The liaison officer also noted how quiet the Reaper was in comparison.[39] Another limit of the Heron was it did not have a tactical datalink, such as Link 16, to share targeting information with ground forces.[40]

Heron A45-253 in Australian skies (Andrew Eddie)

Nonetheless, the introduction of drones into operational service was a significant improvement in the way the RAAF approached ISR and combat support. The Heron proved the value of precise and persistent surveillance in assisting ground forces to achieve their missions and providing critical protection. The ADF also learnt a lot about using leased aircraft in an operational setting. Elements of the lease contract, notably those that affected technical airworthiness, were identified in the lessons learnt after the return of the Herons as matters to be aware of in future leases.[41] In a statement to the 2015 Australian Senate inquiry into the use of drones by the ADF that reflected short-term leasing was a sound approach, defence and strategic policy expert Dr Andrew Carr noted: 'With emergent technologies like unmanned platforms, however, a focus on quick development, testing and replacement is critical until the ADF gains mature knowledge of how best to use these systems.'[42]

In a salutary warning, Air Marshal Binskin noted: 'Other lessons are harder to take away because the air space is not contested in Afghanistan.' Commenting on the proliferation of drones employed there – and hinting at their lack of ability to defend themselves – he added: 'If we start operating in contested air space that might not be the case.' He lamented: 'Over the recent couple of years many people tend to take air superiority as a given.'[43] What drones, then, will the ADF need to maintain its role in the defence of Australia?

AeroGuard

Improving drone technology and the increasing availability of drones to militaries and the general public have inevitably brought challenges for military forces – primarily how to deter, repel or otherwise counter hostile drone activity. While this is a pressing strategic concern for military forces, managing drone activity is similarly important to civilian agencies. A reported sighting of a drone in the vicinity of Heathrow Airport in 2019 temporarily stopped flight departures. A month earlier, a similar sighting at Gatwick Airport left thousands of people stranded for three days due to cancelled flights.[44] Unregulated drone use in public airspace brings very real safety concerns and, in response, aerospace and technology companies are trying to develop robust and reliable countermeasures. Attempts to use ground-based defence and security systems against drones have proved challenging, and the limited effectiveness of these methods has turned attention upwards to begin operating in the drones' realm: the sky.[45] SCI Technology's AeroGuard is an octocopter – it features eight propellers that make the drone faster, more powerful and able to carry heavier loads than other drones.[46] This is essential because the AeroGuard is a drone interdiction system. Launched when an enemy drone is detected, the AeroGuard fires a tethered net to capture it, then tows it to a safe landing zone to avoid dropping debris on bystanders.[47] Where ground-based systems have failed, the AeroGuard and similar airborne drone interdiction systems have continued to demonstrate their effectiveness against other drones.

(SCI Technology)

MQ-4C Triton

Already in use by the United States Navy, the MQ-4C Triton is a broad area maritime surveillance drone scheduled for delivery to the RAAF in 2024. Intended to complement the RAAF's P-8A Poseidon maritime patrol aircraft, the Triton is a high-altitude, long-endurance system capable of conducting missions at an altitude of up to 60,000 feet for longer than 24 hours while surveying more than one million square nautical miles – an area larger than Western Australia.[54] To facilitate these extended mission times and surveillance requirements, the Triton carries a diverse payload that can weigh 1,400 kilograms. This includes a radar, an electro-optical infra-red sensor, an automatic identification system receiver and electronic support measures, as well as communications relay equipment. To protect this equipment, the forward fuselage that houses the Triton's sensors is reinforced and provided with lightning protection and hail and bird-strike resistance.[55] Crucially, strengthening the drone's capacity to operate in a broad range of weather conditions enables the Triton to descend and ascend in harsh maritime environments to offer excellent ISR to commanders.[56] Upon its introduction into service, the Triton squadron's headquarters will be at South Australia's RAAF Base Edinburgh, and they will fly from a forward operating base at RAAF Base Tindal in the Northern Territory.[57] A highly sophisticated and capable drone, the Triton is anticipated to greatly enhance Australia's surveillance and defence of its maritime territories.[58]

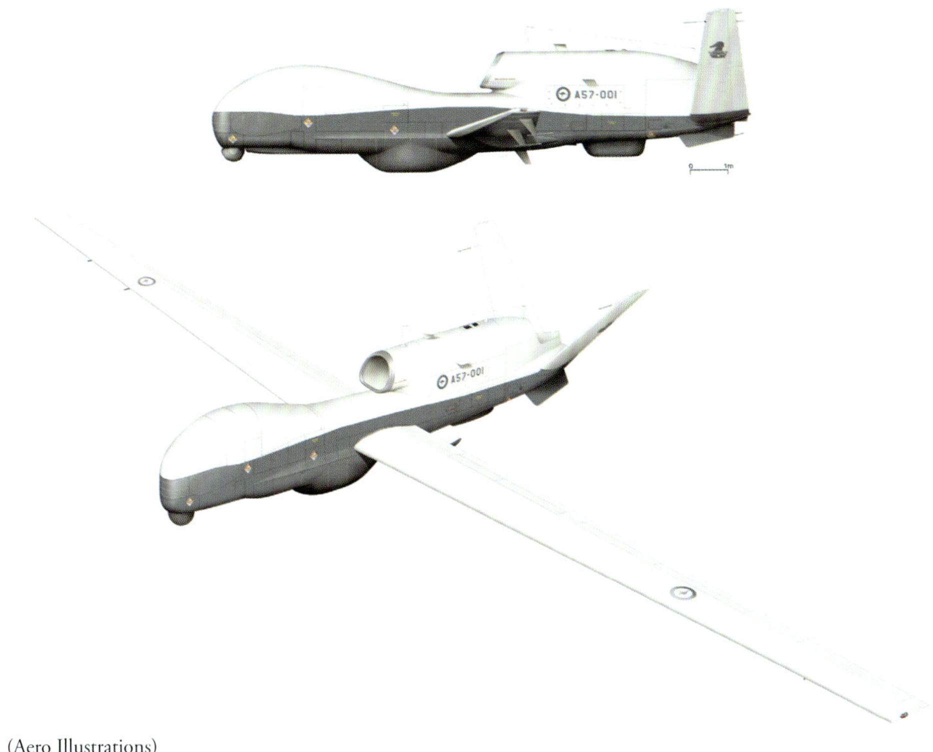

(Aero Illustrations)

Future ADF drones

The ADF recently announced projects that will procure drone capabilities to carry it well into the 21st century. The longest running acquisition project is Project Air 7000-1B. This project determined the Northrop Grumman MQ-4C Triton HALE system is the best drone solution to meet Australia's maritime patrol requirements.[48] The RAAF plans to acquire up to seven Tritons, which will be remotely operated from RAAF Base Edinburgh in South Australia within No 92 Wing as a part of Surveillance and Response Group, with the aircraft themselves being based at RAAF Base Tindal in the Northern Territory.[49] They will be capable of monitoring Australia's maritime approaches, as well as supporting domestic disaster recovery, security operations, maritime patrol, and humanitarian aid and disaster relief internationally.[50] The Triton has de-icing and lightning protection, which will allow it to descend through cloud for low-level observation when required.[51] Air Vice-Marshal Cath Roberts, Head of Air Force Capability, said: 'In terms of persistent surveillance, there isn't anything else out there that can achieve what it can at the altitudes that it works.'[52]

The Tritons will be operated by a re-formed No 9 Squadron. The squadron was first formed in 1939 as a maritime reconnaissance squadron operating Supermarine Seagull Mk V and Walrus flying boats. The squadron saw active service during the Second World War and was disbanded in 1944. It was reformed on 11 June 1962 as a helicopter search and rescue and tactical air transport squadron, seeing active service in Vietnam before being disbanded in 1989. Appropriately, the No 9 Squadron motto is *Videmus nec Videmur* – to see and not be seen.[53]

The Triton is being acquired through a cooperative development model with the United States Navy.[59] This approach to acquisition allows the RAAF to be a partner in the spiral development and upgrade program, ensuring access to the latest modifications and software. The Triton will complement the RAAF fleet of P-8A Poseidon crewed maritime patrol aircraft to conduct long-range surveillance of Australia's maritime approaches and regions of strategic interest. The Triton also has the ability to fly as far as Antarctica.[60] The drone will be equipped with sense-and-avoid radar to ensure its safety while operating in the airspace around Australia and near its home bases in particular. While that system is being introduced, the Triton will operate out of the less-congested airspace of RAAF Base Tindal in the Northern Territory.[61]

The other major defence project that was to involve drones was Project Air 7003. The project aimed to introduce the first medium-altitude, long-endurance (MALE) armed drones into ADF service. The project was to acquire up to 12 General Atomics MQ-9B SkyGuardian systems.[62] However, the Australian Government announced its decision not to proceed with the project in April 2022. While recognising the excellence of the SkyGuardian system, the government noted the changing strategic environment and the need to adjust the range of ADF capabilities to meet new challenges.[63] Cyber-attack poses an increasing threat in the modern strategic environment – as demonstrated in the war in Ukraine – and bolstering Australia's cyber defence capabilities and resilience took priority over acquisition of SkyGuardians drones.

In line with the Heron experience, industry support will play a vital role in the maintenance and future upgrades of the Triton. The ADF is keen to ensure Australian industry will play a major part – in a model dubbed platform stewardship – to develop sensors, software and communications equipment. The Triton will operate in conjunction with other ADF ISR assets, such as the P-8 Poseidon and MC-55A Peregrine electronic warfare support aircraft, to contribute to the Distributed Ground Station Australia (DGS-AUS).[64] To be established under Project Air 3503, the DGS-AUS intelligence unit will collect, analyse and disseminate the intelligence collected from the various RAAF ISR aircraft and other systems. The DGS-AUS will become a critical strategic and operational asset for the protection of Australia's resources and borders, and drones will play a large part in that intelligence gathering.[65]

Artist's impression of the MC-55A Peregrine due to enter service with the RAAF as an intelligence, surveillance, reconnaissance, electronic warfare asset (L3Harris)

In a completely new concept for drones, Australia is leading the way in manned-unmanned teaming, with the design and development of the Boeing Advanced Teaming System – better known as the MQ-28A Ghost Bat. Originally dubbed the Loyal Wingman, the drone is able to provide extra payload for the aircraft it flies with, or it can act in a protective role.[66] It was developed by a partnership that included the RAAF's Program 6014, Boeing Australia, BAE Systems and more than 30 other companies, and the drone and its systems use more than 70% Australian content.[67] The Ghost Bat – about the size of a fighter jet – can carry a wide range of payloads, including EOIR cameras, radar and signals intelligence detectors. While currently in the early stages of innovation and development, the Ghost Bat may also be able to assume an air combat role, with an ability to carry air-to-air and air-to-surface weapons. It may not go into service with the RAAF, but its development in Australia does show a level of indigenous drone engineering ability not seen since the days of the joint project that led to the Jindivik and its successors. In another sign that Australia's long history of investment in drone development is paying dividends, flight testing is being conducted at Woomera.

MQ-28A Ghost Bat

Developed by Boeing Australia in collaboration with Australia's Department of Defence and the RAAF, the Ghost Bat drone (previously named the Boeing Airpower Teaming System or Loyal Wingman) is a semi-autonomous platform intended to integrate with other combat aircraft. At roughly the size of a jet fighter, the drone has a range of 3,700 kilometres.[68] Teaming with Australia's most valuable aircraft such as Lightning IIs, Super Hornets and Growlers, the Ghost Bat is intended to help safeguard and support these platforms.[69] Using artificial intelligence, the drone can fly independently and react to a dynamic battlespace while maintaining a safe distance from the manned aircraft it is teamed with. Doing so allows manned aircraft to gain the benefits of the Ghost Bat's sensor data in real time without the remote command burden.[70] The fuselage is comprised of composite materials created using an advanced resin-infusion process to make it durable and light, qualities deemed essential to the project's goal of fielding an agile, integrated platform. Designed primarily for ISR and tactical early warning missions, the Ghost Bat's integration with other platforms will allow manned aircraft to simultaneously conduct surveillance, navigation and tactical operations.[71] The drone has a reconfigurable payload design with swappable sensors to tailor the aircraft's capabilities for a chosen mission. The Ghost Bat's inaugural flight occurred at the Woomera Range Complex in South Australia on 27 February 2021; the drone followed a pre-programmed route at various speeds and altitudes.[72] Much of the Ghost Bat's specifications and capabilities have not been disclosed for security reasons, but this platform promises to provide a unique and powerful combat multiplier for the RAAF in an evolving modern battlespace.

(Ricky Treloar)

Drone racing

In 2015, drone racing in Australia was an emerging hobby pursued by enthusiasts in empty car parks, abandoned warehouses and parking stations.[75] Since then, Australian drone racing has become a mainstream and popular pursuit. The inaugural Australian Drone Nationals were held in 2016, and by 2019, there are roughly 2,500 competitors across 14 clubs around the country.[76] Races occur inside and outdoors and require racers to wear first-person view goggles that, by means of a camera mounted on the drone, virtually place pilots in the drone's cockpit. From there, competitors use handheld remote controls to send their craft hurtling around the designated course at speeds of up to 150 km/h.[77] The ADF drone racing team made its competitive debut in 2017, and the following year, Australia hosted the first ever Military International Drone Racing Tournament as part of the Invictus Games.[78] Drone racing has continued to gain support within the ADF, a logical progression for the ADF's increased use of these unmanned vehicles in military operations. Participating in competitions offers a recruitment opportunity for Defence, allowing rapid identification of people with the skills to fly military drones or pursue other technical military trades. Racing drones requires pilots to demonstrate incredible agility, hand-eye coordination and fine motor skills, attributes that translate perfectly to piloting drones in support of Australian forces.[79] One Army combat engineer noted in 2018 that the existence of the Australian Army Drone Racing Team also reduced resistance to integrating drone technologies across the Army.[80] As the ADF continues to expand its unmanned aircraft capabilities across all services and down to the lowest tactical levels, developing and maintaining such vital skills remains a high priority.

Flying Officer Jake Dell-O'Sullivan at the Air Force Drone Racing Tournament held at RAAF Base Richmond, 2019 (Casey Forster)

Swarming drones

Also called distributed collective systems, the term 'swarming drones' refers to a small group of drones programmed to move and behave as a cohesive whole with little to no human direction. Swarming drones can gather intelligence and also carry out offensive or defensive actions. Swarming effects are achieved when the gathered individual elements all adhere to a set of simple rules that determine their individual behaviour in ways that can produce complex unified behaviours for the group. To do so, every drone in the swarm must be able to communicate with the others, and all must be identical in their physical characteristics, programming and sensors, as the guiding rules are often environment driven. While a human pilot controls the swarm's overall behaviour, the individual drones respond as a collective, automatically maintaining their form in accordance with their programming. The possibilities offered by swarming are significant, particularly the potential to replace one large expensive platform with numerous smaller and cheaper drones that provide a similar effect.[88] Swarming would, one 2018 United States study noted, make attack drones at least 50% more lethal, while decreasing their losses to defensive fires by the same amount.[89] This technology has inevitably sparked fears in the international defence community about the capacity of artificially intelligent drones learning new behaviours or applying pre-programmed rules in unforeseen ways due to a dynamically changing and unpredictable environment.[90] Also, there is the challenge of autonomous drone swarms outpacing the humans who ostensibly pilot them. AI systems can integrate, process and respond to information far quicker than humans, and some have proposed that, as the technology continues to develop, the only way to ensure effective operation (in a nonlethal capacity) is to allow such drones to operate with less human involvement.[91] As global technology continues to race ahead and battlespaces continue to evolve, such platforms may become essential to the conduct of modern warfare.

(US Air Force Research Laboratory)

Further acquisition projects will deliver new drones for the Army and Navy. The Army's Shadow drones are obsolete, and the replacement process is well under way. Four Australian companies were selected under Project Land 129 Phase 3 to compete to be the prime tenderer.[73] The Australian Government selected Insitu Pacific as the preferred supplier for the Army's tactical uncrewed aerial system requirements. The company will supply 24 Integrator drones and their ground operating and support systems.[74] This is another example of Australian industry rising to the challenges faced in meeting the defence of Australia, and due to its flexible configuration, the technology will have a wide range of applications by other nations. The ADF has also carried out many trials of small drones in recent years, ranging from handheld micro-UAVs to jet-powered models. It has also put some drones into service as military off-the-shelf (MOTS) acquisitions.

In 2009, the Army conducted a trial of American-made AeroVironment Wasp 3 handheld drones. Three were operated by a four-member team during the trial, which included providing support to the enemy team on that year's Exercise *Talisman Sabre*.[81] In 2015, the Army put the RQ-12 WASP AE AeroVironment drone – again made in the United States – into service.[82] In 2017, the PD-100 Black Hornet 2 went into service with the Army, which acquired 161 of these Norwegian-made drones, each weighing only 33 grams and carried and used by individual soldiers for short-range observation.[83] In 2018, the Army began using Chinese-made DJI Phantom 4 drones.[84] It purchased 350 of these off-the-shelf drones for use as a training device to introduce 'drone literacy' into the Army. Inspired by the value of drones to operations in the Middle East – notably the Heron, Shadow 200 and ScanEagle – the Army aims to use drones as a normal part of everyday operations.[85]

In 2019, RAAF airfield defence guards trialled the SkyRanger R70 drone for use in airbase protection at various sites around Australia. The short-range 4.5-kilogram drone has interchangeable payloads and was tested with electro-optic infra-red and high-definition zoom cameras, a payload delivery option and 3D mapping software. The trials included overnight perimeter surveillance during the Avalon International Airshow and, along with detecting 'intruders' and guiding the dog team to their location, demonstrated that small drones assisting in a security role could be integrated successfully into airfield operations.[86]

The Navy trialled an Australian-made jet-powered Phoenix drone in exercises in 2021 to simulate aircraft attack on three ships. At only 2.4 metres long and weighing 66 kilograms, and with an airframe of composite materials, the drone can 'attack' ships at speeds of up to 300 knots (550 km/h) to test their missile and aircraft defence systems. They can fly in formation to simulate typical aircraft attack profiles and can also break formation to make the attack training sequence more dynamic. Made by Air Affairs Australia, these small and versatile drones are launched by catapult and recovered from the water after ditching by parachute.[87]

Innovations in drone technology worldwide are rapid. Artificial intelligence and advances in nanotechnology will allow new drones to perform in ways not previously seen. New drones may have military effects that will change the way battles are fought in future. For example, swarms of micro-drones may be able to destroy jet engines by flying into air intakes, and lethal one-hit drones may be able to seek and kill individual high-value adversaries. In the military aviation arena, a human in the cockpit is likely to be an obsolete notion, but this will not be in the short term. As early as 2013, Boeing and Lockheed Martin each told a RAAF delegation in California the F-35 Lighting II would probably be the last manned fighter they would ever design.[92]

The proliferation of drones in current military use around the world shows they will be part of warfighting for at least the foreseeable – and indeed imaginable – future. The technical developments being applied make them more capable and more effective, providing greater safety for those exposed to the dangers of warfighting. The capabilities of modern military drones will also have benefits in humanitarian aid disaster relief operations, creating faster response times and more effective recovery efforts. For the ADF, the Heron has played a significant part in paving the way for a future with drones. It may not have been the most-capable ISR drone available at the time, and it may not have been the hoped-for panacea to the improvised explosive device scourge in Afghanistan, but it did prove to be of great value to the ADF in the long run.

Heron A45-253 in a hangar at RAAF Base Tindal on the evening before its final flight for Exercise *Diamond Storm*, and for the RAAF, June 2017 (Andrew Eddie)

The ADF's use of the Heron system was a perfect model of air power – it was the application of aviation technology by a wide range of highly skilled people who used their knowledge to achieve air power effects. It showed that rapid acquisition of a MOTS solution to an urgent need is not only feasible but also a way of acting quickly and decisively to protect lives. It demonstrated that the ADF has the tenacity to overcome the natural hurdles in training and operating that rapid acquisition will always bring. The ADF did so quickly and learnt a lot about partnering with contractors and Coalition allies in the process. The Heron proved operations are not a limiting factor in the development, adaptation and innovation of technology, and it reinforced the major role defence industry plays in the defence of Australia and its national interests. Its use as an operational test bed allowed the ADF and Australian defence science and industry to trial new technology and software where it is most often intended to be used – in the battlespace. The Heron also allowed for the first tentative steps towards civilian airspace integration by drones in Australia, a situation that will become part of everyday life soon.

Annex A

NO 5 FLIGHT AND HERON TASK UNIT COMMANDERS

No 5 Flight commanding officers

Dates	Commanding officer
Jan 2010 – Sep 2011	WGCDR Lyle Holt
Sep 2011 – Jun 2015	WGCDR Jonathon McMullan
Jun 2015 – Dec 2016	WGCDR Matthew Bowers
Dec 2016 – Nov 2017	WGCDR Lee Read

Task Unit 633.2.7 commanders

Rotation	Dates	Task unit commander
Cadre	Jul – Dec 2009	WGCDR Jason Gamlin
1	Nov 2009 – May 2010	A/WGCDR Steven Williams
2	Apr – Sep 2010	A/WGCDR Timothy Creevey
3	Aug 2010 – Jan 2011	A/WGCDR Robert Morris
4	Nov 2010 – May 2011	WGCDR Greg Wells
5	Apr – Sep 2011	A/WGCDR Jonathon McMullan
6	Jul – Dec 2011	A/WGCDR Ian Goold
7	Nov 2011 – Apr 2012	WGCDR Jeff Frost
8	Feb – Aug 2012	WGCDR Paul Jarvis
9	Jun – Nov 2012	A/WGCDR Christopher Plain
10	Oct 2012 – Mar 2013	WGCDR Nick Osborne
11	Jan – Jul 2013	WGCDR Adrian Maso
12	May – Oct 2013	A/WGCDR Steven Parsons
13	Sep 2013 – Apr 2014	WGCDR Jonathon McMullan
14	Feb – Jul 2014	WGCDR Matthew Bowers
15	Jun – Dec 2014	A/WGCDR Phillip Parsons

Annex B
HERON AIRFRAMES AND THEIR FATES

The Canadian Department of National Defense (DND) operated its Herons under the designation of CU-170, where CU designates Canadian unmanned types, of which 170 was the next in the series that began with the CU-160 IAI Eagle 1. The numerical markings are, therefore, expressed in six digits as 170xxx, with the final three digits being the Israel Aerospace Industries (IAI) construction number.

The implementing arrangement (IA) between the ADF and the Canadian DND recognised that each defence force was paying contractors MacDonald Dettwiler and Associates (MDA) separately to provide the Herons from a common pool of airframes, parts, tools and technicians.

Regarding airframe registration, the IA stated:

> 7.2.1 MDA will be providing a pool of airframes in KAF [Kandahar Airfield] with unique serial numbers that will not change. In contrast, airframe registration markings can be legally affixed to different airframes at different times by either Participant [ADF and Canadian DND]. …
>
> and
>
> 7.2.3 To support this situation and process, each Participant will provide MDA with a list of registration numbers available for use.
>
> and
>
> 7.2.4 Airframe Paint Scheme. The requirement for national markings to be applied to the airframe when flown by a Participant will be minimised with the intent of enabling MDA to readily switch markings and registrations between airframes. For example, there could be a single cowling appropriately painted for each registration number and national emblem, with the remainder of the airframe having no national markings. Cowlings could then be swapped to match the Participant that was flying that airframe that day.

In reality, swaps of leased airframes between the ADF and Canadian DND did not occur often and were generally only done to cover maintenance and repair shortfalls. Some airframes in the list below may not have been flown by the ADF despite being placed on the State Register.

The table below shows all Heron aircraft with an Australian military connection.

IAI construction number	Australian registration	Canadian registration	Comment	Fate
046	VH-BRP		Demonstrator for Border Protection Command 2007	Returned to Israel
169	VH-BJJ		Demonstrator for Border Protection Command 2008	Returned to Israel
251	A45-251	CU-170251	Canadian leased	Flown in Afghanistan and returned to Israel
252	A45-252	CU-170252	Canadian leased	Flown in Afghanistan and returned to Israel
253	A45-253	CU-170253	Canadian leased, transferred to Australian lease	Flown in Canada then Australia and returned to Israel
254	A45-254	CU-170254	Canadian leased	Flown in Afghanistan and returned to Israel
255	A45-255	CU-170255	Canadian leased	Destroyed 16 July 2010 in Canada
262	A45-262		Australian leased	Flown in Afghanistan then Australia and returned to Israel
265	A45-265		Australian leased	Flown in Afghanistan and returned to Israel
274	A45-274		Australian leased	Flown in Afghanistan and returned to Israel

Annex C

HERON AIRFRAME MARKING SCHEME

This drawing, dating from September 2009, is an amended version of the original Canadian Heron paint scheme that indicates the markings for ADF-leased Herons. It was used by MDA contractors to mark Australian-leased Herons and to re-mark Canadian-leased airframes for Australian missions.

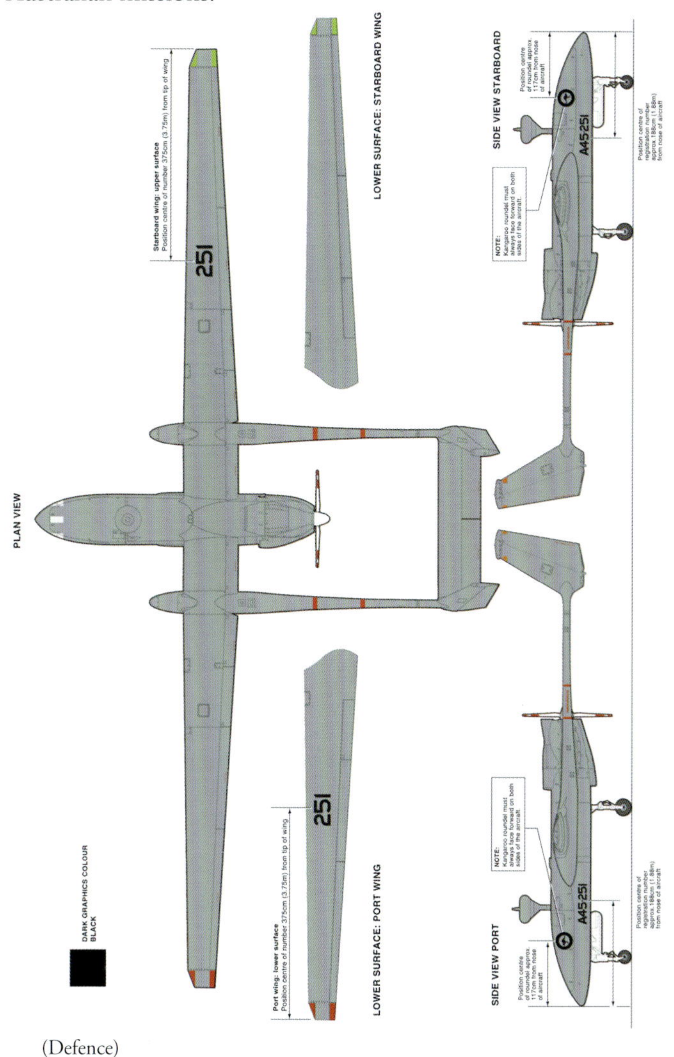

(Defence)

BIBLIOGRAPHY

Interview transcripts

Meier, John, *John Meier interviews Jonathon McMullan* [unpublished interview transcript], Royal Australian Air Force, 6 November 2014.

——, *John Meier interviews Sean McClure* [unpublished interview transcript], Royal Australian Air Force, 6 November 2014.

Note: An additional 13 unpublished transcripts of interviews conducted by the Royal Australian Air Force during 2014 and 2015 are referred to but are not identified here due to privacy restrictions.

Government documents

Airservices Australia, 'AIP Supplement H58/15', Airservices Australia, 22 June 2015.

Civil Aviation Safety Authority, 'Meeting Information', South Queensland RAPAC, 15 April 2015.

Department of Defence, '5FLT Unit History Record', Royal Australian Air Force, April 2011.

——, '5FLT Unit History Record', Royal Australian Air Force, June 2015.

——, '5FLT Unit History Record', Royal Australian Air Force, July 2015.

——, '5FLT Unit History Record', Royal Australian Air Force, October 2015.

——, '5FLT Unit History Record', Royal Australian Air Force, November 2015.

——, '5FLT Unit History Record', Royal Australian Air Force, April 2016.

——, '5FLT Unit History Record', Royal Australian Air Force, August 2016.

——, '5FLT Unit History Record', Royal Australian Air Force, January 2017.

——, Administrative Instruction No 05/2015, 'Heron Deployment to Exercise Iron Moon 2015', Royal Australian Air Force, 31 August 2015.

——, Administrative Instruction No 06/2011, 'Heron Practical Unmanned Aerial System (UAS) Training – Roto 5', Royal Australian Air Force, 18 February 2011.

——, Administrative Instruction No 09/2011, 'Operational Upgrade Training 11–12 Apr 11 and Heron GIA Training 13 Apr 11', Royal Australian Air Force, 4 April 2011.

——, Administrative Instruction No 11/2011, 'Motion Imagery Exploitation Course 9–13 May 2011', Royal Australian Air Force, 29 April 2011.

——, Administrative Instruction No 12/2010, 'Heron UAS Rotation 5 – Theory Training 17 Jan to 11 Feb 11', Royal Australian Air Force, 26 November 2010.

——, Air Force Organisational Directive 2009-07, 'Number 5 Flight', Royal Australian Air Force, 3 February 2010.

——, Air Force Organisational Directive 2013-01, 'Change of Command and Control of Number 5 Flight', Royal Australian Air Force, 27 March 2013.

——, Air Force Organisational Directive 2017-08, 'Disbandment of Number 5 Flight', Royal Australian Air Force, 19 February 2018.

——, Aviation Safety Occurrence Report 5 Flight UAV-024-2010-SASOR 1, 'Human / Aircrew / Engine Cut on Final Approach', Royal Australian Air Force, 4 June 2010.

——, Aviation Safety Occurrence Report 5 Flight UAV-038-2011, 'Materiel / Engine / Loss of Oil Pressure Leading to Engine Fire', Royal Australian Air Force, 2 May 2011.

——, Aviation Safety Occurrence Report 5 Flight UAV-045-2010-SASOR 1, 'Materiel / Landing Gear and Braking System / Landing with NLG locked in up position', Royal Australian Air Force, 28 September 2010.

——, 'CAF Message – Reformation of Number 9 Squadron', Royal Australian Air Force, 16 March 2023.

——, 'Chief of Air Force Commendation – Number 5 Flight', Royal Australian Air Force, 18 April 2015.

——, DEFGRAM 137/2002, 'Decision not to proceed with AIR 7003 Ph1 – MQ-9B SkyGuardian', Royal Australian Air Force, 4 April 2022.

——, 'Implementing Arrangement 01/09 Between the Canadian Forces and the Australian Department of Defence Concerning the Operation of the Heron Unmanned Aerial System in Afghanistan', Royal Australian Air Force, February 2010.

——, 'Memorandum of Understanding Between the Canadian Forces and the Australian Department of Defence Concerning Cooperation in the Development and Operation of the Heron Unmanned Aerial System in Afghanistan', Royal Australian Air Force, 17 August 2009.

——, 'RPAS Strategic Communication Plan', Royal Australian Air Force, 2020.

——, 'Unmanned Aircraft System Operating Permit 001/2015', Defence Aviation Authority, 11 June 2015.

Reports

Foreign Affairs, Defence and Trade References Committee, *Use of unmanned air, maritime and land platforms by the Australian Defence Force*, Australian Government, June 2015. https://www.aph.gov.au/Parliamentary_Business/Committees/Senate/Foreign_Affairs_Defence_and_Trade/Defence_Unmanned_Platform/Report

Hobbs, Alan and Stanley Herwitz, *Human Challenges in the Maintenance of Unmanned Aircraft Systems*, Washington, Federal Aviation Administration Human Factors Research and Engineering Division and National Aeronautics and Space Administration Aeronautical Safety and Human Factors, May 2006. https://human-factors.arc.nasa.gov/publications/UAV_interimreport_Hobbs_Herwitz.pdf

Hobbs, Alan and Stanley Herwitz, *Maintenance Challenges of Small Unmanned Aircraft Systems – A Human Factors Perspective*, Federal Aviation Administration, 2008. https://human-factors.arc.nasa.gov/publications/Maint_Chall_Small_Unman_Aircraft_Human_Factors_Persp.pdf

Joint Standing Committee on Foreign Affairs, Defence and Trade, *Defence Sub-Committee visit to the Middle East Area of Operations: Report of the Delegation to the MEAO 14 to 18 May 2011*, Australian Government, March 2012. https://www.aph.gov.au/Parliamentary_Business/Committees/Joint/Completed_Inquiries/jfadt/DefenceDelegation2011/report

KPMG, *Australia's Aerospace Industry Capability: Research and Economic Modelling of the Aircraft Manufacturing and Repair Services Industry in Australia*, KPMG, 2019.

Royal Australian Air Force, *Implications for Future ISREW UAS Capability Planning: Lesson Learned from Interim MDA Heron Unmanned Aerial Systems Capability Contract (Heron)*, 2nd report, Department of Defence, July 2017, unpublished.

——, *Lessons Learned from Operations of the Heron Unmanned Aircraft System*, Department of Defence, n.d., unpublished.

——, *No. 3 SECFOR SQN Unmanned Aircraft Systems Trial October 2019*, Department of Defence, 23 October 2019, unpublished.

Journal and magazine articles

Australian Defence Magazine, 'Avatar Jacks up connectivity', *Australian Defence Magazine*, 10 January 2008. https://www.australiandefence.com.au/D358D750-F806-11DD-8DFE0050568C22C9

——, 'From the Source: Air Marshal Mark Binskin, AO', *Australian Defence Magazine*, 1 February 2011. https://www.australiandefence.com.au/news/from-the-source-air-marshal-mark-binskin-ao

——, 'From the Source: Air Marshal Mark Binskin, AO (Part 2)', *Australian Defence Magazine*, 1 February 2011. https://www.australiandefence.com.au/archive/from-the-source-air-marshal-mark-binskin-ao-part-2-adm-feb-2011

——, 'JP129 Tactical UAV project terminated', *Australian Defence Magazine*, 15 September 2008. https://www.australiandefence.com.au/3A1028E0-F807-11DD-8DFE0050568C22C9

Blenkin, Max, 'Northrop Grumman demonstrates Triton gateway capability', *Australian Defence Magazine*, 16 February 2023. https://www.australiandefence.com.au/news/northrop-grumman-demonstrates-triton-gateway-capability

Borg, Stefan, 'Assembling Israel Drone Warfare: Loitering Surveillance and Operational Sustainability', *Security Dialogue*, 17 November 2020. https://journals.sagepub.com/doi/full/10.1177/0967010620956796

Brouwers, Josho, 'From horsemen to Hoplites: Some Remarks on Archaic Greek Warfare', *BABesch*, 2007, 82:305–19.

Canadian–American Strategic Review, 'Australia to lease Heron UAVs from McDonald Dettwiler – Is Oz Following CF Lead or did the ADF inspire DND's Project Noctua?', *Canadian–American Strategic Review*, 7 September 2009.

Christiuk, Karen, 'Learning to Fly the Heron', *Defense Aerospace*, May 2009. https://www.defense-aerospace.com/articles-view/release/3/105079/canadian-troops-work-ip-on-heron-uav.html

Egozi, Arie, 'Canada receives first Heron UAV system', *Flight Global*, 25 October 2008. https://www.flightglobal.com/canada-receives-first-heron-uav-system/83543.article

Flight Global, 'Aerosonde in military role', *Flight Global*, 29 July 2003. https://www.flightglobal.com/aerosonde-in-military-role/50042.article

Grant, Rebecca, 'The Bekaa Valley War', *Air Force Magazine*, June 2002.

Hambling, David, 'Drone Swarms Are Getting Too Fast For Humans To Fight, U.S. General Warns,' *Forbes*, 27 January 2021. https://www.forbes.com/sites/davidhambling/2021/01/27/drone-swarms-are-getting-too-fast-for-humans-too-fight-us-general-warns/

——, David, 'What Are Drone Swarms And Why Does Every Military Suddenly Want One?', *Forbes*, 1 March 2021. https://www.forbes.com/sites/davidhambling/2021/03/01/what-are-drone-swarms-and-why-does-everyone-suddenly-want-one/

Haynes, Fred, 'Queen Bee – Radio-Controlled Target Aircraft of the 1930s', *Naval Historical Review*, June 2002. https://www.navyhistory.org.au/queen-bee-radio-controlled-target-aircraft-of-the-1930s/

Jenkins, John, 'The operational role of the Heron remotely-piloted aircraft in the Royal Australian Air Force', *United Service*, December 2013, 64(4).

Jones, Spencer, 'Scouting for Soldiers: Reconnaissance and the British Cavalry, 1899–1914', *War in History*, 2011, 18(4):495–513.

Keane, John and Stephen Carr, 'A Brief History of Early Unmanned Aircraft', *John Hopkins APL Technical Digest*, 2013, 32(3):558–71.

Lachow, Irving, 'The Upside and Downside of Swarming Drones', *Bulletin of the Atomic Scientists*, 2017, 73(2): 96–101. https://www.tandfonline.com/action/showCitFormats?doi=10.1080/00963402.2017.1290879

Langford, Ian, 'Australian Special Forces in Afghanistan', *Australian Army Journal*, Autumn 2010, VII(I).

Levick, Ewen, 'Army target drone literacy with Phantom delivery', *Australian Defence Magazine*, 23 August 2018. https://www.australiandefence.com.au/land/army-targets-drone-literacy-with-phantom-delivery

Low, Archibald, 'The First Guided Missile', *Flight*, 3 October 1952.

McLaughlin, Andrew, 'Insitu Pacific selected for Australian Army's LAND 129 Phase 3 TUAS', *Australian Defence Business Review*, 14 March 2022. https://adbr.com.au/insitu-pacific-selected-for-australian-armys-land-129-phase-3-tuas/

——, 'RAAF UAS Projects AI.R Power', *Australian Defence Business Review*, May–June 2020. https://issuu.com/adbr5/docs/adbr_may-june/s/10734656

Naval Aviation News, 'Aerial Targets', *Naval Aviation News*, November 1945. https://www.history.navy.mil/content/dam/nhhc/research/histories/naval-aviation/Naval%20Aviation%20News/1940/pdf/1nov45.pdf

Popular Mechanics, 'Pilotless Photo Drone Takes Aerial Pictures', *Popular Mechanics*, June 1956.

Reim, Garrett, 'General Atomics teases new addition to its portfolio of air-launched effects', *FlightGlobal*, 21 May 2021. https://www.flightglobal.com/military-uavs/general-atomics-teases-new-addition-to-its-portfolio-of-air-launched-effects/143847.article

Rogers, Ann, 'Investigating the Relationship Between Drone Warfare and Civilian Casualties in Gaza', *Journal of Strategic Security*, 2014, 7(4): 94–107.

Wallace, Duncan, and J Costello, 'Eye in the sky: Understanding the mental health of unmanned aerial vehicle operators', *Journal of Military and Veterans' Health*, 2017, 25(3).

Wastnage, Justin, 'BAE Systems Tests HERTI UAV over South Australia', *Flight Global*, 31 January 2007. https://www.flightglobal.com/articles/2007/01/31/211860/picture-bae-systems-tests-herti-uav-over-south-australia.html

Media reports and articles

Air Force News, 'Controllers guide UAVs', *Air Force News*, Vol 45 No 16, 11 September 2003.

BBC News, 'Heathrow airport: Drone sighting halts departures', *BBC News*, 8 January 2019. https://www.bbc.com/news/uk-46803713

Callinan, Rory, 'Inquiry into the death of Lieutenant Marcus Case leaves unanswered questions over chopper crash', *Sydney Morning Herald*, 11 December 2014. https://www.smh.com.au/national/inquiry-into-the-death-of-lieutenant-marcus-case-leaves-unanswered-questions-over-chopper-crash-20141209-1234xz.html

CTV News, 'Unmanned aircraft crashes near CFB Suffield', *CTV News*, 16 July 2010. https://calgary.ctvnews.ca/unmanned-aircraft-crashes-near-cfb-suffield-1.533153

Dodd, Mark, 'Expanded military role for drones no risk to pilot jobs', *Australian*, 25 September 2009.

Gordon, Jason, 'Enduring survivor's guilt', *Newcastle Herald*, 24 April 2015. https://www.newcastleherald.com.au/story/3034652/enduring-survivors-guilt/

Greene, Andrew, 'Australian-made Loyal Wingman air combat drone with AI-driven targeting system completes first test flight', *ABC News*, 2 March 2021. https://www.abc.net.au/news/2021-03-02/loyal-wingman-first-flight-australia-boeing/13207388

Griffiths, Emma, 'Australian soldiers complete withdrawal from Afghanistan's Uruzgan province', *ABC News*, 17 December 2013. https://www.abc.net.au/news/2013-12-16/australian-soldiers-pull-out-of-uruzgan-province/5159220?nw=0

Hartley, Anna, 'Advanced RAAF drone takes flight in Ipswich', *Courier Mail*, 20 April 2016. https://www.couriermail.com.au/news/queensland/ipswich/watch-advanced-raaf-drone-takes-flight-in-ipswich/news-story/e7eb0ff76796244bd892d4f2b949e838

Hawkes, Rebecca, 'Post-traumatic stress disorder is higher in drone operators', *Telegraph*, 30 May 2015.

Hoffmann, Lars, 'Germany to Lease Israeli "Heron" Drone for Mali Operations', *Defense News*, 22 July 2016. https://www.defensenews.com/air/2016/07/22/germany-to-lease-israeli-heron-drone-for-mali-operations/

Insinna, Valerie, 'Boeing rolls out Australia's first 'Loyal Wingman' combat drone', *Defense News*, 5 May 2020. https://www.defensenews.com/air/2020/05/04/boeing-rolls-out-australias-first-loyal-wingman-combat-drone/

——, Valerie, 'Australia makes another order for Boeing's Loyal Wingman drones after a successful first flight', *Defense News*, 3 March 2021. https://www.defensenews.com/air/2021/03/02/australia-makes-another-order-for-boeing-made-loyal-wingman-drones-after-a-successful-first-flight/

Joyce, Keirin, 'The Australian Army and Unmanned Aerial Vehicles… 20 Years On and Nothing In-service', *RAA Liaison Letter 2010*, Autumn edn, Royal Regiment of Australian Artillery, Puckapunyal, 2010. https://australianartilleryassociation.com/liaison_letter/2010/raa-liaison-letter-2010-autumn/

Leigh, N, 'Australian Special Operations Forces War Crimes in Afghanistan Confirmed', *Overt Defense*, 19 November 2020. https://www.overtdefense.com/2020/11/19/australian-special-forces-war-crimes-in-afghanistan-confirmed/

Marsden, William, 'The allies' eyes in the skies', *Vancouver Sun*, 23 July 2011. https://www.pressreader.com/canada/vancouver-sun/20110723/286976831214645

McDonald, Susan, 'Lieutenant Marcus Case', *ABC News*, 18 December 2014. https://www.abc.net.au/news/2014-12-18/aircraft-fault-pilot-error-partly-to-blame-for-fatal-crash/5977144

News.com.au, 'Dead soldier honoured in Afghanistan', *News.com.au*, 5 June 2011. https://www.news.com.au/world/dead-soldier-honoured-in-afghanistan/news-story/b36942066ea6dc8e08610ee5eab002c9

Om, Jason, 'Drone Racing Champs: Australia's Fastest Crowned at Weekend of Speed', *ABC News*, 22 August 2016. https://www.abc.net.au/news/2016-08-22/australian-drone-nationals-championships/7771864

——, 'Game of Drones', *ABC News*, 12 June 2015. https://www.abc.net.au/news/2015-06-11/the-underground-world-of-drone-racing/6532896?nw=0

Royal Regiment of Australian Artillery, '131st STA Battery', *RAA Liaison Letter 2003*, Spring edn, Royal Regiment of Australian Artillery, Puckapunyal, 2003. http://www.artilleryhistory.org/todays_gunline/liaison_letter/documents/raa_liaison_letter_2003_spring.pdf

Sundstrom, Kathy and Daniel Prosser, 'Drone Racing Camps the Answer for School-age Teens Seeking New Pilots to Compete With', *ABC News*, 11 January 2019. https://www.abc.net.au/news/2019-01-11/drone-racing-camp-for-teens-with-no-one-to-race-with/10703044

Vogelaar, Rob, 'Contract Extended for Israel Aerospace Industries UAV Serving Australian Air Force in Afghanistan', *Aviation News*, 13 August 2010.

Walters, Patrick, 'Heron on the wing to guide Diggers', *Australian*, 8 September 2009.

Media releases

Australian War Memorial, *ScanEagle UAV to be a significant feature in new exhibition, Afghanistan: the Australian story* [media release], 11 June 2013.

Boeing Australia, *Boeing Australia to Provide Australia's First Tactical Unmanned Aerial Vehicle Capability* [media release], 15 December 2006.

Boeing Australia, *ScanEagle Backgrounder* [media release], 31 July 2013.

Defense Security Cooperation Agency, *Australia – RQ-7B SHADOW 200 Unmanned Aircraft System* [media release], 6 May 2010.

Department of Defence, *AIR 7003* [media release], 4 April 2022.

——, *Air Force to begin operating its first unmanned aerial system* [media release], Minister for Defence, MIN2509/09, 7 September 2009.

——, *Australia extends Heron mission in southern Afghanistan* [media release], 10 December 2013.

——, *Heron takes to Afghan skies* [media release], 13 January 2010.

——, *Heron UAV to Support Australian Troops in Afghanistan* [media release], 13 January 2010.

——, *Pilotless Aircraft Deploy to Solomon Islands* [media release], 9 August 2003.

——, *Response to Nigel Pittaway* [media release], 9 September 2009.

——, *Shadow Tactical Unmanned Aerial System commences Afghan operations* [media release], 4 May 2012.

——, *UAV accident in Dili* [media release], 10 May 2007.

Web pages

ADF Serials, 'A43 AAI Corporation RQ-7B Shadow 200 UAV', ADF Serials, n.d. http://www.adf-serials.com.au/3a43.htm

——, 'MSPA 512/2010 3 November 2010', 8 August 2011. http://www.adf-messageboard.com.au/invboard/index.php?showtopic=1724

——, 'RAN N28 MQM-107E Kalkara', ADF Serials, n.d. www.adf-serials.com.au/n28.htm

Aerosonde, 'Aerosonde Background Information', Aerosonde, n.d. https://www.ctie.monash.edu/hargrave/ael_avalon/ael_avalon_05_bkgrnd_info.pdf

Air Force Technology, 'Heron/Machatz 1 Unmanned Aerial Vehicle (UAV)', Air Force Technology, 28 July 2021. https://www.airforce-technology.com/projects/heron-uav/

——, 'Loyal wingman Unmanned Aircraft', Air Force Technology, 22 May 2020. https://www.airforce-technology.com/projects/loyal-wingman-unmanned-aircraft/

Amazon. 'First Prime Air Delivery', Amazon, 15 December 2016. https://www.youtube.com/watch?v=vNySOrI2Ny8&ab_channel=amazon

Amnesty International, 'Gaza: Operation "Cast Lead"', Amnesty International UK, 2017. https://www.amnesty.org.uk/gaza-operation-cast-lead

Atkinson, Leigh, 'RAAF's thin end of the wedge', Aviation Spotters Online, 17 May 2016. http://aviationspottersonline.com/raafs-thin-end-of-the-wedge/

Attar, Moshe, Elias Wahnon and Doron Chaimovitz, 'Advanced Flight Control Technologies for UAVs', September 2003. https://www.researchgate.net/publication/268569936_Advanced_Flight_Control_Technologies_for_UAVs

Australian Aircraft Restoration Group, 'GAF Jindivik A92-492', Australian Aircraft Restoration Group, n.d. https://www.aarg.com.au/gaf-jindivik.html

Australian Army, 'Australian Army in Afghanistan', Department of Defence, n.d. https://www.army.gov.au/our-heritage/history/history-focus/australian-army-afghanistan

——, 'Unmanned Aerial Vehicles', Department of Defence, n.d. https://www.army.gov.au/our-work/equipment-uniforms/equipment/surveillance/unmanned-aerial-vehicles

Australian War Memorial, 'UH-60L Black Hawk Engine Cowling', *3D Treasures*, n.d. https://www.awm.gov.au/3dtreasures/items/blackhawk-cowling/

BAE Systems, 'Airspeed AS30 Queen Wasp', BAE Systems, n.d. https://www.baesystems.com/en/heritage/airspeed-as30-queen-wasp

Bardoe, Baz, 'Drones and Defence: The ADF and Unmanned Aerial Systems', *Australian Aviation*, 7 December 2019. https://australianaviation.com.au/2019/12/drones-and-defence-the-adf-and-unmanned-aerial-systems/

Barnard Microsystems, 'First Atlantic crossing by an Unmanned Aircraft', Barnard Microsystems, n.d. https://barnardmicrosystems.com/UAV/milestones/atlanticc_crossing_1.html

Blenkin, Max, 'Unmanned Systems Finally Taking Off in ADF Service', *Australian Aviation*, 5 April 2018. https://australianaviation.com.au/2018/04/unmanned-systems-finally-taking-off-in-adf-service/

Budanovic, Nikola, 'The Early Days Of Drones – Unmanned Aircraft From World War One And World War Two', *War History Online*, 15 January 2017. https://www.warhistoryonline.com/military-vehicle-news/short-history-drones-part-1.html

Carey, Bill, 'Australia Will Use Heron as Training Bridge to MQ-4C Triton', *AINonline*, 3 November 2014. https://www.ainonline.com/aviation-news/2014-11-03/australia-will-use-heron-training-bridge-mq-4c-triton

Cision, 'SCI Technology's AeroGuard Named 2018 Drone Security New Product of the Year by Security Today Magazine', *PR Newswire*, 24 September 2018. https://www.prnewswire.com/news-releases/sci-technologys-aeroguard-named-2018-drone-security-new-product-of-the-year-by-security-today-magazine-300716969.html

City of Greater Geelong, 'UAV Trials - Unlocking the Potential of Low-Altitude Airspace', City of Greater Geelong, n.d. https://www.geelongaustralia.com.au/smartcity/article/item/8d87a7639ed61ce.aspx

Contact, 'Meritorious Unit Citation for Heron UAV unit', Contact, 13 September 2016. https://www.contactairlandandsea.com/2016/09/13/heron_uav/

Corrigan, Fintan, '10 Thermal Vision Cameras For Drones And How Thermal Imaging Works', DroneZone, 27 February 2020. https://www.dronezon.com/learn-about-drones-quadcopters/9-heat-vision-cameras-for-drones-and-how-thermal-imaging-works/

CQ Plane Spotting, 'Tuesday's Highlights at Rockhampton Airport', CQ Plane Spotting, 7 July 2015. http://cqplanespotting.blogspot.com/2015/07/tuesdays-highlights-at-rockhampton_7.html

Crotty, David, 'GAF Turana Guided Missile', Collections, Museums Victoria, 2010. https://collections.museumsvictoria.com.au/articles/3663

De Havilland Aircraft Museum, 'De Havilland DH82B Queen Bee', De Havilland Aircraft Museum, n.d. https://www.dehavillandmuseum.co.uk/aircraft/de-havilland-dh82b-queen-bee/

Defence Connect, 'Sydney to host first Military International Drone Racing Tournament', *Defence Connect*, 22 October 2018. https://www.defenceconnect.com.au/key-enablers/3042-sydney-to-host-first-military-international-drone-racing-tournament

Defence Today, 'Australian Army builds drone air force', *Defence Today*, 10 September 2018. https://www.defence-today.com.au/australian-army-builds-drone-air-force

Defense World, 'Australian Air Force Withdraws Heron UAVs From Service', Defense World, 9 August 2017. https://www.defenseworld.net/news/20203/Australian_Air_Force_Withdraws_Heron_UAVs_From_Service#.YTGiG44zauU

Department of Defence, 'AIR7003 Phase 1 MQ-9B SkyGuardian Armed Remotely Piloted Aircraft System', Australian Government, n.d. https://www1.defence.gov.au/project/air7003-skyguardian-armed-remotely-piloted-aircraft-system

——, 'Lieutenant Marcus Sean Case', Australian Government, n.d. https://www.defence.gov.au/Vale/LtCase.asp

——, 'Kestral Aerial Surveillance System', Australian Government, n.d. https://www.dst.defence.gov.au/ctd-success-story/kestral-aerial-surveillance-system

——, 'Personal details of Lieutenant Marcus Sean Case', Australian Government, n.d. https://www.defence.gov.au/Vale/LtCase/default.asp

——, 'Triton Remotely Piloted Unmanned Aircraft System', Australian Government, December 2020. https://www1.defence.gov.au/project/triton-remotely-piloted-unmanned-aircraft-system

Department of Industry Science, and Resources, 'Review of Australia's Space Industry Capability', Australian Government, March 2018. https://www.industry.gov.au/data-and-publications/review-of-australias-space-industry-capability

Drone Wars, 'Drone Crash Database', Drone Wars, n.d. https://dronewars.net/drone-crash-database/

Evans, Hannah, 'Sending Our Women to War: The Role of Women in the Australian Army from 2000 to Today', *Australian Policy and History*, 13 November 2017. https://aph.org.au/2017/11/sending-our-women-to-war-the-role-of-women-in-the-australian-army-from-2000-to-today/

Federation of American Scientists, 'History of Remote Sensing', Federation of American Scientists, n.d. https://fas.org/irp/imint/docs/rst/Intro/Part2_7.html

Ferguson, Gregor, 'Surveillance: BAE Systems eyes UAV opportunities', *Australian Defence Magazine*, 1 June 2009. https://www.australiandefence.com.au/71E446CE-7C05-11DE-83AF0050568C22C9

Fleet Air Arm Association of Australia, 'GAF Jindivik Pilotless Target Aircraft', Fleet Air Arm Association of Australia, n.d. https://www.faaaa.asn.au/our-heritage-unmanned-target-aircraft/

——, 'PTA – Radioplane', Fleet Air Arm Association of Australia, n.d. https://www.faaaa.asn.au/uav-radioplane/

——, 'PTA – Turana', Fleet Air Arm Association of Australia, n.d. https://www.faaaa.asn.au/uav-turana/

Flynt, Joseph, 'Differences Between Hexacopters, Quadcopters and Octocopters', 3DInsider, 9 July 2017. https://3dinsider.com/hexacopters-quadcopters-octocopters/

French, Sally, 'Ready for Takeoff', *Slate*, 7 August 2018. https://slate.com/technology/2018/08/australias-military-drone-racing-team-hopes-to-stage-a-comeback-at-the-invictus-games.html

Hargrave Remote Piloted Aerial Vehicles, 'The "Aerial Target" and "Aerial Torpedo" in Australia', Hargrave, 25 January 2006. https://www.ctie.monash.edu/hargrave/rpav_jindivik.html

InSitu Pacific, 'Backgrounder: ScanEagle Unmanned Aircraft Systems', Boeing Australia, n.d. http://www.boeing.com/farnborough2014/pdf/BDS/ScanEagle%20Backgrounder%200114.pdf

——, 'Versatile and agile multi-domain UAS solutions', Boeing Australia, n.d. https://insitupacific.com.au/

Israel Aerospace Industries, 'Heron Multi-Role MALE UAS', Israel Aerospace Industries, n.d. https://www.iai.co.il/p/heron

——, 'History: IAI and the Security of Israel', Israel Aerospace Industries, n.d. https://www.iai.co.il/about/history

——, 'MOSP3000-HD', Israel Aerospace Industries, n.d. https://www.iai.co.il/p/mosp

la Franchi, Peter, 'Flight International unmanned air vehicle (UAV) directory 2006', *Flight Global*, 22 August 2006. https://www.flightglobal.com/flight-international-unmanned-air-vehicle-uav-directory-2006/69097.article

Kerr, Julian, 'EW and UAVs: Aerosonde: From Local to International Success', *Australian Defence Magazine*, May 2013. https://www.australiandefence.com.au/news/ew-and-uavs-aerosonde-from-local-to-international-success-adm-may-2013

——, 'Land Surveillance: JP129 – Surveillance in the Land domain post-Afghanistan', *Australian Defence Magazine*, 2 September 2014. https://www.australiandefence.com.au/news/land-surveillance-jp129-surveillance-in-the-land-domain-post-afghanistan-adm-july-2014

Layton, Peter, 'The Australian Army's drone air force', *The Interpreter*, 5 November 2018. https://www.lowyinstitute.org/the-interpreter/australian-army-drone-air-force

Legacy, 'Lieutenant Marcus Sean Case', Legacy, n.d. https://www.legacy.com/obituaries/heraldsun-au/obituary.aspx?n=marcus-sean-case&pid=151418858

Maksel, Rebecca, 'The World's First Warplane', *Smithsonian Magazine*, 21 October 2011. https://www.smithsonianmag.com/air-space-magazine/the-worlds-first-warplane-115175678/

Menzies, Robert, 'Australian Federal Electoral Speeches', Australian Government, 1951. https://electionspeeches.moadoph.gov.au/speeches/1951-robert-menzies

Military, 'RQ-11B Raven', Military, n.d. https://www.military.com/equipment/rq-11b-raven

Military Factory, 'Radioplane OQ-2: Aerial Target Drone (1941)', Military Factory, 19 January 2017. https://www.militaryfactory.com/aircraft/detail.php?aircraft_id=331

Muir, Tom, 'The ADF's love affair with tactical UAVs', *Australian Defence Magazine*, 19 March 2015. https://www.australiandefence.com.au/news/the-adf-s-love-affair-with-tactical-uavs

National Army Museum, 'Cavalry roles', National Army Museum, n.d. https://www.nam.ac.uk/explore/cavalry-roles

National Museum of the United States Air Force, 'Radioplane OQ-2A', United States Air Force, n.d. https://www.nationalmuseum.af.mil/Visit/Museum-Exhibits/Fact-Sheets/Display/Article/196292/radioplane-oq-2a/

Naval Technology, 'MQ-4C Triton Broad Area Maritime Surveillance (BAMS) UAS', Naval Technology, 18 September 2021. https://www.naval-technology.com/projects/mq-4c-triton-bams-uas-us/

New Mexico Museum of Space History, 'Archibald M. Low', New Mexico Museum of Space History, 2021. https://www.nmspacemuseum.org/inductee/archibald-m-low/

Newdick, Thomas and Tyler Rogoway, 'Russia's Predator-Style Drone With Big Export Potential Has Launched Its First Missiles', *The Warzone*, 28 December 2020. https://www.thedrive.com/the-war-zone/38446/russias-predator-style-drone-with-big-export-potential-has-launched-its-first-missiles

Nicholson, Brendan, 'ADF Women are Already "In Combat"', *The Strategist*, Australian Strategic Policy Institute, 24 March 2017. https://www.aspistrategist.org.au/adf-women-already-combat/

Northrop Grumman, 'MQ-4C Triton', Northrop Grumman, n.d. https://www.northropgrumman.com/what-we-do/air/triton/

O'Malley, Dave, 'The Mother of All Drones', Vintage Wings of Canada, n.d. http://www.vintagewings.ca/VintageNews/Stories/tabid/116/articleType/ArticleView/articleId/484/The-Mother-of-All-Drones.aspx

Parsch, Andreas, 'GAF Jindivik', *Directory of U.S. Military Rockets and Missiles*, 2004. http://www.designation-systems.net/dusrm/app4/jindivik.html

Pittaway, Nigel, 'Land Warfare 2011: UAVs – operations and aspirations', *Australian Defence Magazine*, 1 October 2011. https://www.australiandefence.com.au/archive/land-warfare-2011-uavs-operations-and-aspirations-adm-october-2011

——, 'Triton program delayed by US budget cuts', *Australian Defence Magazine*, 29 April 2021. https://www.australiandefence.com.au/defence/air/triton-program-delayed-by-us-budget-cuts

Roberts, Peter, 'Air Affair's Phoenix Jet Drone Deployed in Navy Exercises', AuManufacturing, 21 January 2021. https://www.aumanufacturing.com.au/air-affairss-phoenix-jet-drone-deployed-in-navy-exercises

Royal Australian Air Force, 'Heron', Air Force, Department of Defence, n.d. https://www.airforce.gov.au/technology/aircraft/intelligence-surveillance-and-reconnaissance/heron

——, 'MQ-4C Triton Unmanned Aircraft System', Department of Defence, n.d. https://www.airforce.gov.au/technology/aircraft/intelligence-surveillance-and-reconnaissance/mq-4c-triton-unmanned-aircraft

Royal Australian Navy, '822X Squadron', Department of Defence, n.d. https://www.navy.gov.au/about/organisation/fleet-air-arm/822x-squadron

——, 'BAE Kalkara Unmanned Aerial Target', Department of Defence, n.d. https://www.navy.gov.au/aircraft/bae-kalkara-unmanned-aerial-target

——, 'GAF Jindivik Pilotless Target Aircraft', Department of Defence, n.d. https://www.navy.gov.au/aircraft/gaf-jindivik-pilotless-target-aircraft

——, 'HMAS Australia (II)', Department of Defence, n.d. https://www.navy.gov.au/hmas-australia-ii

——, 'ScanEagle', Department of Defence, n.d. https://www.navy.gov.au/unmanned-systems/scaneagle

——, 'Supermarine Seagull V (Walrus)', Department of Defence, n.d. https://www.navy.gov.au/aircraft/supermarine-seagull-v-walrus

Schiebel, 'Camcopter S-100 Unmanned Air System' Schiebel, n.d. https://schiebel.net/products/camcopter-s-100/

Schiebel, 'Camcopter S-100 Unmanned Air System: Specifications', Schiebel, n.d. https://schiebel.net/products/camcopter-s-100-system-2/

Selinger, Marc, 'Counterdrone Challenges', *Aerospace America*, May 2019. https://aerospaceamerica.aiaa.org/features/counterdrone-challenges/

Sentient Vision, 'Kestrel', Sentient, n.d. https://www.sentientvision.com/prodcuts/kestrel-land-mti/

Shell, Jason, 'How the IED Won: Dispelling the Myth of Tactical Success and Innovation', Texas National Security Review, 1 May 2017. https://warontherocks.com/2017/05/how-the-ied-won-dispelling-the-myth-of-tactical-success-and-innovation/

South Australian Aviation Museum, 'Shelduck', South Australian Aviation Museum, n.d. https://www.saam.org.au/shelduck/

SpaceWar, 'Kestrel Support Project NANKEEN in Afghanistan', SpaceWar, 11 November 2010. https://www.spacewar.com/reports/Kestrel_Supports_Project_NANKEEN_In_Afghanistan_999.html

Tanter, Richard, 'Mentoring Task Force', Nautilus Institute for Security and Sustainability, 14 August 2010. https://nautilus.org/publications/books/australian-forces-abroad/afghanistan/mentoring-task-force/

——, 'Unmanned aerial vehicles (UAVs)', Nautilus Institute for Security and Sustainability, 18 January 2011. https://nautilus.org/publications/books/australian-forces-abroad/afghanistan/unmanned-aerial-vehicle-uav-detachment/

——, '131 Surveillance and Target Acquisition Battery', Nautilus Institute for Security and Sustainability, n.d. https://nautilus.org/publications/books/australian-forces-abroad/solomon-islands/131-surveillance-and-target-acquisition-battery/

The Horse and its Heritage, '1870: from combat cavalry to reconnaissance cavalry', *The Horse and its Heritage*, n.d. http://www.cheval.culture.fr/en/page/1870_from_combat_cavalry_to_reconnaissance_cavalry

Vyas, Kashyap, 'A Brief History of Drones: The Remote Controlled Unmanned Aerial Vehicles (UAVs)', *Interesting Engineering*, 30 June 2020. https://interestingengineering.com/a-brief-history-of-drones-the-remote-controlled-unmanned-aerial-vehicles-uavs

Western Museum of Flight, 'Radioplane RP-5A Target Drone', Western Museum of Flight, 2010. https://www.wmof.com/rp5a.htm

World of Aviation, 'BAE Taranis UCAV Breaks Cover', *World of Aviation*, 6 February 2014. https://worldofaviation.com/2014/02/bae-taranis-ucav-breaks-cover/

Yeo, Mike, 'Four companies short listed for Project LAND 129 Phase 3 to replace Shadow UAS', *Asia–Pacific Defence Reporter*, 20 March 2020. https://asiapacificdefencereporter.com/four-companies-shortlisted-for-project-land-129-phase-3-to-replace-shadow-uas/

Ziesing, Katherine, 'Air Power: Heron in Woomera this year', *Australian Defence Magazine*, 1 February 2011.

——, 'Project Nankeen: A Heron by any other name', *Australian Defence Magazine*, 1 February 2011.

Published works

Allen, Terry, *Reconnaissance by Horse Cavalry Regiments and Smaller Units*. Pennsylvania: The Military Service Publishing Company, 1939.

Bridgman, Leonard (ed), *Jane's All the World's Aircraft 1952–53*. New York: McGraw-Hill, 1953.

Cole, Chris, *Accidents will Happen: a review of military drone crash data as the UK considers allowing large military drone flights in its airspace*. Oxford: Drone Wars UK, 2019.

Dennis, Peter, Jeffrey Grey, Ewan Morris, Robin Prior and Jean Bou, *The Oxford Companion to Australian Military History* (2nd edn). Melbourne: Oxford University Press, 2008.

Dolan, Hugh, *36 Days: The Untold Story Behind the Gallipoli Landings*. Sydney: Macmillan, 2010.

Ehrhard, Thomas, *Air Force UAVs: The Secret History*. Washington: Mitchell Institute for Airpower Studies, 2010.

Fishstein, Paul and Andrew Wilder, *Winning Hearts and Minds? Examining the Relationship between Aid and Security in Afghanistan*. Boston: Feinstein International Center, 2012.

Gettinger, Dan, *The Drone Databook*. New York: The Center for the Study of the Drone at Bard College, 2019.

Johnson, David, *Hard Fighting: Israel in Lebanon and Gaza*. Santa Monica: RAND Corporation, 2011.

Joyce, Keirin, 'The Australian Army and Unmanned Aerial Vehicles… 20 Years and Finally In-service', *28th International Congress of the Aeronautical Sciences* [conference presentation], Brisbane, 23–28 September 2012.

McGrath, John, *Scouts Out! The Development of Reconnaissance Units in Modern Armies*. Kansas: Combat Studies Institute Press, 2010.

Mckelvey, Ben, *Mosul: Australia's secret war inside the ISIS caliphate*. Sydney: Hachette, 2020.

McMullan, Jonathan and Matthew Lunnay, 'Civilian/Military Integration – Afghanistan: The Afghan RPAS Success Story', *International Civil Aviation Organization Remotely Piloted Aircraft Systems (RPAS) Symposium* [conference presentation], Montreal, 23–25 March 2015.

McPhedran, Ian, *Air Force: Inside Australia's Air Wars: Bali to Baghdad and Beyond*. Sydney: Harper Collins, 2013.

Miles, John and John Pescott, *Testing Times*. Geelong: Neptune Press, 1979.

Mills, Steve, *The Dawn of the Drone: from the back-room boys of World War One*. Oxford: Casemate, 2019.

Morton, Peter, *Fire Across the Desert: Woomera and the Anglo-Australian Joint Project 1946–80*. Canberra: Australian Government Publishing Service, 1989.

Overton, Iain, Roger Davies and Louise Tumchewics, *Improvised Explosive Devices: past, present and future* London: Action on Armed Violence, 2020.

Royal Australian Air Force, *Australian Air Publication 1000–D: The Air Power Manual*, 6th edn. Canberra: Air Power Development Centre, 2013.

Sun Tzu, *The Art of War: The Oldest Military Treatise in the World – Translated from the Chinese with Introduction and Critical Notes*, (Lionel Giles trans). London: Luzac, 1910.

Thompson, Holland, *The World's Greatest War from the Outbreak of the war to the Treaty of Versailles*. New York: Grolier, 1921.

Von Richthofen, Manfred. *Red Fighter Pilot: The Autobiography of the Red Baron*. Florida: Red and Black, 2007.

Werrell, Kenneth, *The Evolution of the Cruise Missile. Alabama:* Air University Press, *1985.*

ENDNOTES

Chapter 1

1 Australian War Memorial, 'UH-60L Black Hawk Engine Cowling', *3D Treasures*, n.d. https://www.awm.gov.au/3dtreasures/items/balckhawk-cowling/
2 Meier, Unpublished interview transcript with undisclosed interviewee.
3 Sun Tzu, *The Art of War: The Oldest Military Treatise in the World – Translated from the Chinese with Introduction and Critical Notes*, (Lionel Giles trans). London: Luzac, 1910, chap XIII para 4.
4 John McGrath, *Scouts Out! The Development of Reconnaissance Units in Modern Armies*. Kansas: Combat Studies Institute Press, 2010, p 1.
5 The Horse and its Heritage, '1870: from combat cavalry to reconnaissance cavalry'. http://www.cheval.culture.fr/en/page/1870_from_combat_cavalry_to_reconnaissance_cavalry
6 Terry Allen, *Reconnaissance by Horse Cavalry Regiments and Smaller Units*. Pennsylvania: The Military Service Publishing Company, 1939.
7 Manfred von Richthofen, *Red Fighter Pilot: The Autobiography of the Red Baron*. Florida: Red and Black, 2007, p 49.
8 Josho Brouwers, 'From Horsemen to Hoplites: Some Remarks on Archaic Greek Warfare', *BABesch*, 2007, 82:305–19.
9 National Army Museum, 'Cavalry roles'. https://www.nam.ac.uk/explore/cavalry-roles
10 McGrath, *Scouts Out!*
11 Spencer Jones, 'Scouting for Soldiers: Reconnaissance and the British Cavalry, 1899–1914', *War in History*, 2011, 18(4):495–513.
12 McGrath, *Scouts Out!*, p 1.
13 Thompson, Holland, *The World's greatest war from the outbreak of the war to the Treaty of Versailles*. New York: Grolier, 1921, p 243.
14 Federation of American Scientists, 'History of Remote Sensing'. https://fas.org/irp/imint/docs/rst/Intro/Part2_7.html
15 Rebecca Maksel, 'The World's First Warplane', Air & Space Magazine, 21 October 2011. https://www.smithsonianmag.com/air-space-magazine/the-worlds-first-warplane-115175678/
16 Hugh Dolan, *36 Days: The Untold Story Behind the Gallipoli Landings*. Sydney: Macmillan, 2010, p 384.
17 John Stanaway, *P-38 Lightning Aces of the ETO/MTO*, New York: Osprey, 1998.
18 War History Online, 'The Early Days Of Drones – Unmanned Aircraft From World War One And World War Two'. https://www.warhistoryonline.com/military-vehicle-news/short-history-drones-part-1.html
19 Steve Mills, *The Dawn of the Drone: from the back-room boys of World War One*. Oxford: Casemate, 2019, pp 182, 150–1; Arthur Low, 'The First Guided Missile', *Flight*, 3 October 1952, p 436.
20 Vyas, Kashyap, 'A Brief History of Drones: The Remote Controlled Unmanned Aerial Vehicles (UAVs)', *Interesting Engineering*, 30 June 2020. https://interestingengineering.com/a-brief-history-of-drones-the-remote-controlled-unmanned-aerial-vehicles-uavs
21 New Mexico Museum of Space History, 'Archibald M. Low', New Mexico Museum of Space History, 2021. https://www.nmspacemuseum.org/inductee/archibald-m-low/
22 Kenneth Werrell, *The Evolution of the Cruise Missile.* Alabama: Air University Press, 1985, p 18.
23 De Havilland Aircraft Museum, 'De Havilland DH82B Queen Bee'. https://www.dehavillandmuseum.co.uk/aircraft/de-havilland-dh82b-queen-bee/

24 BAE Systems, 'Airspeed AS30 Queen Wasp'. https://www.baesystems.com/en/heritage/airspeed-as30-queen-wasp
25 De Havilland Aircraft Museum, 'De Havilland DH82B Queen Bee'.
26 Dave O'Malley, 'The Mother of All Drones', Vintage Wings of Canada, n.d. http://www.vintagewings.ca/VintageNews/Stories/tabid/116/articleType/ArticleView/articleId/484/The-Mother-of-All-Drones.aspx
27 De Havilland Aircraft Museum, 'De Havilland DH82B Queen Bee'.
28 John Keane and Stephen Carr, 'A Brief History of Early Unmanned Aircraft', *John Hopkins APL Technical Digest*, 2013, 32(3):558–71; O'Malley, 'The Mother of All Drones'.
29 Western Museum of Flight, 'Radioplane RP-5A Target Drone', Western Museum of Flight, 2010. https://www.wmof.com/rp5a.htm
30 Keane and Carr, 'A Brief History of Early Unmanned Aircraft'.
31 Western Museum of Flight, 'Radioplane RP-5A Target Drone'.
32 National Museum of the United States Air Force, 'Radioplane OQ-2A', United States Air Force, n.d. https://www.nationalmuseum.af.mil/Visit/Museum-Exhibits/Fact-Sheets/Display/Article/196292/radioplane-oq-2a/; Military Factory, 'Radioplane OQ-2: Aerial Target Drone (1941)', Military Factory, 19 January 2017. https://www.militaryfactory.com/aircraft/detail.php?aircraft_id=331
33 Western Museum of Flight, 'Radioplane RP-5A Target Drone'.
34 'Pilotless Photo Drone Takes Aerial Pictures', *Popular Mechanics*, June 1956, p 144.
35 Thomas Ehrhard, *Air Force UAVs: The Secret History*. Washington: Mitchell Institute for Airpower Studies, 2010.
36 Rebecca Grant, 'The Bekaa Valley War', *Air Force Magazine Online*, June 2002.
37 Amazon. 'First Prime Air Delivery', Amazon, 15 December 2016. https://www.youtube.com/watch?v=vNySOrI2Ny8&ab_channel=amazon
38 Fintan Corrigan, '10 Thermal Vision Cameras For Drones And How Thermal Imaging Works', DroneZone.com,
27 February 2020. https://www.dronezon.com/learn-about-drones-quadcopters/9-heat-vision-cameras-for-drones-and-how-thermal-imaging-works/
39 Royal Australian Air Force (RAAF), *Australian Air Publication 1000–D: The Air Power Manual*, 6th edn. Canberra: Air Power Development Centre, 2013, p 70.
40 RAAF, *The Air Power Manual*, p 70.
41 David Johnson, *Hard Fighting: Israel in Lebanon and Gaza*. Santa Monica: RAND Corporation, 2011, p 96.
42 Amnesty International, 'Gaza: Operation "Cast Lead"', Amnesty International UK, 2017. https://www.amnesty.org.uk/gaza-operation-cast-lead
43 Stefan Borg, 'Assembling Israel Drone Warfare: Loitering Surveillance and Operational Sustainability', *Security Dialogue*, 17 November 2020. https://journals.sagepub.com/doi/full/10.1177/0967010620956796
44 Rogers, 'Investigating the Relationship Between Drone Warfare and Civilian Casualties in Gaza', pp 102–3.
45 RAN, 'HMAS *Australia* (II)', Department of Defence, n.d. https://www.navy.gov.au/hmas-australia-ii.
46 Fred Haynes, 'Queen Bee – Radio-Controlled Target Aircraft of the 1930s', *Naval Historical Review*, June 2002. https://www.navyhistory.org.au/queen-bee-radio-controlled-target-aircraft-of-the-1930s/; RAN, 'Supermarine Seagull V (Walrus)', Department of Defence, n.d. https://www.navy.gov.au/aircraft/supermarine-seagull-v-walrus
47 Haynes, 'Queen Bee – Radio-Controlled Target Aircraft of the 1930s'.
48 Robert Menzies, Speech given at Canterbury, Victoria, 1951. https://electionspeeches.moadoph.gov.au/speeches/1951-robert-menzies

49 Peter Morton, *Fire Across the Desert: Woomera and the Anglo-Australian Joint Project 1946–80*. Canberra: Australian Government Publishing Service, 1989, p 7.
50 Morton, *Fire Across the Desert*, p 371.
51 Morton, *Fire Across the Desert*, p 372; Directory of U.S. Military Rockets and Missiles, 'GAF Jindivik'. http://www.designation-systems.net/dusrm/app4/jindivik.html
52 Naval Aviation News, 'Aerial Targets', *Naval Aviation News*, November 1945. https://www.history.navy.mil/content/dam/nhhc/research/histories/naval-aviation/Naval%20Aviation%20News/1940/pdf/1nov45.pdf
53 Royal Australian Navy (RAN), 'GAF Jindivik Pilotless Aircraft'. https://www.navy.gov.au/aircraft/gaf-jindivik-pilotless-target-aircraft
54 Hargrave RPAV, "The Aerial Target' and 'Aerial Torpedo' in Australia'. https://www.ctie.monash.edu/hargrave/rpav_jindivik.html
55 Directory of U.S. Military Rockets and Missiles, 'GAF Jindivik'.
56 Hargrave RPAV, "The Aerial Target' and 'Aerial Torpedo' in Australia'.
57 RAN, 'GAF Jindivik Pilotless Target Aircraft', Department of Defence, n.d. https://www.navy.gov.au/aircraft/gaf-jindivik-pilotless-target-aircraft
58 Hargrave RPAV, "The Aerial Target' and 'Aerial Torpedo' in Australia'.
59 Leonard Bridgman (ed), *Jane's All the World's Aircraft 1952–53*. New York: McGraw-Hill, 1953, pp 91–2.
60 John Miles and John Pescott, *Testing Times*. Geelong: Neptune Press, 1979, pp 90, 140.
61 Miles and Pescott, *Testing Times*, pp 141–2.
62 RAN, 'GAF Jindivik Pilotless Target Aircraft'.
63 Australian Aircraft Restoration Group, 'GAF Jindivik A92-492', Australian Aircraft Restoration Group, n.d. https://www.aarg.com.au/gaf-jindivik.html
64 Miles and Pescott, *Testing Times*, p 50.
65 Fleet Air Arm Association of Australia, 'GAF Jindivik Pilotless Target Aircraft', Fleet Air Arm Association of Australia, n.d. https://www.faaaa.asn.au/our-heritage-unmanned-target-aircraft/
66 Morton, *Fire Across the Desert*, pp 369–70.
67 Fleet Air Arm Association, 'PTA – Radioplane', Fleet Air Arm Association of Australia, n.d. https://www.faaaa.asn.au/uav-radioplane/
68 Fleet Air Arm Association of Australia, 'PTA — Radioplane'.
69 South Australian Aviation Museum, 'Shelduck', South Australian Aviation Museum, n.d. https://www.saam.org.au/shelduck/
70 Fleet Air Arm Association, 'PTA – Radioplane'.
71 Fleet Air Arm Association, 'PTA – Radioplane'.
72 Museum Victoria, 'GAF Turana Guided Missile', Collections, Museum Victoria, n.d. https://collections.museumsvictoria.com.au/articles/3663#:~:text=Developed%20from%20the%20Ikara%20anti,Royal%20Australian%20Navy%20(RAN).
73 'PTA – Turana', Fleet Air Arm Association of Australia, n.d. https://www.faaaa.asn.au/uav-turana/
74 KPMG, Australia's Aerospace Industry Capability: Research and Economic Modelling of the Aircraft Manufacturing and Repair Services Industry in Australia, report 12 June 2019, pp 6, 54–5.
75 BAE Systems Australia, 'Review of Australia's Space Industry Capability'. file:///C:/Users/RICT/Downloads/BAE-Systems-Submission.pdf
76 RAN, 'BAE Kllkara Unmanned Aerial Target'. https://www.navy.gov.au/aircraft/bae-kalkara-unmanned-aerial-target
77 RAN, 'BAE Kllkara Unmanned Aerial Target'.
78 Hargrave RPAV, "The Aerial Target' and 'Aerial Torpedo' in Australia'.
79 Hargrave RPAV, "The Aerial Target' and 'Aerial Torpedo' in Australia'.
80 ADF Serials, 'RAN N28 MQM-107E Kalkara'. www.adf-serials.com.au/n28.htm

81 Hargrave RPAV, "'The Aerial Target' and 'Aerial Torpedo' in Australia'; ADF Serials, 'RAN N28 MQM-107E Kalkara'; RAN, 'BAE Kllkara Unmanned Aerial Target'.

82 Keirin Joyce, 'The Australian Army and Unmanned Aerial Vehicles… 20 Years On and Nothing In-service', *RAA Liaison Letter*, Autumn 2010, Royal Regiment of Australian Artillery, Puckapunyal, p 55. https://australianartilleryassociation.com/liaison_letter/2010/raa-liaison-letter-2010-autumn/

83 Joyce, 'The Australian Army and Unmanned Aerial Vehicles', p 56.

84 Joyce, 'The Australian Army and Unmanned Aerial Vehicles', p 56.

85 Joyce, 'The Australian Army and Unmanned Aerial Vehicles', p 57.

86 Joyce, 'The Australian Army and Unmanned Aerial Vehicles', p 57.

87 Boeing Australia, *Boeing Australia to Provide Australia's First Tactical Unmanned Aerial Vehicle Capability* [media release], 15 December 2006.

88 Australian Defence Magazine, 'JP129 Tactical UAV project terminated', *Australian Defence Magazine*, 15 September 2008. https://www.australiandefence.com.au/3A1028E0-F807-11DD-8DFE0050568C22C9; Joyce, 'The Australian Army and Unmanned Aerial Vehicles', p 58.

89 'Directory: unmanned air vehicles' *Flight International*, August 2006, p 42.

90 Joyce, 'The Australian Army and Unmanned Aerial Vehicles', p 58.

91 'Directory: unmanned air vehicles' *Flight International*, August 2006, p 43; Joyce, 'The Australian Army and Unmanned Aerial Vehicles', pp 43, 58.

92 Australian Defence Magazine, 'Avatar Jacks up connectivity', *Australian Defence Magazine*, 10 January 2008. https://www.australiandefence.com.au/D358D750-F806-11DD-8DFE0050568C22C9

93 Barnard Microsystems, 'First Atlantic crossing by an Unmanned Aircraft'. https://barnardmicrosystems.com/UAV/milestones/atlanticc_crossing_1.html

94 Department of Defence, *Pilotless Aircraft Deploy to Solomon Islands* [media release], 9 August 2003; *Flight Global*, 'Aerosonde in military role', 29 July 2003. https://www.flightglobal.com/aerosonde-in-military-role/50042.article; Richard Tanter, 'Unmanned aerial vehicles (UAVs)', Nautilus Institute for Security and Sustainability, 18 January 2011. https://nautilus.org/publications/books/australian-forces-abroad/solomon-islands/unmanned-aerial-vehicles-uavs/

95 *Flight Global*, 'Aerosonde in military role'; Department of Defence, *Pilotless Aircraft Deploy to Solomon Islands*.

96 Nautilus Institute for Security and Sustainability, '131 Surveillance and Target Acquisition Battery'. https://nautilus.org/publications/books/australian-forces-abroad/solomon-islands/131-surveillance-and-target-acquisition-battery/

97 Department of Defence, *Pilotless Aircraft Deploy to Solomon Islands*.

98 *Air Force News*, 'Controllers guide UAVs', Vol 45 no 16, 11 September 2003.

99 Department of Defence, *Pilotless Aircraft Deploy to Solomon Islands*; Aerosonde, 'Background Information' [pamphlet], n.d.

100 Royal Regiment of Australian Artillery, '131st STA Battery', *RAA Liaison Letter 2003*, Spring edn, Royal Regiment of Australian Artillery, Puckapunyal, 2003, p 36–8. http://www.artilleryhistory.org/todays_gunline/liaison_letter/documents/raa_liaison_letter_2003_spring.pdf

101 Joyce, 'The Australian Army and Unmanned Aerial Vehicles', p 54.

102 Royal Regiment of Australian Artillery, '131st STA Battery'.

103 Julian Kerr, 'EW and UAVs: Aerosonde: From Local to International Success', *Australian Defence Magazine*, May 2013. https://www.australiandefence.com.au/news/ew-and-uavs-aerosonde-from-local-to-international-success-adm-may-2013

104 Max Blenkin, 'Unmanned Systems Finally Taking Off in ADF Service', Australian Aviation, 5 April 2018. https://australianaviation.com.au/2018/04/unmanned-systems-finally-taking-off-in-adf-service/

105 Joyce, 'The Australian Army and Unmanned Aerial Vehicles', p 59.

106 Military.com, 'RQ-11B Raven'. https://www.military.com/equipment/rq-11b-raven

107 'Australian Army builds drone air force', *Defence Today*, 10 September 2018. https://www.defence-today.com.au/australian-army-builds-drone-air-force

108 Joyce, 'The Australian Army and Unmanned Aerial Vehicles', p 59.

109 Joyce, 'The Australian Army and Unmanned Aerial Vehicles', p 59; Department of Defence, *UAV accident in Dili* [media release], 10 May 2007.

110 'Australian Army builds drone air force', *Defence Today*; 'Directory: unmanned air vehicles' *Flight International*, p 42; Dan Gettinger, *The Drone Databook*. New York: The Center for the Study of the Drone at Bard College, 2020, p 8.

111 Joyce, 'The Australian Army and Unmanned Aerial Vehicles', p 59.

112 InSitu Pacific, 'Defence Services'. https://insitupacific.com.au/

113 Australian War Memorial, *ScanEagle UAV to be a significant feature in new exhibition: Afghanistan: the Australian story* [media release], 11 June 2013. https://www.awm.gov.au/media/press-releases/scaneagle-uav-be-significant-feature-new-exhibition-afghanistan-australian-story; Joyce, 'The Australian Army and Unmanned Aerial Vehicles', p 60; Gettinger, *The Drone Databook*, p 8.

114 Joyce, 'The Australian Army and Unmanned Aerial Vehicles', p 60.

115 InSitu Pacific, 'Versatile and agile multi-domain UAS solutions'. https://insitupacific.com.au/

116 Keirin Joyce (personal correspondence) 11 January 2022; Defense Security Cooperation Agency, *Australia – RQ-7B SHADOW 200 Unmanned Aircraft System* [media release] 6 May 2010. https://www.dsca.mil/sites/default/files/mas/australia_10-19_0.pdf

117 ADF Serials, 'A43 AAI Corporation RQ-7B Shadow 200 UAV'. http://www.adf-serials.com.au/3a43.htm

118 Gettinger, *The Drone Databook*, p 6.

119 Australian Army, 'Unmanned Aerial Vehicles'. https://www.army.gov.au/our-work/equipment-uniforms/equipment/surveillance/unmanned-aerial-vehicles

120 Australian Defence Magazine, 'The ADF's love affair with tactical UAVs'. https://www.australiandefence.com.au/news/the-adf-s-love-affair-with-tactical-uavs

121 Joyce, 'The Australian Army and Unmanned Aerial Vehicles… 20 Years and Finally In-service' [conference presentation], *28th International Congress of the Aeronautical Sciences*, Brisbane, 23–28 September 2012. https://www.icas.org/ICAS_ARCHIVE/ICAS2012/PAPERS/176.PDF

122 Julian Kerr, 'Land Surveillance: JP129 – Surveillance in the Land domain post-Afghanistan', *Australian Defence Magazine*, July 2014. https://www.australiandefence.com.au/news/land-surveillance-jp129-surveillance-in-the-land-domain-post-afghanistan-adm-july-2014

123 Department of Defence, *Shadow Tactical Unmanned Aerial System Commences Afghan Operations* [media release], 4 May 2012. https://news.defence.gov.au/media/media-releases/shadow-tactical-unmanned-aerial-system-commences-afghan-operations

124 Foreign Affairs, Defence and Trade References Committee, *Use of unmanned air, maritime and land platforms by the Australian Defence Force*, Australian Government, June 2015, chap 2. https://www.aph.gov.au/Parliamentary_Business/Committees/Senate/Foreign_Affairs_Defence_and_Trade/Defence_Unmanned_Platform/Report

125 InSitu Pacific, 'Backgrounder: ScanEagle Unmanned Aircraft Systems'. http://www.boeing.com/farnborough2014/pdf/BDS/ScanEagle%20Backgrounder%20014.pdf

126 RAN, '822X Squadron'. https://www.navy.gov.au/about/organisation/fleet-air-arm/822x-squadron

127 Keirin Joyce (personal correspondence) 11 January 2022.

128 RAN, '822X Squadron'.

129 RAN, 'ScanEagle'. https://www.navy.gov.au/unmanned-systems/scaneagle

130 RAN, '822X Squadron'.

131 Scheibel 'Camcopter S-100 Unmanned Air System'. https://schiebel.net/products/camcopter-s-100/

132 Scheibel, 'Camcopter S-100 Unmanned Air System Specifications'. https://schiebel.net/products/camcopter-s-100-system-2/

133 RAN, 'ScanEagle'.
134 Justin Wastnage, 'BAE Systems Tests HERTI UAV Over South Australia', *Flight Global*, 31 January 2007. https://www.flightglobal.com/articles/2007/01/31/211860/picture-bae-systems-tests-herti-uav-over-south-australia.html
135 Andrew McLaughlin, 'RAAF UAS Projects AI.R Power', *Australian Defence Business Review*, May–June 2020. https://issuu.com/adbr5/docs/adbr_may-june/s/10734656
136 World of Aviation, 'BAE Taranis UCAV Breaks Cover', World of Aviation, 6 February 2014. https://worldofaviation.com/2014/02/bae-taranis-ucav-breaks-cover/
137 Foreign Affairs, Defence and Trade References Committee, *Use of unmanned air, maritime and land platforms by the Australian Defence Force*, chap 6.

Chapter 2

1 Australian Army, 'Australian Army in Afghanistan', Department of Defence, n.d. https://www.army.gov.au/our-heritage/history/history-focus/australian-army-afghanistan
2 Paul Fishstein and Andrew Wilder, *Winning Hearts and Minds? Examining the Relationship between Aid and Security in Afghanistan*. Boston: Feinstein International Center, 2012.
3 Richard Tanter, 'Mentoring Task Force', Nautilus Institute for Security and Sustainability, 14 August 2010. https://nautilus.org/publications/books/australian-forces-abroad/afghanistan/mentoring-task-force/
4 Iain Overton, Roger Davies and Louise Tumchewics, *Improvised Explosive Devices: past, present and future*. London: Action on Armed Violence, 2020, p 10–11.
5 *Australian Defence Magazine*, 'JP129 Tactical UAV project terminated'.
6 RAAF, *Lessons Learned from Operations of the Heron Unmanned Aircraft System*, Department of Defence, n.d., unpublished, p 1; David Riddel (personal correspondence) 8–9 September 2021.
7 Ian McPhedran, *Air Force: Inside Australia's Air Wars: Bali to Baghdad and Beyond*. Sydney: Harper Collins, 2013, p 234.
8 ADF emails (details withheld).
9 ADF email (details withheld).
10 Meier, Unpublished interview transcript with undisclosed interviewee.
11 Gregor Ferguson, 'Surveillance: BAE Systems eyes UAV opportunities', *Australian Defence Magazine*, 1 June 2009. https://www.australiandefence.com.au/71E446CE-7C05-11DE-83AF0050568C22C9
12 McLaughlin, 'RAAF UAS Projects AI.R Power'; David Riddel (personal correspondence) 8–9 September 2021; Meier, Unpublished interview transcript with undisclosed interviewee.
13 Meier, Unpublished interview transcript with undisclosed interviewee; ADF email (details withheld).
14 ADF email (details withheld).
15 David Riddel (personal correspondence) 8–9 September 2021.
16 Robert Coorey (personal correspondence) 6–7 March 2023.
17 Robert Coorey (personal correspondence) 6–7 March 2023.
18 David Riddel (personal correspondence) 8–9 September 2021.
19 Katherine Ziesing, 'Project Nankeen: A Heron by any other name', *Australian Defence Magazine*, 1 February 2011; ADF email (details withheld).
20 Ziesing, 'Project Nankeen: A Heron by any other name'.
21 ADF emails (details withheld).
22 ADF email (details withheld).
23 ADF email (details withheld).
24 Department of Defence, *Response to Nigel Pittaway* [media release], 9 September 2009.
25 Mark Dodd, 'Expanded military role for drones no risk to pilot jobs', *Australian*, 25 September 2009.
26 Ziesing, 'Project Nankeen: A Heron by any other name'.
27 David Riddel (personal correspondence) 8–9 September 2021.

28 Ziesing, 'Project Nankeen: A Heron by any other name'.
29 Arie Egozi, 'Canada receives first Heron UAV system', *Flight Global*, 25 October 2008. https://www.flightglobal.com/canada-receives-first-heron-uav-system/83543.article
30 David Riddel (personal correspondence) 8–9 September 2021.
31 Peter la Franchi, 'Flight International unmanned air vehicle (UAV) directory 2006', *Flight Global*, 22 August 2006. https://www.flightglobal.com/flight-international-unmanned-air-vehicle-uav-directory-2006/69097.article
32 Email (Unclassified) Riddel/Coorey, 21 March 2009 1105hL; David Riddel (personal correspondence) 8–9 September 2021.
33 RAAF, *Implications for Future ISREW UAS Capability Planning: Lesson Learned from Interim MDA Heron Unmanned Aerial Systems Capability Contract (Heron)*, 2nd report, July 2017, p 2.
34 David Riddel (personal correspondence) 8–9 September 2021.
35 ADF email (details withheld).
36 Ziesing, 'Project Nankeen: A Heron by any other name'.
37 David Riddel (personal correspondence) 8–9 September 2021.
38 David Riddel (personal correspondence) 15 September 2021.
39 David Riddel (personal correspondence) 15 September 2021.
40 Department of Defence, Heron Unit History.
41 ADF email (details withheld).
42 Ziesing, 'Project Nankeen: A Heron by any other name'; Email (Unclassified) Meighan/Quinn, 29 April 2009 0431hK.
43 Letter, OCAF/OUT/800/2009, 2009/1011345/3, 1 May 2009.
44 ADF email (details withheld).
45 David Riddel (personal correspondence) 8–9 September 2021.
46 ADF email (details withheld).
47 RAAF, *Implications for Future ISREW UAS Capability Planning*, p 3 para 10.
48 RAAF, *Implications for Future ISREW UAS Capability Planning*, p 7 para 34.
49 Department of Defence, *Response to Nigel Pittaway*.
50 McPhedran, *Air Force*, p 232.
51 John Meier, *John Meier interviews Sean McClure* [unpublished interview transcript], RAAF, 6 November 2014, p 12.
52 Boeing Australia, *ScanEagle Backgrounder* [media release], 31 July 2013.
53 Canadian–American Strategic Review, 'Australia to lease Heron UAVs from McDonald Dettwiler – Is Oz Following CF Lead or did the ADF inspire DND's Project Noctua?', *Canadian–American Strategic Review*, 7 September 2009.
54 Lars Hoffmann, 'Germany to Lease Israeli "Heron" Drone for Mali Operations', *Defense News*, 22 July 2016. https://www.defensenews.com/air/2016/07/22/germany-to-lease-israeli-heron-drone-for-mali-operations/
55 Department of Defence, 'Memorandum of Understanding Between the Canadian Forces and the Australian Department of Defence Concerning Cooperation in the Development and Operation of the Heron Unmanned Aerial System in Afghanistan', RAAF, 17 August 2009.
56 Department of Defence, 'Implementing Arrangement 01/09 Between the Canadian Forces and the Australian Department of Defence Concerning the Operation of the Heron Unmanned Aerial System in Afghanistan', RAAF, February 2010.
57 McPhedran, *Air Force*, p 232.
58 Ziesing, 'Project Nankeen: A Heron by any other name'; Department of Defence, *Air Force to begin operating its first unmanned aerial system* [media release], Minister for Defence, MIN2509/09, 7 September 2009.
59 David Riddel (personal correspondence) 8–9 September 2021.

60 Department of Defence, *Air Force to begin operating its first unmanned aerial system.*
61 David Riddel (personal correspondence) 8–9 September 2021; Ziesing, 'Project Nankeen: A Heron by any other name'.
62 David Riddel (personal correspondence) 8–9 September 2021.
63 Department of Defence, *Heron takes to Afghan skies* [media release], 13 January 2010; Department of Defence, *Air Force to begin operating its first unmanned aerial system.*
64 Email Binskin/Riddel, 3 January 2010.
65 Israel Aerospace Industries, 'History: IAI and the Security of Israel', Israel Aerospace Industries, n.d. https://www.iai.co.il/about/history
66 Department of Defence, Heron Unit History.
67 Israel Aerospace Industries, 'MOSP3000-HD', n.d. https://www.iai.co.il/p/mosp
68 Israel Aerospace Industries, 'MOSP3000-HD'; David Riddel, 'Air Force Project NANKEEN', PowerPoint presentation, 13 October 2009.
69 Riddel, 'Air Force Project NANKEEN'.
70 SpaceWar, 'Kestrel Support Project NANKEEN in Afghanistan', SpaceWar, 11 November 2010. https://www.spacewar.com/reports/Kestrel_Supports_Project_NANKEEN_In_Afghanistan_999.html; Sentient Vision, 'Kestrel', https://www.sentientvision.com/prodcuts/kestrel-land-mti/; Ziesing, 'Project Nankeen: A Heron by any other name'.
71 SpaceWar, 'Kestrel Support Project NANKEEN in Afghanistan'.
72 Tanter, 'Unmanned aerial vehicles (UAVs)'; Department of Defence, 'Kestral Aerial Surveillance System', Australian Government, n.d. https://www.dst.defence.gov.au/ctd-success-story/kestral-aerial-surveillance-system
73 SpaceWar, 'Kestrel Support Project NANKEEN in Afghanistan'.
74 Ziesing, 'Project Nankeen: A Heron by any other name'.
75 Meier, Unpublished interview transcript with undisclosed interviewee.
76 Meier, Unpublished interview transcript with undisclosed interviewee.
77 Department of Defence, *Heron takes to Afghan skies.*
78 Ziesing, 'Project Nankeen: A Heron by any other name'.

Chapter 3

1 Sean McClure (personal correspondence) 26 May 2023.
2 ADF email (details withheld).
3 Department of Defence, Air Force Organisational Directive 2009-07, 'Number 5 Flight', RAAF, 3 February 2010; Katherine Ziesing, 'Air Power: Heron in Woomera this year', *Australian Defence Magazine*, 1 February 2011.
4 John Meier, *John Meier interviews Jonathon McMullan* [unpublished interview transcript], RAAF, 7 November 2014, p 28.
5 Meier, Unpublished interview transcript with undisclosed interviewee.
6 Ziesing, 'Air Power: Heron in Woomera this year'; John Jenkins, 'The operational role of the Heron remotely-piloted aircraft in the Royal Australian Air Force', *United Service*, December 2013, 64(4), p 23.
7 Meier, *John Meier interviews Sean McClure*, p 23; Meier, Unpublished interview transcript with undisclosed interviewee; McPhedran, *Air Force*, p 234.
8 McPhedran, *Air Force*, p 234.
9 Karen Christiuk, 'Learning to Fly the Heron', *Defense Aerospace*, May 2009. https://www.defense-aerospace.com/articles-view/release/3/105079/canadian-troops-work-ip-on-heron-uav.html
10 RAAF, 'Heron', n.d. https://www.airforce.gov.au/technology/aircraft/intelligence-surveillance-and-reconnaissance/heron
11 Meier, Unpublished interview transcript with undisclosed interviewee.

12 Meier, Unpublished interview transcript with undisclosed interviewee.
13 ADF email (details withheld).
14 Meier, *John Meier interviews Sean McClure*, p 27.
15 Meier, Unpublished interview transcript with undisclosed interviewee.
16 ADF email (details withheld).
17 Email (Unclassified) Riddel/Quinn, 'Re: Project NANKEEN visit', 24 April 2009.
18 Meier, Unpublished interview transcript with undisclosed interviewee.
19 Meier, *John Meier interviews Sean McClure*, pp 4–6.
20 Meier, Unpublished interview transcript with undisclosed interviewee.
21 Meier, Unpublished interview transcript with undisclosed interviewee.
22 Meier, Unpublished interview transcript with undisclosed interviewee.
23 Andrew Earl (personal correspondence) 9 September 2021.
24 Ziesing, 'Air Power: Heron in Woomera this year'.
25 Meier, Unpublished interview transcript with undisclosed interviewee.; ADF email (details withheld).
26 Meier, Unpublished interview transcript with undisclosed interviewee.
27 Meier, Unpublished interview transcript with undisclosed interviewee.
28 Meier, Unpublished interview transcript with undisclosed interviewee.
29 RAAF, *Implications for Future ISREW UAS Capability Planning*, p 10 para 50.
30 Meier, Unpublished interview transcript with undisclosed interviewee.
31 Meier, *John Meier interviews Sean McClure*, pp 6–7.
32 Meier, Unpublished interview transcript with undisclosed interviewee.
33 CTV News, 'Unmanned aircraft crashes near CFB Suffield', *CTV News*, 16 July 2010. https://calgary.ctvnews.ca/unmanned-aircraft-crashes-near-cfb-suffield-1.533153
34 CTV News, 'Unmanned aircraft crashes near CFB Suffield'.
35 Canadian Minister of National Defence, Flight Safety Occurrence Report 143377.
36 Meier, *John Meier interviews Sean McClure*, p 24.
37 Meier, Unpublished interview transcript with undisclosed interviewee; Sean McClure (personal correspondence) 30 September 2021.
38 RAAF, *Implications for Future ISREW UAS Capability Planning*, p 2 para 4.
39 RAAF, *Implications for Future ISREW UAS Capability Planning*, p 3 para 11.
40 Meier, Unpublished interview transcript with undisclosed interviewee.
41 RAAF, *Lessons Learned from Operations of the Heron Unmanned Aircraft System*, p 6.
42 Meier, *John Meier interviews Sean McClure*, p 9.
43 Meier, *John Meier interviews Sean McClure*, p 11; Meier, Unpublished interview transcripts with undisclosed interviewees.
44 Meier, *John Meier interviews Jonathon McMullan*, p 18.
45 Department of Defence, Administrative Instruction No 06/2011, 'Heron Practical Unmanned Aerial System (UAS) Training – Roto 5', RAAF, 18 February 2011.
46 Department of Defence, Administrative Instruction No 12/2010, 'Heron UAS Rotation 5 – Theory Training 17 Jan to 11 Feb 11', RAAF, 26 November 2010; Department of Defence, Administrative Instruction No 06/2011; Meier, *John Meier interviews Jonathon McMullan*, pp 24–5.
47 Meier, Unpublished interview transcript with undisclosed interviewee.
48 Meier, Unpublished interview transcript with undisclosed interviewee.
49 Meier, Unpublished interview transcript with undisclosed interviewee.
50 Meier, *John Meier interviews Sean McClure*, p 28.
51 Meier, *John Meier interviews Sean McClure*, p 29.
52 Meier, Unpublished interview transcript with undisclosed interviewee.
53 Meier, Unpublished interview transcript with undisclosed interviewee.
54 Meier, Unpublished interview transcript with undisclosed interviewee.

55 Meier, Unpublished interview transcript with undisclosed interviewee.
56 Department of Defence, Administrative Instruction No 11/2011, 'Motion Imagery Exploitation Course 9–13 May 2011', RAAF, 29 April 2011.
57 Meier, Unpublished interview transcript with undisclosed interviewee.
58 Meier, Unpublished interview transcript with undisclosed interviewee.
59 Meier, Unpublished interview transcript with undisclosed interviewee.
60 Meier, *John Meier interviews Jonathon McMullan*, pp 25–6.
61 Department of Defence, Administrative Instruction No 09/2011, 'Operational Upgrade Training 11-12 Apr 11 and Heron GIA Training 13 Apr 11', RAAF, 4 April 2011; Meier, *John Meier interviews Sean McClure*, pp 29–30; Meier, Unpublished interview transcript with undisclosed interviewee.
62 Meier, Unpublished interview transcript with undisclosed interviewee.
63 Meier, Unpublished interview transcript with undisclosed interviewee.
64 Meier, *John Meier interviews Jonathon McMullan*, p 28.
65 Meier, Unpublished interview transcript with undisclosed interviewee.
66 Meier, *John Meier interviews Sean McClure*, p 29.
67 Meier, Unpublished interview transcript with undisclosed interviewee.
68 Meier, Unpublished interview transcript with undisclosed interviewee.
69 Ziesing, 'Air Power: Heron in Woomera this year'.
70 Meier, Unpublished interview transcript with undisclosed interviewee.
71 Meier, Unpublished interview transcript with undisclosed interviewee.
72 Meier, Unpublished interview transcript with undisclosed interviewee.
73 Meier, Unpublished interview transcript with undisclosed interviewee.
74 Meier, Unpublished interview transcript with undisclosed interviewee.
75 Meier, Unpublished interview transcript with undisclosed interviewee.
76 Meier, Unpublished interview transcript with undisclosed interviewee.
77 Ziesing, 'Air Power: Heron in Woomera this year'.
78 Meier, *John Meier interviews Jonathon McMullan*, pp 40, 42.
79 Meier, Unpublished interview transcript with undisclosed interviewee.
80 Meier, Unpublished interview transcript with undisclosed interviewee.
81 Meier, *John Meier interviews Jonathon McMullan*, p 48.
82 Meier, Unpublished interview transcript with undisclosed interviewee.
83 Meier, Unpublished interview transcript with undisclosed interviewee.
84 Meier, Unpublished interview transcript with undisclosed interviewee.
85 Andrew Earl (personal correspondence) 9 September 2021.
86 Meier, Unpublished interview transcript with undisclosed interviewee.
87 Brendan Nicholson, 'ADF Women are Already "In Combat"', *The Strategist*, Australian Strategic Policy Institute, 24 Mar 2017. URL: https://www.aspistrategist.org.au/adf-women-already-combat/
88 Hannah Evans, 'Sending Our Women to War: The Role of Women in the Australian Army from 2000 to Today', *Australian Policy and History*, 13 November 2017. https://aph.org.au/2017/11/sending-our-women-to-war-the-role-of-women-in-the-australian-army-from-2000-to-today/
89 Department of Defence, *Shadow Tactical Unmanned Aerial System Commences Afghan Operations*.
90 Meier, Unpublished interview transcripts with undisclosed interviewees.
91 Meier, Unpublished interview transcript with undisclosed interviewee.
92 Meier, Unpublished interview transcript with undisclosed interviewee.
93 Meier, Unpublished interview transcript with undisclosed interviewee.
94 Meier, *John Meier interviews Sean McClure*, p 20.
95 Meier, *John Meier interviews Sean McClure*; Meier, Unpublished interview transcript with undisclosed interviewee.
96 Meier, Unpublished interview transcript with undisclosed interviewee.

97 Meier, Unpublished interview transcript with undisclosed interviewee.
98 Meier, Unpublished interview transcript with undisclosed interviewee.
99 Meier, Unpublished interview transcripts with undisclosed interviewees.
100 Department of Defence, Heron Unit History.
101 Meier, *John Meier interviews Jonathon McMullan*, p 42.
102 Meier, Unpublished interview transcript with undisclosed interviewee.
103 Meier, Unpublished interview transcript with undisclosed interviewee.
104 Department of Defence, Heron Unit History.
105 Joint Standing Committee on Foreign Affairs, *Defence and Trade, Defence Sub-Committee visit to the Middle East Area of Operations Report of the Delegation to the MEAO 14 to 18 May 2011*, Australian Government, March 2012. https://www.aph.gov.au/Parliamentary_Business/Committees/Joint/Completed_Inquiries/jfadt/DefenceDelegation2011/report
106 Meier, Unpublished interview transcript with undisclosed interviewee.
107 Meier, Unpublished interview transcript with undisclosed interviewee.
108 Meier, Unpublished interview transcript with undisclosed interviewee.
109 Meier, Unpublished interview transcript with undisclosed interviewee.
110 Meier, Unpublished interview transcript with undisclosed interviewee.
111 Meier, Unpublished interview transcript with undisclosed interviewee.
112 Meier, Unpublished interview transcript with undisclosed interviewee.
113 Department of Defence, Heron Unit History.
114 Meier, Unpublished interview transcript with undisclosed interviewee.
115 Meier, Unpublished interview transcript with undisclosed interviewee; Department of Defence, Heron Unit History.
116 Department of Defence, Heron Unit History.
117 Meier, Unpublished interview transcript with undisclosed interviewee.
118 Meier, Unpublished interview transcript with undisclosed interviewee.
119 Meier, Unpublished interview transcripts with undisclosed interviewees.
120 Meier, Unpublished interview transcript with undisclosed interviewee.
121 Meier, Unpublished interview transcript with undisclosed interviewee.
122 Meier, Unpublished interview transcript with undisclosed interviewee.
123 Meier, Unpublished interview transcript with undisclosed interviewee.
124 RAAF, *Lessons Learned from Operations of the Heron Unmanned Aircraft System*, p 5.
125 Meier, *John Meier interviews Jonathon McMullan*, p 13; Meier, Unpublished interview transcript with undisclosed interviewee.
126 Meier, *John Meier interviews Jonathon McMullan*, pp 20, 34.
127 Meier, Unpublished interview transcript with undisclosed interviewee.
128 Meier, Unpublished interview transcript with undisclosed interviewee.
129 Meier, Unpublished interview transcript with undisclosed interviewee.
130 Meier, Unpublished interview transcript with undisclosed interviewee.
131 Meier, Unpublished interview transcript with undisclosed interviewee.
132 Ziesing, 'Project Nankeen: A Heron by any other name'; Meier, Unpublished interview transcript with undisclosed interviewee.
133 Meier, Unpublished interview transcript with undisclosed interviewee.
134 Meier, Unpublished interview transcript with undisclosed interviewee.
135 Meier, Unpublished interview transcripts with undisclosed interviewees.
136 Meier, Unpublished interview transcript with undisclosed interviewee.
137 RAAF, *Implications for Future ISREW UAS Capability Planning*, p 5 para 18.
138 Meier, Unpublished interview transcript with undisclosed interviewee.
139 Department of Defence, Heron Unit History.

140 Meier, Unpublished interview transcript with undisclosed interviewee.
141 RAAF, *Implications for Future ISREW UAS Capability Planning*, p 3 para 11.
142 RAAF, *Implications for Future ISREW UAS Capability Planning*, p 6 para 26.
143 Meier, Unpublished interview transcript with undisclosed interviewee.
144 Alan Hobbs and Stanley Herwitz, *Human Challenges in the Maintenance of Unmanned Aircraft Systems*, Federal Aviation Administration Human Factors Research and Engineering Division and National Aeronautics and Space Administration Aeronautical Safety and Human Factors, May 2006. https://human-factors.arc.nasa.gov/publications/UAV_interimreport_Hobbs_Herwitz.pdf; Hobbs, Alan and Stanley Herwitz, *Maintenance Challenges of Small Unmanned Aircraft Systems – A Human Factors Perspective*, Federal Aviation Administration, 2008. https://human-factors.arc.nasa.gov/publications/Maint_Chall_Small_Unman_Aircraft_Human_Factors_Persp.pdf
145 Meier, Unpublished interview transcript with undisclosed interviewee.
146 Meier, Unpublished interview transcript with undisclosed interviewee.
147 Meier, Unpublished interview transcript with undisclosed interviewee.
148 Department of Defence, '5FLT Unit History Record', RAAF, April 2011.
149 Department of Defence, 'Lieutenant Marcus Sean Case', Australian Government, n.d. https://www.defence.gov.au/Vale/LtCase.asp.
150 Meier, *John Meier interviews Jonathon McMullan*, p 43.
151 Susan McDonald, 'Lieutenant Marcus Case', *ABC News*, 18 December 2014. https://www.abc.net.au/news/2014-12-18/aircraft-fault-pilot-error-partly-to-blame-for-fatal-crash/5977144; Legacy, 'Lieutenant Marcus Sean Case', Legacy, n.d. https://www.legacy.com/obituaries/heraldsun-au/obituary.aspx?n=marcus-sean-case&pid=151418858
152 Meier, *John Meier interviews Jonathon McMullan*, pp 44–7.
153 Department of Defence, 'Personal details of Lieutenant Marcus Sean Case', Australian Government, n.d. https://www.defence.gov.au/Vale/LtCase/default.asp
154 Rory Callinan, 'Inquiry into the death of Lieutenant Marcus Case leaves unanswered questions over chopper crash', *Sydney Morning Herald*, 11 December 2014. https://www.smh.com.au/national/inquiry-into-the-death-of-lieutenant-marcus-case-leaves-unanswered-questions-over-chopper-crash-20141209-1234xz.html
155 Meier, *John Meier interviews Jonathon McMullan*, pp 48, 52.
156 News.com.au, 'Dead soldier honoured in Afghanistan', *News.co.au*, 5 June 2011. https://www.news.com.au/world/dead-soldier-honoured-in-afghanistan/news-story/b36942066ea6dc8e08610ee5eab002c9; Meier, *John Meier interviews Jonathon McMullan*, p 55.
157 Jonathon McMullan (personal correspondence) 30 September 2021.
158 Meier, Unpublished interview transcript with undisclosed interviewee.
159 Meier, Unpublished interview transcript with undisclosed interviewee.
160 Meier, Unpublished interview transcript with undisclosed interviewee.
161 Australian War Memorial, 'UH-60L Black Hawk Engine Cowling'; Meier, Unpublished interview transcript with undisclosed interviewee.
162 Andrew Earl (personal correspondence) 9 September 2021.
163 Meier, Unpublished interview transcript with undisclosed interviewee.
164 Meier, Unpublished interview transcript with undisclosed interviewee.
165 Meier, Unpublished interview transcript with undisclosed interviewee.
166 Meier, Unpublished interview transcript with undisclosed interviewee.
167 Meier, Unpublished interview transcript with undisclosed interviewee.
168 Meier, Unpublished interview transcript with undisclosed interviewee.
169 RAAF, *Lessons Learned from Operations of the Heron Unmanned Aircraft System*, p 6.
170 Foreign Affairs, Defence and Trade References Committee, *Use of unmanned air, maritime and land platforms by the Australian Defence Force*, p 64.

171 Rebecca Hawkes, 'Post-traumatic stress disorder is higher in drone operators', *Telegraph*, 30 May 2015.
172 Sean McClure (personal correspondence) 30 September 2021.
173 Jason Gordon, 'Enduring survivor's guilt', *Newcastle Herald*, 24 April 2015. https://www.newcastleherald.com.au/story/3034652/enduring-survivors-guilt/
174 Meier, Unpublished interview transcript with undisclosed interviewee.
175 Duncan Wallace and J Costello, 'Eye in the sky: Understanding the mental health of unmanned aerial vehicle operators', *Journal of Military and Veterans' Health*, 2017, 25(3), p 58.
176 Meier, *John Meier interviews Jonathon McMullan*, 29.
177 Meier, Unpublished interview transcript with undisclosed interviewee.
178 Meier, *John Meier interviews Jonathon McMullan*, p 33.

Chapter 4

1 McPhedran, *Air Force*, p 233.
2 Ziesing, 'Project Nankeen: A Heron by any other name'.
3 Ziesing, 'Project Nankeen: A Heron by any other name'.
4 Ziesing, 'Project Nankeen: A Heron by any other name'.
5 Ziesing, 'Air Power: Heron in Woomera this year'; Ziesing, 'Project Nankeen: A Heron by any other name'.
6 Department of Defence, *Heron UAV to Support Australian Troops in Afghanistan.*
7 Department of Defence, *Heron UAV to Support Australian Troops in Afghanistan.*
8 Patrick Walters, *The Australian*, 'Heron on the wing to guide Diggers', 8 September 2009.
9 Australian Defence Magazine, 'From the Source: Air Marshal Mark Binskin, AO (part 2)', *Australian Defence Magazine*, 1 February 2011. https://www.australiandefence.com.au/archive/from-the-source-air-marshal-mark-binskin-ao-part-2-adm-feb-2011
10 Rob Vogelaar, 'Contract Extended for Israel Aerospace Industries UAV Serving Australian Air Force in Afghanistan', *Aviation News*, 13 August 2010.
11 Meier, Unpublished interview transcript with undisclosed interviewee.
12 Jenkins, 'The operational role of the Heron remotely-piloted aircraft in the Royal Australian Air Force', p 23.
13 Meier, Unpublished interview transcript with undisclosed interviewee.
14 Meier, Unpublished interview transcript with undisclosed interviewee.
15 Meier, Unpublished interview transcript with undisclosed interviewee.
16 Meier, Unpublished interview transcript with undisclosed interviewee.
17 Air Force Technology, 'Heron/Machatz 1 Unmanned Aerial Vehicle (UAV)', Air Force Technology, 28 July 2021. https://www.airforce-technology.com/projects/heron-uav/
18 Meier, Unpublished interview transcript with undisclosed interviewee.
19 Meier, Unpublished interview transcript with undisclosed interviewee.
20 Keirin Joyce (personal correspondence) 11 January 2022; Meier, Unpublished interview transcript with undisclosed interviewee.
21 Ziesing, 'Project Nankeen: A Heron by any other name'.
22 Ziesing, 'Project Nankeen: A Heron by any other name'.
23 Jonathan McMullan and Matthew Lunnay, 'Civilian/Military Integration – Afghanistan: The Afghan RPAS Success Story' [slide presentation], Royal Australian Air Force, 18 March 2015.
24 Meier, Unpublished interview transcript with undisclosed interviewee.
25 Anna Hartley, 'Advanced RAAF drone takes flight in Ipswich', *Courier Mail*, 20 April 2016. https://www.couriermail.com.au/news/queensland/ipswich/watch-advanced-raaf-drone-takes-flight-in-ipswich/news-story/e7eb0ff76796244bd892d4f2b949e838
26 Meier, *John Meier interviews Sean McClure*, p 21.
27 RAAF, *Lessons Learned from Operations of the Heron Unmanned Aircraft System*, p 6.
28 Australian Defence Magazine, 'From the Source: Air Marshal Mark Binskin, AO (part 2)'.

29 Meier, Unpublished interview transcript with undisclosed interviewee; RAAF, *Lessons Learned from Operations of the Heron Unmanned Aircraft System*, p 3.
30 RAAF, *Lessons Learned from Operations of the Heron Unmanned Aircraft System*, p 3.
31 Andrew Earl (personal correspondence) 9 September 2021.
32 Andrew Earl (personal correspondence) 9 September 2021.
33 Australian Defence Magazine, 'From the Source: Air Marshal Mark Binskin, AO (part 2)'.
34 Australian Defence Magazine, 'From the Source: Air Marshal Mark Binskin, AO (part 2)'.
35 Jenkins, 'The operational role of the Heron remotely-piloted aircraft in the Royal Australian Air Force', p 23.
36 RAAF, *Lessons Learned from Operations of the Heron Unmanned Aircraft System*, p 2; Meier, Unpublished interview transcripts with undisclosed interviewees.
37 Meier, Unpublished interview transcripts with undisclosed interviewees.
38 Meier, Unpublished interview transcript with undisclosed interviewee.
39 Meier, Unpublished interview transcript with undisclosed interviewee.
40 Meier, Unpublished interview transcript with undisclosed interviewee.
41 Meier, Unpublished interview transcript with undisclosed interviewee.
42 Meier, Unpublished interview transcript with undisclosed interviewee.
43 Meier, *John Meier interviews Sean McClure*, p 36; Meier, Unpublished interview transcript with undisclosed interviewee.
44 Meier, Unpublished interview transcript with undisclosed interviewee; RAAF, *Lessons Learned from Operations of the Heron Unmanned Aircraft System*, pp 4–5.
45 Australian Defence Magazine, 'From the Source: Air Marshal Mark Binskin, AO (part 2)'.
46 Meier, Unpublished interview transcript with undisclosed interviewee; Department of Defence, Heron Unit History.
47 Meier, Unpublished interview transcript with undisclosed interviewee.
48 Meier, Unpublished interview transcript with undisclosed interviewee; RAAF, *Lessons Learned from Operations of the Heron Unmanned Aircraft System*, p 2.
49 Meier, Unpublished interview transcript with undisclosed interviewee; Department of Defence, Heron Unit History.
50 Meier, *John Meier interviews Sean McClure*, p 25; Meier, Unpublished interview transcript with undisclosed interviewee.
51 Meier, Unpublished interview transcript with undisclosed interviewee.
52 Meier, Unpublished interview transcript with undisclosed interviewee.
53 Meier, Unpublished interview transcript with undisclosed interviewee.
54 Meier, Unpublished interview transcript with undisclosed interviewee.
55 Meier, Unpublished interview transcript with undisclosed interviewee.
56 RAAF, *Lessons Learned from Operations of the Heron Unmanned Aircraft System*, p 2.
57 Meier, *John Meier interviews Sean McClure*, p 39; Jenkins, 'The operational role of the Heron remotely-piloted aircraft in the Royal Australian Air Force', p 23.
58 Meier, Unpublished interview transcript with undisclosed interviewee.
59 Chris Cole, *Accidents will Happen: a review of military drone crash data as the UK considers allowing large military drone flights in its airspace*. Oxford: UK Drone Wars, 2019, p 20; Meier, Unpublished interview transcript with undisclosed interviewee.
60 Meier, Unpublished interview transcript with undisclosed interviewee; Andrew Earl (personal correspondence) 9 September 2021.
61 Meier, Unpublished interview transcript with undisclosed interviewee.
62 Meier, Unpublished interview transcript with undisclosed interviewee.
63 RAAF, *Lessons Learned from Operations of the Heron Unmanned Aircraft System*, p 2.
64 Department of Defence, Heron Unit History.

65 Meier, Unpublished interview transcript with undisclosed interviewee.
66 Department of Defence, Heron Unit History.
67 Meier, Unpublished interview transcript with undisclosed interviewee.
68 Meier, Unpublished interview transcript with undisclosed interviewee.
69 Meier, Unpublished interview transcript with undisclosed interviewee.
70 Meier, Unpublished interview transcript with undisclosed interviewee.
71 Meier, Unpublished interview transcript with undisclosed interviewee.
72 Meier, Unpublished interview transcript with undisclosed interviewee.
73 Meier, Unpublished interview transcript with undisclosed interviewee.
74 Department of Defence, Aviation Safety Occurrence Report 5 Flight UAV-024-2010-SASOR 1, 'Human / Aircrew / Engine Cut on Final Approach', Royal Australian Air Force, 4 June 2010; Meier, Unpublished interview transcript with undisclosed interviewee.
75 Meier, Unpublished interview transcript with undisclosed interviewee.
76 Department of Defence, Aviation Safety Occurrence Report 5 Flight UAV-024-2010-SASOR 1.
77 Meier, Unpublished interview transcript with undisclosed interviewee.
78 Meier, Unpublished interview transcript with undisclosed interviewee.
79 Meier, Unpublished interview transcript with undisclosed interviewee.
80 Ziesing, 'Project Nankeen: A Heron by any other name'.
81 Meier, Unpublished interview transcript with undisclosed interviewee.
82 Department of Defence, Heron Unit History.
83 Department of Defence, Aviation Safety Occurrence Report 5 Flight UAV-045-2010-SASOR 1, 'Materiel / Landing Gear and Braking System / Landing with NLG locked in up position', Royal Australian Air Force, 28 September 2010.
84 Department of Defence, Heron Unit History.
85 Department of Defence, Heron Unit History.
86 ADF Serials, 'MSPA 512/2010 3 November 2010', ADF Serials, 8 August 2011. http://www.adf-messageboard.com.au/invboard/index.php?showtopic=1724
87 Department of Defence, Aviation Safety Occurrence Report 5 Flight UAV-038-2011, 'Materiel / Engine / Loss of Oil Pressure Leading to Engine Fire', Royal Australian Air Force, 2 May 2011.
88 Meier, *John Meier interviews Jonathon McMullan*, p 36.
89 Meier, *John Meier interviews Jonathon McMullan*, p 20.
90 Andrew Earl (personal correspondence) 9 September 2021.
91 Meier, *John Meier interviews Jonathon McMullan*, p 14.
92 Meier, *John Meier interviews Jonathon McMullan*, pp 12–13.
93 Meier, Unpublished interview transcript with undisclosed interviewee.
94 Department of Defence, Heron Unit History.
95 William Marsden, 'The allies' eyes in the skies', *Vancouver Sun*, 23 July 2011. https://www.pressreader.com/canada/vancouver-sun/20110723/286976831214645
96 Meier, Unpublished interview transcript with undisclosed interviewee.
97 RAAF, *Implications for Future ISREW UAS Capability Planning*, p 9 para 44.
98 Meier, Unpublished interview transcript with undisclosed interviewee.
99 Meier, *John Meier interviews Sean McClure*, p 40; Meier, Unpublished interview transcript with undisclosed interviewee.
100 Meier, *John Meier interviews Sean McClure*, p 32; Meier, Unpublished interview transcript with undisclosed interviewee.
101 Nigel Pittaway, 'Land Warfare 2011: UAVs – operations and aspirations', *Australian Defence Magazine*, 1 October 2011. https://www.australiandefence.com.au/archive/land-warfare-2011-uavs-operations-and-aspirations-adm-october-2011
102 Ziesing, 'Project Nankeen: A Heron by any other name'.

103 Meier, *John Meier interviews Sean McClure*, p 42.
104 Meier, Unpublished interview transcript with undisclosed interviewee.
105 David Riddel (personal correspondence) 8–9 September 2021; Meier, Unpublished interview transcript with undisclosed interviewee.
106 Meier, Unpublished interview transcript with undisclosed interviewee.
107 Meier, Unpublished interview transcript with undisclosed interviewee.
108 Meier, *John Meier interviews Sean McClure*, p 34.
109 Meier, *John Meier interviews Sean McClure*, p 33.
110 Meier, *John Meier interviews Sean McClure*, pp 34–5.
111 Meier, Unpublished interview transcript with undisclosed interviewee; Jenkins, 'The operational role of the Heron remotely-piloted aircraft in the Royal Australian Air Force', p 23.
112 Meier, Unpublished interview transcript with undisclosed interviewee.
113 Meier, *John Meier interviews Sean McClure*, p 13; Meier, Unpublished interview transcript with undisclosed interviewee.
114 Meier, *John Meier interviews Sean McClure*, p 14.
115 Meier, Unpublished interview transcript with undisclosed interviewee.
116 Department of Defence, Heron Unit History.
117 Meier, *John Meier interviews Sean McClure*, p 16.
118 Ben Mckelvey, *Mosul: Australia's secret war inside the ISIS caliphate*. Sydney: Hachette, 2020; N Leigh, 'Australian Special Operations Forces War Crimes in Afghanistan Confirmed', *Overt Defense*, 19 November 2020. https://www.overtdefense.com/2020/11/19/australian-special-forces-war-crimes-in-afghanistan-confirmed/
119 Leigh, 'Australian Special Operations Forces War Crimes in Afghanistan Confirmed'; Ian Langford, 'Australian Special Forces in Afghanistan', *Australian Army Journal*, Autumn 2010, VII(I), p 22; Meier, Unpublished interview transcript with undisclosed interviewee.
120 Meier, *John Meier interviews Jonathon McMullan*, p 58; Meier, Unpublished interview transcripts with undisclosed interviewees.
121 Meier, Unpublished interview transcripts with undisclosed interviewees.
122 Meier, *John Meier interviews Sean McClure*, p 17; Meier, *John Meier interviews Jonathon McMullan*, p 57; Meier, Unpublished interview transcripts with undisclosed interviewees.
123 Meier, Unpublished interview transcripts with undisclosed interviewees.
124 Meier, Unpublished interview transcript with undisclosed interviewee.
125 Meier, Unpublished interview transcript with undisclosed interviewee; Meier, *John Meier interviews Sean McClure*, p 17.
126 Meier, *John Meier interviews Jonathon McMullan*, p 57; Meier, Unpublished interview transcript with undisclosed interviewee; Meier, *John Meier interviews Sean McClure*, p 17.
127 Meier, Unpublished interview transcript with undisclosed interviewee.
128 Department of Defence, Heron Unit History.
129 Meier, *John Meier interviews Sean McClure*, p 37.
130 Meier, Unpublished interview transcript with undisclosed interviewee.
131 Meier, *John Meier interviews Sean McClure*, pp 13, 41.
132 Meier, Unpublished interview transcript with undisclosed interviewee.
133 Meier, Unpublished interview transcript with undisclosed interviewee.
134 Jenkins, 'The operational role of the Heron remotely-piloted aircraft in the Royal Australian Air Force', p 23.
135 McPhedran, *Air Force*, p 233.
136 Meier, *John Meier interviews Jonathon McMullan*, pp 59–60.
137 Department of Defence, Air Force Organisational Directive 2013-01, 'Change of Command and Control of Number 5 Flight', RAAF, 27 March 2013.

138 Emma Griffiths, 'Australian soldiers complete withdrawal from Afghanistan's Uruzgan province', *ABC News*, 17 December 2013. https://www.abc.net.au/news/2013-12-16/australian-soldiers-pull-out-of-uruzgan-province/5159220?nw=0
139 Department of Defence, *Australia extends Heron mission in southern Afghanistan* [media release], 10 December 2013.
140 Meier, Unpublished interview transcript with undisclosed interviewee.
141 Meier, Unpublished interview transcript with undisclosed interviewee.
142 Meier, Unpublished interview transcript with undisclosed interviewee.
143 Jonathan McMullan (personal correspondence) 14 March 2023.
144 Meier, Unpublished interview transcripts with undisclosed interviewees; Meier, *John Meier interviews Sean McClure*, p 53.
145 Jonathan McMullan (personal correspondence) 14 March 2023.
146 Andrew Earl (personal correspondence) 9 September 2021; Meier, *John Meier interviews Sean McClure*, p 46; Meier, Unpublished interview transcripts with undisclosed interviewees.
147 Meier, Unpublished interview transcript with undisclosed interviewee.
148 Meier, Unpublished interview transcript with undisclosed interviewee.
149 Meier, Unpublished interview transcript with undisclosed interviewee.
150 Meier, Unpublished interview transcript with undisclosed interviewee.
151 Meier, Unpublished interview transcript with undisclosed interviewee; Meier, *John Meier interviews Sean McClure*, p 48; Andrew Earl (personal correspondence) 17 May 2021.
152 Meier, Unpublished interview transcript with undisclosed interviewee.
153 Meier, *John Meier interviews Sean McClure*, p 49.
154 Andrew Earl (personal correspondence) 17 May 2021.
155 Meier, Unpublished interview transcript with undisclosed interviewee; Andrew Earl (personal correspondence) 9 September 2021.
156 Australian Defence Magazine, 'From the Source: Air Marshal Mark Binskin, AO (part 2)'.
157 Andrew Earl (personal correspondence) 17 May 2021.
158 Meier, Unpublished interview transcript with undisclosed interviewee.
159 Meier, *John Meier interviews Sean McClure*, p 48.
160 Meier, Unpublished interview transcripts with undisclosed interviewees.
161 Meier, Unpublished interview transcript with undisclosed interviewee.
162 Meier, Unpublished interview transcript with undisclosed interviewee.
163 Meier, Unpublished interview transcript with undisclosed interviewee.
164 Meier, *John Meier interviews Sean McClure*, p 53; Meier, Unpublished interview transcript with undisclosed interviewee.
165 Foreign Affairs, Defence and Trade References Committee, *Use of unmanned air, maritime and land platforms by the Australian Defence Force*, chap 2.
166 RAAF, 'RPAS Strategic Communication Plan', RAAF, 2020, Annex D; McLaughlin, 'RAAF UAS Projects AI.R Power'.
167 Contact, 'Meritorious Unit Citation for Heron UAV unit', Contact, 13 September 2016. https://www.contactairlandandsea.com/2016/09/13/heron_uav/
168 Contact, 'Meritorious Unit Citation for Heron UAV unit'.
169 Contact, 'Meritorious Unit Citation for Heron UAV unit'.

Chapter 5

1 RAAF, *Implications for Future ISREW UAS Capability Planning*, p 2 para 5.
2 Foreign Affairs, Defence and Trade References Committee, *Use of unmanned air, maritime and land platforms by the Australian Defence Force*, chap 2.
3 McLaughlin, 'RAAF UAS Projects AI.R Power'.

4 Foreign Affairs, Defence and Trade References Committee, *Use of unmanned air, maritime and land platforms by the Australian Defence Force*, chap 2.
5 RAAF, *Lessons Learned from Operations of the Heron Unmanned Aircraft System*, p 1.
6 Meier, Unpublished interview transcript with undisclosed interviewee.
7 Department of Defence, 'Unmanned Aircraft System operating Permit 001/2015', Defence Aviation Authority, 11 June 2015.
8 McLaughlin, 'RAAF UAS Projects AI.R Power'; RAAF, *Implications for Future ISREW UAS Capability Planning*, p 2.
9 Leigh Atkinson, 'RAAF's thin end of the wedge', Aviation Spotters Online, 17 May 2016. http://aviationspottersonline.com/raafs-thin-end-of-the-wedge/
10 Department of Defence, '5FLT Unit History Record', July 2015; McLaughlin, 'RAAF UAS Projects AI.R Power'.
11 RAAF, *Lessons Learned from Operations of the Heron Unmanned Aircraft System*, p 1.
12 Airservices Australia, 'AIP Supplement H58/15', Airservices Australia, 22 June 2015, pp 1–2.
13 Civil Aviation Safety Authority, 'Meeting Information', South Queensland RAPAC, 15 April 2015, p 12.
14 CQ Plane Spotting, 'Tuesday's Highlights at Rockhampton Airport', CQ Plane Spotting, 7 July 2015. http://cqplanespotting.blogspot.com/2015/07/tuesdays-highlights-at-rockhampton_7.html
15 Department of Defence, '5FLT Unit History Record', June 2015.
16 Department of Defence, '5FLT Unit History Record', October 2015; Department of Defence, Administrative Instruction No 05/2015, 'Heron Deployment to Exercise Iron Moon 2015', RAAF, 31 August 2015.
17 RAAF, *Lessons Learned from Operations of the Heron Unmanned Aircraft System*, p 1; Atkinson, 'RAAF's thin end of the wedge'; Department of Defence, '5FLT Unit History Record', April 2016.
18 Department of Defence, '5FLT Unit History Record', November 2015; Department of Defence, 'Chief of Air Force Commendation – Number 5 Flight', Royal Australian Air Force, 18 April 2015.
19 RAAF, *Lessons Learned from Operations of the Heron Unmanned Aircraft System*, p 1.
20 Department of Defence, '5FLT Unit History Record', August 2016.
21 Department of Defence, '5FLT Unit History Record', January 2017.
22 McLaughlin, 'RAAF UAS Projects AI.R Power'.
23 Bill Carey, 'Australia Will Use Heron as Training Bridge to MQ-4C Triton', *AINonline*, 3 November 2014. https://www.ainonline.com/aviation-news/2014-11-03/australia-will-use-heron-training-bridge-mq-4c-triton; McLaughlin, 'RAAF UAS Projects AI.R Power'.
24 RAAF, *Lessons Learned from Operations of the Heron Unmanned Aircraft System*, p 2.
25 McLaughlin, 'RAAF UAS Projects AI.R Power'.
26 Department of Defence, Air Force Organisational Directive 2017-08, 'Disbandment of Number 5 Flight', Royal Australian Air Force, 19 February 2018.
27 Defense World, 'Australian Air Force Withdraws Heron UAVs From Service', Defense World, 9 August 2017. https://www.defenseworld.net/news/20203/Australian_Air_Force_Withdraws_Heron_UAVs_From_Service#.YTGiG44zauU
28 Foreign Affairs, Defence and Trade References Committee, *Use of unmanned air, maritime and land platforms by the Australian Defence Force*, chap 2; McLaughlin, 'RAAF UAS Projects AI.R Power'.
29 Sean McClure (personal correspondence) 30 September 2021.
30 RAAF, *Lessons Learned from Operations of the Heron Unmanned Aircraft System*, p 2.
31 Australian Defence Magazine, 'From the Source: Air Marshal Mark Binskin, AO (part 2)'.
32 Hartley, 'Advanced RAAF drone takes flight in Ipswich', *Courier Mail*.
33 Australian Defence Magazine, 'From the Source: Air Marshal Mark Binskin, AO (part 2)'.
34 RAAF, *Lessons Learned from Operations of the Heron Unmanned Aircraft System*, p 5.
35 RAAF, *Lessons Learned from Operations of the Heron Unmanned Aircraft System*, p 5.

36 Meier, Unpublished interview transcript with undisclosed interviewee.
37 Meier, Unpublished interview transcript with undisclosed interviewee.
38 Meier, Unpublished interview transcript with undisclosed interviewee.
39 Meier, Unpublished interview transcript with undisclosed interviewee.
40 RAAF, *Lessons Learned from Operations of the Heron Unmanned Aircraft System*, p 3.
41 RAAF, *Implications for Future ISREW UAS Capability Planning*, p 6.
42 Foreign Affairs, Defence and Trade References Committee, *Use of unmanned air, maritime and land platforms by the Australian Defence Force*, chap 6.
43 Australian Defence Magazine, 'From the Source: Air Marshal Mark Binskin, AO (part 2)'.
44 BBC News, 'Heathrow airport: Drone sighting halts departures', *BBC* News, 8 January 2019. https://www.bbc.com/news/uk-46803713
45 Cision, 'SCI Technology's AeroGuard Named 2018 Drone Security New Product of the Year by Security Today Magazine', *PR Newswire*, 24 September 2018. https://www.prnewswire.com/news-releases/sci-technologys-aeroguard-named-2018-drone-security-new-product-of-the-year-by-security-today-magazine-300716969.html
46 Joseph Flynt, 'Differences Between Hexacopters, Quadcopters and Octocopters', 3DInsider, 9 July 2017. https://3dinsider.com/hexacopters-quadcopters-octocopters/
47 Marc Selinger, 'Counterdrone Challenges', *Aerospace America*, May 2019. https://aerospaceamerica.aiaa.org/features/counterdrone-challenges/
48 RAAF, 'RPAS Strategic Communication Plan', Annex E.
49 Max Blenkin, 'Northrop Grumman demonstrates Triton gateway capability', *Australian Defence Magazine*, 16 February 2023. https://www.australiandefence.com.au/news/northrop-grumman-demonstrates-triton-gateway-capability
50 RAAF, 'RPAS Strategic Communication Plan', Annex F.
51 RAAF, 'MQ-4C Triton Unmanned Aircraft System', n.d. https://www.airforce.gov.au/technology/aircraft/intelligence-surveillance-and-reconnaissance/mq-4c-triton-unmanned-aircraft
52 McLaughlin, 'RAAF UAS Projects AI.R Power'.
53 Department of Defence, 'CAF Message – Reformation of Number 9 Squadron', Royal Australian Air Force, 16 March 2023.
54 Department of Defence, 'Triton Remotely Piloted Unmanned Aircraft System', Australian Government, December 2020. https://www1.defence.gov.au/project/triton-remotely-piloted-unmanned-aircraft-system
55 Naval Technology, 'MQ-4C Triton Broad Area Maritime Surveillance (BAMS) UAS', *Naval Technology*, 18 September 2021. https://www.naval-technology.com/projects/mq-4c-triton-bams-uas-us/
56 Northrop Grumman, 'MQ-4C Triton', Northrop Grumman, n.d. https://www.northropgrumman.com/what-we-do/air/triton/
57 Nigel Pittaway, 'Triton Program Delayed by US Budget Cuts', *Australian Defence Magazine*, 29 April 2021. https://www.australiandefence.com.au/defence/air/triton-program-delayed-by-us-budget-cuts
58 Baz Bardoe, 'Drones and Defence: The ADF and Unmanned Aerial Systems', *Australian Aviation*, 7 December 2019. https://australianaviation.com.au/2019/12/drones-and-defence-the-adf-and-unmanned-aerial-systems/
59 McLaughlin, 'RAAF UAS Projects AI.R Power'.
60 McLaughlin, 'RAAF UAS Projects AI.R Power'.
61 McLaughlin, 'RAAF UAS Projects AI.R Power'.
62 Department of Defence, 'AIR7003 Phase 1 MQ-9B SkyGuardian Armed Remotely Piloted Aircraft System', Australian Government, n.d. https://www1.defence.gov.au/project/air7003-skyguardian-armed-remotely-piloted-aircraft-system
63 Department of Defence, *AIR 7003* [media release], 4 April 2022; Department of Defence, DEFGRAM 137/2002, 'Decision not to proceed with AIR 7003 Ph1 – MQ-9B SkyGuardian', Royal Australian Air Force, 4 April 2022.

64 McLaughlin, 'RAAF UAS Projects AI.R Power'.
65 RAAF, 'RPAS Strategic Communication Plan', Annex J; RAAF, *Lessons Learned from Operations of the Heron Unmanned Aircraft System*, p 4; RAAF, 'RPAS Strategic Communication Plan', Annex F.
66 McLaughlin, 'RAAF UAS Projects AI.R Power'.
67 McLaughlin, 'RAAF UAS Projects AI.R Power'.
68 Andrew Greene, 'Australian-made Loyal Wingman air combat drone with AI-driven targeting system completes first test flight', *ABC News*, 2 March 2021. https://www.abc.net.au/news/2021-03-02/loyal-wingman-first-flight-australia-boeing/13207388
69 Air Force Technology, 'Loyal wingman Unmanned Aircraft', Air Force Technology, 22 May 2020. https://www.airforce-technology.com/projects/loyal-wingman-unmanned-aircraft/
70 Air Force Technology, 'Loyal wingman Unmanned Aircraft'; Valerie Insinna, 'Boeing rolls out Australia's first 'Loyal Wingman' combat drone', *Defense News*, 5 May 2020. https://www.defensenews.com/air/2020/05/04/boeing-rolls-out-australias-first-loyal-wingman-combat-drone/
71 Air Force Technology, 'Loyal wingman Unmanned Aircraft'.
72 Greene, 'Australian-made Loyal Wingman air combat drone with AI-driven targeting system completes first test flight'; Valerie Insinna, 'Australia makes another order for Boeing's Loyal Wingman drones after a successful first flight', *Defense News*, 3 March 2021. https://www.defensenews.com/air/2021/03/02/australia-makes-another-order-for-boeing-made-loyal-wingman-drones-after-a-successful-first-flight/
73 Mike Yeo, 'Four companies short listed for Project LAND 129 Phase 3 to replace Shadow UAS', *Asia–Pacific Defence Reporter*, 20 March 2020. https://asiapacificdefencereporter.com/four-companies-shortlisted-for-project-land-129-phase-3-to-replace-shadow-uas/
74 Andrew McLaughlin, 'Insitu Pacific selected for Australian Army's LAND 129 Phase 3 TUAS', *Australian Defence Business Review*, 14 March 2022. https://adbr.com.au/insitu-pacific-selected-for-australian-armys-land-129-phase-3-tuas/
75 Jason Om, 'Game of Drones', *ABC News*, 12 June 2015. https://www.abc.net.au/news/2015-06-11/the-underground-world-of-drone-racing/6532896?nw=0
76 Jason Om, 'Drone Racing Champs: Australia's Fastest Crowned at Weekend of Speed', *ABC News*, 22 August 2016. https://www.abc.net.au/news/2016-08-22/australian-drone-nationals-championships/7771864; Kathy Sundstrom and Daniel Prosser, 'Drone Racing Camps the Answer for School-age Teens Seeking New Pilots to Compete With', *ABC News*, 11 January 2019. https://www.abc.net.au/news/2019-01-11/drone-racing-camp-for-teens-with-no-one-to-race-with/10703044
77 Sundstrom and Prosser, 'Drone Racing Camps the Answer for School-age Teens Seeking New Pilots to Compete With'.
78 Sally French, 'Ready for Takeoff', *Slate*, 7 August 2018. https://slate.com/technology/2018/08/australias-military-drone-racing-team-hopes-to-stage-a-comeback-at-the-invictus-games.html; Defence Connect, 'Sydney to host first Military International Drone Racing Tournament', *Defence Connect*, 22 October 2018. https://www.defenceconnect.com.au/key-enablers/3042-sydney-to-host-first-military-international-drone-racing-tournament
79 French, 'Ready for Takeoff'.
80 Defence Connect, 'Sydney to host first Military International Drone Racing Tournament'.
81 Keirin Joyce, 'The Australian Army and Unmanned Aerial Vehicles', p 61.
82 Gettinger, *The Drone Databook*, p 5; Peter Layton, 'The Australian Army's drone air force', *The Interpreter*, 5 November 2015. https://www.lowyinstitute.org/the-interpreter/australian-army-drone-air-force
83 Gettinger, *The Drone Databook*, p 5; Layton, 'The Australian Army's drone air force'.
84 Gettinger, *The Drone Databook*, p 5.
85 Ewen Levick, 'Army target drone literacy with Phantom delivery', *Australian Defence Magazine*, 23 August 2018. https://www.australiandefence.com.au/land/army-targets-drone-literacy-with-phantom-delivery

86 RAAF, No. 3 *SECFOR SQN Unmanned Aircraft Systems Trial October 2019*, Department of Defence, 23 October 2019, unpublished.
87 Peter Roberts, 'Air Affair's Phoenix Jet Drone Deployed in Navy Exercises', AuManufacturing, 21 January 2021. https://www.aumanufacturing.com.au/air-affairss-phoenix-jet-drone-deployed-in-navy-exercises
88 Irving Lachow, 'The Upside and Downside of Swarming Drones', *Bulletin of the Atomic Scientists*, 73(2): 96–101. https://www.tandfonline.com/action/showCitFormats?doi=10.1080/00963402.2017.1290879
89 David Hambling, 'What Are Drone Swarms And Why Does Every Military Suddenly Want One?', *Forbes*, 1 March 2021. https://www.forbes.com/sites/davidhambling/2021/03/01/what-are-drone-swarms-and-why-does-everyone-suddenly-want-one/
90 Lachow, 'The Upside and Downside of Swarming Drones'.
91 David Hambling, 'Drown Swarms are Getting too Fast for Humans to Fight, U.S. General Warns,' *Forbes*, 27 January 2021. https://www.forbes.com/sites/davidhambling/2021/01/27/drone-swarms-are-getting-too-fast-for-humans-too-fight-us-general-warns/
92 McPhedran, *Air Force*, p 230.

INDEX